"It would be an understatement t ...
evangelical tradition. Emerson puts our eyes back on this imp...
demonstrates how it is biblical, historical, and clarifies and informs other doctrines. Once you see the descent, it is hard to go back to neglecting it. This book shines a helpful light on this derelict doctrine. *Tolle lege.*"

Patrick Schreiner, assistant professor of New Testament language and literature, Western Seminary

"Matthew Emerson has ably recovered a theology of Holy Saturday, Christ's descent into the place of death, for churches that are normally suspicious about ancient creeds. He shows that it is biblical, theologically necessary, integral to the work of Christ, and even intrinsic to the very identity of the God we worship. A concise and convincing account of a contested topic."

Michael F. Bird, academic dean and lecturer in theology at Ridley College in Melbourne, Australia

"A treasure trove of biblical and theological wisdom! Matthew Emerson has read everything on the subject. For Catholics, his correction of Balthasar needs to be listened to—especially given that, with Balthasar and the creedal tradition, he insists upon the profound importance of Christ's descent to the dead. This book is a word that needs saying in our death-despairing age."

Matthew Levering, James N. and Mary D. Perry Jr. Chair of Theology, Mundelein Seminary

"Emerson's book retrieves a seriously neglected yet helpful doctrine—Christ's descent to the dead—with exegetical insight, theological acumen, and a pastoral heart. I highly recommend it."

Walter R. Strickland II, associate vice president for Kingdom Diversity Initiatives and assistant professor, Southeastern Baptist Theological Seminary

"I can't recall the last time I read a new book that gave me so much insight into an event from the mission of Jesus Christ. In this retrieval of the doctrine of Christ's descent to the dead, Emerson clears away misconceptions, corrects erroneous interpretations, establishes solid foundations, and explores the vast implications of this single line of the classic creed. This book deserves a wide readership but will be especially helpful for evangelicals who have mumbled their way through, or have misunderstood, the creedal descent clause."

Fred Sanders, professor at the Torrey Honors Institute, Biola University

"Matthew Emerson has given us here a major study of the historic, but too often distorted and neglected, doctrine of the descent of Jesus Christ to the dead. In doing so, he demonstrates the coinherence of biblical and historical theology and their relevance for the Christian life."

Timothy George, founding dean of Beeson Divinity School of Samford University and general editor of the Reformation Commentary on Scripture

"This is a tour de force! Emerson has given us a superbly written, incisively argued volume that makes the case for a doctrine that is often neglected or rejected outright by Protestants, illuminating many facets of its theological, liturgical, and pastoral importance along the way. Not everyone will agree with all the details, but this is an outstanding biblical, historical, and theological survey of Christ's descent to the dead. I expect it to become the benchmark Protestant account of the subject for years to come, and it also opens up rich and fruitful avenues for further exploration."

Suzanne McDonald, professor of systematic and historical theology at Western Theological Seminary

"HE DESCENDED TO THE DEAD"

AN EVANGELICAL THEOLOGY OF HOLY SATURDAY

MATTHEW Y. EMERSON

IVP Academic

An imprint of InterVarsity Press
Downers Grove, Illinois

InterVarsity Press
P.O. Box 1400, Downers Grove, IL 60515-1426
ivpress.com
email@ivpress.com

InterVarsity Press® is the book-publishing division of InterVarsity Christian Fellowship/USA®, a movement of students and faculty active on campus at hundreds of universities, colleges, and schools of nursing in the United States of America, and a member movement of the International Fellowship of Evangelical Students. For information about local and regional activities, visit intervarsity.org.

Scripture quotations, unless otherwise noted, are from The Holy Bible, English Standard Version, copyright © 2001 by Crossway Bibles, a division of Good News Publishers. Used by permission. All rights reserved.

Figure 3.1 Icon of the Resurrection / Surgun100, Wikimedia Commons
Figure 5.1 Icon showing baptism of Christ / Wikimedia Commons

Cover design and image composite: David Fassett
Interior design: Jeanna Wiggins
Images: recycled cardstock texture: © Zakharova_Natalia / iStock / Getty Images Plus
    gold foil texture: © Katsumi Murouchi / Moment Collection / Getty Images
    Resurrection by Mikhail Aleksandrovich Vrubel at Museum of Russian Art, Kiev, Ukraine / Bridgeman Images

ISBN 978-0-8308-5258-1 (print)
ISBN 978-0-8308-7053-0 (digital)

Printed in the United States of America ∞

Library of Congress Cataloging-in-Publication Data
A catalog record for this book is available from the Library of Congress.

P	25	24	23	22	21	20	19	18	17	16	15	14	13	12	11	10	9	8	7	6	5	4	3	2	1
Y	39	38	37	36	35	34	33	32	31	30	29	28	27	26	25	24	23	22	21	20	19				

For B, Grandma, Aunt Jane,

and all those in the communion of the saints who are,

though absent from the body,

now present with the Lord

(2 Cor 5:8)

CONTENTS

PREFACE

No worst, there is none. Pitched past pitch of grief,
More pangs will, schooled at forepangs, wilder wring.
Comforter, where, where is your comforting?
Mary, mother of us, where is your relief?
My cries heave, herds-long; huddle in a main, a chief
Woe, world-sorrow; on an age-old anvil wince and sing—
Then lull, then leave off. Fury had shrieked 'No ling-
ering! Let me be fell: force I must be brief.'

O the mind, mind has mountains; cliffs of fall
Frightful, sheer, no-man-fathomed. Hold them cheap
May who ne'er hung there. Nor does long our small
Durance deal with that steep or deep. Here! creep,
Wretch, under a comfort serves in a whirlwind: all
Life death does end and each day dies with sleep.

GERARD MANLEY HOPKINS, "NO WORST,
THERE IS NONE, PITCHED PAST PITCH OF GRIEF"

A contemporary example of this kind of reflection on the inevitability of death, namely the refrain, "We're all gonna die," echoes throughout Sufjan Stevens's "Fourth of July," a song in the middle of his elegiac album, *Carrie and Lowell*. Stevens, "Fourth of July," track 6 on *Carrie and Lowell*, Asthmatic Kitty, 2015. See also Langston Hughes's poem, "Drum," in *Selected Poems of Langston Hughes* (New York: Vintage Classics, 1959), 87.

This haunting poem reminds us that death is inevitable for human beings. And while we may want to avoid acknowledging this pervasive reality, we all know it is true. We are bombarded daily, hourly, with grim news from both home and abroad. The list of celebrities who died in the past year, usually posthumously paraded via images at the Oscars, seems to grow longer and closer to home each year. Cancer, unforeseen accidents, murder, and plain old age take those acquaintances, distant relatives, coworkers, friends, spouses, parents, and children so often that it is easy to become numb to it. And yet despite all our attempts at avoidance and even with the growing numbness, one day we, too, will face the fact that our lives are about to end. In short, Death comes for us all. This pervasive reality, one to which the Bible bears witness and even personifies as one of God's most ardent enemies, is apparent in the world around us. It is apparent in our own experience. When I first wrote this preface, my Aunt Jane was dying of ovarian cancer. After battling it for eight years (much longer than expected), she was facing her end in this present life. She could not eat or drink, and soon after passed away into eternity. And as I wrote this book, I thought of an acquaintance who lost twins in childbirth. This then reminded me of another friend who has lost a child at birth and his father to suicide, and who will one day lose his wife to a debilitating and chronic tumor on her spine. Death is all around us.

What, as Christians, can we say to those who face death, either their own or that of their loved ones? We certainly can give them the hope of Christ's resurrection, if they or their loved one has trusted Christ in repentance and faith. We can also assure them that they do not grieve without hope because they, if they and their loved ones are Christ-followers, will one day see that loved one again. But here is what faces us in the meantime: the twin realizations that—unless we too pass on soon—we will not see them face to face for a long time and that this is because our loved ones no longer live bodily on this earth. Yes, they and we will be raised with Christ one day; yes, we have hope in the resurrection; and yes, they are with Christ. But on this last note, perhaps there is some further hope we can offer. Perhaps there is something more immediate than Christ's second coming and believers' resurrection to eternal life that we can preach to those grieving but not without hope. The hope that is more immediate, and one that is descriptive of our departed loved ones' eternal state right now, not just some distant day, is that Christ, too, has experienced death. He did not just experience dying only to rise again moments later, but he actually remained dead in the grave. He did not simply have his breath expire and then immediately rise to glory, but his body was buried and his soul departed to the place of the dead. And because he is God in the flesh, he defeated the place of the dead and the grave by descending into them and then rising again on the third day. In the Christian tradition, this hope is known as the doctrine of Christ's *descensus*—his descent to the dead.

Descents are everywhere. From Hercules and Orpheus venturing into Hades, to Harry Potter following the pipes down into the Chamber of Secrets, to the Sheriff and Joyce Byers frantically searching for Will in the Upside Down (in the Netflix series *Stranger Things*), we want our heroes to descend into the underworld, defeat the enemy, and rescue their loved ones. We want Maui to enter the Realm of Monsters and defeat Tamatoa in the Disney film *Moana*. We love seeing Doctor Strange enter the Dark Dimension, experience death *ad infinitum*, and thereby trick and defeat Mordo at the end of the film named after him. Our hearts swell while reading *The Silver Chair* as Jill and Eustace rescue Prince Rilian from Underland, and in *The Lord of the Rings* as Gandalf descends into the depths of Moria, gives up his own life to defeat the Balrog, and then rises again to save Middle-Earth. There is something fascinating about—a shared yearning for—a hero who can enter the underworld, defeat our enemies, and bring the dead back to life.[1]

---

[1] For an older study of the descent motif in both biblical and nonbiblical literature, see J. A. MacCulloch, *The Harrowing of Hell: A Comparative Study of an Early Christian Doctrine* (Edinburgh: T & T Clark, 1930), esp. 1-44 for a sort of "global history" of descent stories. See

This descent motif, so popular in ancient and modern mythology, is also found in the historic events of the Bible, climaxing in Christ's descent to the dead between his death and resurrection. It might seem like an odd thing to meditate on the fact that Jesus remained dead for three days, and yet that is what I have done for the past two years, nearly daily, many times hourly and by the minute. It may seem even stranger to hear that, over the course of that time, this doctrine has become a source of comfort, amazement, and worship of our Triune God for me. That God himself would descend in the incarnate Son to take on human flesh and all that entails, including not only dying but remaining dead, in order to redeem us from the curse of sin, is at the heart of the good news. God the Son first descended when he took on flesh, and in doing so he experienced all that humanity experiences, including death and its temporal state. What good news is this, that God vicariously experiences not only life but also death with us through the incarnate Son? What gospel do Christians proclaim, except that Jesus has defeated all rulers, authorities, principalities, and powers, including death itself, and that he does so through dying for sin, remaining dead, and rising from the dead? And what hope do Christians have for those who, unlike those who read these words, no longer live? We who follow Christ have the hope that Jesus already experienced death, the state of being dead, with and for those who trust in his atoning death and victorious resurrection. This doctrine moves me to be comforted in the face of death. This doctrine comforts me as I grieve with those who grieve and as I remember those to whom I've dedicated this book. And it moves me to worship and praise as I comprehend more deeply each day what it means for God the Son to take on human flesh "for us and for our salvation."

And yet this doctrine has been nearly abandoned in many circles, particularly conservative evangelical ones. While the descent is making

---

also his article, "Descent to Hades (Ethnic)," in *Encyclopedia of Religion and Ethics*, vol. 4, *Confirmation–Drama*, ed. James Hastings (1912; Edinburgh: T&T Clark, 1981), 648–54.

a bit of a comeback these days,[2] it remains either under fire or ignored in many evangelical circles. Some demand its excision from the Apostles' Creed,[3] while others call for its radical revision to the point that it is redundant with "he died, and was buried." In many evangelical colleges and seminaries, the phrase "he descended to the dead" is trounced as a capitulation to misguided Roman Catholic notions of the intermediate state, purgatory, and justification. The motivation for writing this book arose out of my ever-growing appreciation for the doctrine in the face of what seems like an increasingly full-on assault of the doctrine's biblical and systematic viability. I began my inquiry into what the descent might mean if we recovered it as Protestant evangelicals in a paper at the 2015 Los Angeles Theology Conference, and my appreciation for and desire to recover the doctrine for evangelicals has grown since then. I hope in this book to show the biblical and historical warrant for the descent so that, in turn, we can see how vital this doctrine is for the confession and ministry of the church.

A Collect for Holy Saturday

O God, Creator of heaven and earth: Grant that, as the crucified body of thy dear Son was laid in the tomb and rested on this holy Sabbath, so we may await with him the coming of the third day, and rise with him to newness of life; who now liveth and reigneth with thee and the Holy Spirit, one God, for ever and ever. *Amen.*[4]

---

[2] See especially the works of Justin Bass, Michael Bird, and Jeffrey Hamm, discussed extensively in the rest of the book.

[3] The phrase also occurs in the so-called Athanasian Creed, although this is used much less frequently by evangelicals (if at all) and so has escaped scrutiny with respect to the descent doctrine.

[4] "Collects: Traditional," BCP Online, accessed May 19, 2019, www.bcponline.org/Collects /seasonst.html.

ACKNOWLEDGMENTS

In writing this book I owe a debt of gratitude to many, the first of whom is my wife. I thank God for Alicia, particularly for her patience with me on this project. Many times, academics' spouses assume that the toil of research and writing is over after the dissertation is done, but Alicia has not only been patient with this post-dissertation book but also persistent in encouraging me to do what I love—to read, write about, and teach God's Word to his people. I also owe thanks to my children, who remind me each day how beautiful life is and how God has blessed me.

With respect to the arguments that follow, I am grateful for the almost constant dialogue with Luke Stamps. Luke challenges me, points me to better resources, and is always willing to listen. I would not have been able to conceive of this book, much less write it, without Luke. I am also grateful to Craig Bartholomew, Heath Thomas, and Chris Morgan, each of whom is a mentor in my pursuit of an academic vocation and ministry. Particularly on this project, Craig was instrumental in helping me to conceive of and pitch the book. I also want to thank all those who read a draft of the entirety or select chapters of this book: Alan Bandy, Patrick Schreiner, Fred Sanders, Brandon Smith, Luke Stamps, and Heath Thomas. This is a much better book because of their help. In that regard, I am grateful to my student workers at OBU, Andrew Tucker and Chandler Warren, both of whom assisted in finding sources. Finally, I owe many thanks to the editors at IVP Academic, especially David McNutt. They, too, have made this an exponentially better book through their careful review of the manuscript. Of course, whatever deficiencies remain are exclusively my responsibility.

ABBREVIATIONS

PRIMARY SOURCES

Antichr.	*De Antrichristo*
Apoll.	*On the Incarnation Against Apollinaris*
Ascen. Isa.	*Ascension of Isaiah*
C. Ar.	*Orations Against the Arians*
Cels.	*Against Celsus*
Comm. Jo.	*Commentary on John*
Comm. Matt.	*Commentary on Matthew*
Dial.	*Dialogue with Trypho*
1 En.	*1 Enoch*
2 En.	*2 Enoch*
Boniface, *Ep.*	Boniface, *Epistle*
Gregory, *Ep.*	Gregory the Great, *Epistle*
Ep. Epict.	*Letter to Epictetus*
Epid.	*Demonstration of the Apostolic Preaching*
Exc.	*Excerpts from Theodotus*
Fr. Luc.	*Fragmenta in Lucam*
Gos. Bart.	*Gospel of Bartholomew*
Augustine, *Haer.*	*On Heresies*
Irenaeus, *Haer.*	*Against Heresies*

Herm. *Sim.*	Shepherd of Hermas, *Similitude*
Hom. 1 Reg.	*Homilies on 1 Kings*
Hom. Exod.	*Homilies on Exodus*
Hom. Lev.	*Homilies on Leviticus*
Ign. *Eph.*	Ignatius, *Epistle to the Ephesians*
Ign. *Magn.*	Ignatius, *Epistle to the Magnesians*
Ign. *Trall.*	Ignatius, *Epistle to the Trallians*
Odes Sol.	*Odes of Solomon*
Pol. *Phil.*	Polycarp, *Epistle to the Philippians*
Pr Man	Prayer of Manasseh
Spir. Sanct.	*De Spiritu Sancto*
Strom.	*Miscellanies*
T. Dan	Testament of Dan
Teach. Silv.	*Teachings of Silvanus*
Tg. Psalms	*Targum to the Psalms*
Trin.	*De Trinitate*
Wisd Sol	Wisdom of Solomon

MODERN TRANSLATIONS AND SECONDARY SOURCES

AB	Anchor Bible
ACCS	Ancient Christian Commentary on Scripture
AGJU	Arbeiten zur Geschichte des antiken Judentums und des Urchristentums
ANF	*Ante-Nicene Fathers*
BCOTWP	Baker Commentary on the Old Testament Wisdom and Psalms
BDAG	Danker, Bauer, Arndt, and Gingrich. *A Greek-English Lexicon of the New Testament and Other Early Christian Literature*
BECNT	Baker Exegetical Commentary on the New Testament
Bib	*Biblia*

CBQ	*Catholic Biblical Quarterly*
CCSA	Corpus Christianorum: Series Apocryphorum
CCSG	Corpus Christianorum: Series Graeca
CCSL	Corpus Christianorum: Series Latina
CHRC	*Church History and Religious Culture*
CTR	*Criswell Theological Review*
EvQ	*Evangelical Quarterly*
ExpTim	*Expository Times*
HBM	Hebrew Bible Monographs
IBC	Interpretation: A Biblical Commentary for Teaching and Preaching
ICC	International Critical Commentary
IJST	*International Journal of Systematic Theology*
IPM	Instrumenta Patristica et Mediaevalia
IVPNTC	IVP New Testament Commentary
JETS	*Journal of the Evangelical Theological Society*
JHS	*Journal of Hebrew Scriptures*
JRT	*Journal of Reformed Theology*
JSNTSup	Journal for the Study of the New Testament Supplement
JSOT	Journal for the Study of the Old Testament
LNTS	Library of New Testament Studies
ModTheo	*Modern Theology*
NAC	New American Commentary
NICGT	New International Commentary on the Greek Text
NICNT	New International Commentary on the New Testament
NICOT	New International Commentary on the Old Testament
NKZ	*Neue kirchliche Zeitschrift*
NovTSup	Novum Testamentum Supplement

NPNF¹	*Nicene and Post-Nicene Fathers*, Series 1
NPNF²	*Nicene and Post-Nicene Fathers*, Series 2
NSBT	New Studies in Biblical Theology
PG	Patrologia Graeca
PNTC	Pillar New Testament Commentary
PO	Patrologia Orientalis
RevExp	*Review and Expositor*
RFP	*Reformed Faith & Practice*
RRR	*Reformation and Renaissance Review*
RTR	*The Reformed Theological Review*
SBET	*Scottish Bulletin of Evangelical Theology*
SBJT	*Southern Baptist Journal of Theology*
SBL	Society of Biblical Literature
SBT	Studies in Biblical Theology
SC	Sources Chrétiennes
SJT	*Scottish Journal of Theology*
SNTS	Society for New Testament Studies Monographs
STR	*Southeastern Theological Review*
TDNT	*Theological Dictionary of the New Testament*
TrinJ	*Trinity Journal*
TOTC	Tyndale Old Testament Commentary
TS	*Theological Studies*
VCSup	Vigiliae Christianae Supplement
WBC	Word Biblical Commentary
WTJ	*Westminster Theological Journal*
ZKT	*Zeitschrift für katholische Theologie*
ZNW	*Zeitschrift für die neutestamentliche Wissenschaft*

PART ONE

BIBLICAL, HISTORICAL, AND THEOLOGICAL FOUNDATIONS

"I BELIEVE"

Evangelicalism, Creedal Authority, and the Descent

The descent clause of the Apostles' and Athanasian creeds—"he descended into hell"—has come under fire over the last two decades, primarily from within American evangelicalism. By "evangelical" and "evangelicalism" I do not mean a particular political voting bloc in the United States but rather the Christian movement that (1) began in the late eighteenth century, (2) is most concentrated in North America, and (3) is characterized by David Bebbington's quadrilateral of commitment to biblical authority ("Biblicism"), a focus on the cross as the center of Christ's work ("crucicentrism"), the need for personal conversion ("conversionism"), and the importance of sharing one's faith in evangelism and engagement with the public square ("activism").[1] It is out of this tradition primarily that I write. Although this group's boundaries are fuzzy, it is from within this movement that much of the doubt regarding the clause "he descended into hell" has come. One point requiring absolute clarity is that "descended into hell" did not mean, until Calvin, "descend into the place of torment." The creedal Latin

---

[1]See David Bebbington, *Evangelicalism in Modern Britain: A History from the 1730s to the 1980s* (Grand Rapids: Baker, 1989).

varies between *ad inferna* ("descended into hell") and *ad inferos* ("descended to the dead [ones]), but these are synonyms until the Reformation. While *ad inferna* is certainly much more widely attested, there are still variants with *ad inferos* in the Apostles' Creed's development.[2] And, given the later clarification of the terms in ecclesiastical Latin, the content of the original phrase is more accurately rendered by *ad inferos* than by *ad inferna*.[3] In any case, while this recent debate about the clause may seem to have come from left field, the clause has been under scrutiny since the Reformation.[4] Most critics of the phrase fall into one of two camps: either the clause is redundant with "he was buried" (since it is simply stating that Jesus died) or the clause is teaching something unbiblical if it is referring to any of the variations of the "Harrowing of Hell" doctrine. In doing so, some have called for an alteration of the creeds by excising the phrase,[5] while others have called for an alteration of the creeds via an alteration of the phrase itself.[6] What does this willingness of evangelicals (as well as Protestants since the Reformation) to call into question the biblical warrant for the phrase and thus to call for its creedal excision, say about

---

[2]See on this Liuwe H. Westra, *The Apostles' Creed; Origin, History, and Some Early Commentaries*, IPM 43 (Turnhout: Brepols, 2002), 539-62.

[3]See on this Catherine Ella Laufer, *Hell's Destruction: An Exploration of Christ's Descent to the Dead* (Surrey: Ashgate, 2013), 30, and Alyssa Lyra Pitstick, *Light in Darkness: Hans Urs von Balthasar and the Catholic Doctrine of Christ's Descent into Hell* (Grand Rapids: Eerdmans, 2013). For more on the historic meaning of the phrase and the terminology used, see chapter three.

[4]See Justin W. Bass's explanation of the rise of Calvin's and Bucer's idiosyncratic views in his *The Battle for the Keys: Revelation 1:18 and Christ's Descent into the Underworld*, Paternoster Biblical Monographs (Eugene, OR: Wipf and Stock, 2014), 17-19. See also the older work of John Yates, "'He Descended into Hell': Creed, Article and Scripture Part I," *Churchman* 102.3 (1988): 240-50; and Yates, "'He Descended into Hell': Creed, Article and Scripture Part II," *Churchman* 102.4 (1988): 303-15. While I disagree with some of Yates's exegesis, he makes the same point about Calvin's and Bucer's views.

[5]Wayne Grudem takes both of these objections in his essay calling for the excision of the creedal phrase. See Wayne A. Grudem, "He Did Not Descend into Hell: A Plea for Following Scripture Instead of the Apostles' Creed," *JETS* 34.1 (1991): 103-13. See also similar comments by Michael Williams in his "He Descended into Hell? An Issue of Confessional Integrity," *Presbyterion* 25.2 (1999): 80-90.

[6]This is anecdotal. I have heard pastors suggest a complete alteration of the phrase, inserting something like "He suffered the wrath of God for us." I do not know of anyone who has made this kind of suggestion in print.

evangelicals' view of creedal authority? More importantly, what should an evangelical view of authority be?

DERIVATIVE CREEDAL AUTHORITY

Evangelicals, in my experience, have a strange relationship with both the three ecumenical creeds—Nicene, Apostles', and Athanasian—and with a particular affirmation of the latter two: that Jesus "descended to the dead." Regarding creedal authority, evangelicals seem to understand intuitively the importance of creedal affirmations. Evangelicals want to defend the doctrine of the Trinity, the direction of the Father in creation, the necessity of the Son's work for salvation, the activity of the Spirit in the church, and the hope of Christ's return. And yet evangelicals are also Protestants and so want to recognize the supreme authority of Holy Scripture over tradition in matters of faith and practice. When it comes to the creeds, then, evangelicals sense their importance and their truthfulness but are also reluctant to call them "authoritative."[7]

Of course, there are different kinds of evangelicals, some who value tradition more than others. Evangelical Anglicans, Lutherans, Presbyterians, and Methodists, in various ways and to various degrees, affirm the three ecumenical creeds. And yet within evangelicalism, these denominations are only a portion of the larger group. Many evangelicals are free church, baptistic, and nondenominational. Further, within all of these groups, free church or not, "traditional" or not, the modern rejection of tradition and the postmodern tendency toward communal authority rather than historic authority have led evangelicals to two disparate means of rejecting creedal authority. On the one hand, many evangelicals distort *sola Scriptura* into *solo* or *nuda Scriptura*. As Timothy George puts it,

> Bible-church Christians, restorationists, and some Baptists, among others, have elevated this expression ["No creed but the Bible"] to a fundamental

---

[7]On evangelicals' suspicion of the creeds and their authority, as well as historical, theological, and practical reasons to continue to affirm them, see Carl R. Trueman, *The Creedal Imperative* (Wheaton, IL: Crossway, 2012).

article of the faith. 'We have no creed but the Bible,' they say—thus making a creed out of their commitment to creedless Christianity![8]

This distortion of confessionalism,[9] combined with modernism's suspicion of tradition, leads many evangelicals simply to reject creedal statements outright. For instance, there are a number of philosophical and systematic theologians who have called into question the doctrine of the eternal generation of the Son,[10] a key affirmation of the Nicene Creed. The descent doctrine has also come under fire in the twentieth century.[11]

The rationale given in such instances is that these creedal statements are unbiblical, or at least not explicitly taught in Scripture, and therefore not required as matters of faith. Often the rejection of particular creedal statements as unbiblical is based on exegesis of particular passages supposed to be lynchpins of those doctrines. So Wayne Grudem has based his doubt of eternal generation on his own exegesis of Proverbs 8:22-31,[12] while his rejection of the descent doctrine arises out of his exegesis of 1 Peter 3:18-22.[13] Methodologically, this approach is many times based

---

[8]Timothy George, "Introduction," xvii-xxiv in *Evangelicals and Nicene Faith: Reclaiming the Apostolic Witness*, ed. Timothy George (Grand Rapids: Baker Academic, 2011), xxi.

[9]To be sure, "no creed but the Bible" is a distortion of the Reformation cry of *sola Scriptura*. We should acknowledge, however, that there is an important and necessary denial of credalism—the idea that creeds or confessions are on par with Scripture and not merely accurate summaries of its doctrinal content—in this expression of "no creed but the Bible." On both of these points, see George, "Introduction," xxi.

[10]For examples of this, see Kevin Giles's defense of the doctrine, *The Eternal Generation of the Son: Maintaining Orthodoxy in Trinitarian Theology* (Downers Grove, IL: IVP Academic, 2012), 36-37. Giles here gives six reasons for why some evangelicals reject eternal generation, most of which revolve around exegetical arguments. For an example of that to which Giles refers, see John S. Feinberg's questioning of eternal generation in his *No One Like Him: The Doctrine of God* (Wheaton: Crossway, 2006), 488-92.

[11]This kind of creedal suspicion is not only evident within evangelicalism; see also, for instance, reflection on the virgin birth by Andrew T. Lincoln, *Born of a Virgin? Reconceiving Jesus in the Bible, Tradition, and Theology* (Grand Rapids: Eerdmans, 2013).

[12]For his doubt of the doctrine of eternal generation, see Wayne Grudem, *Systematic Theology: An Introduction to Biblical Doctrine* (Grand Rapids: Zondervan, 1994), 1233-34. For his discussion of Prov 8:22-31, see Grudem, *Systematic Theology*, 229-30. It should be noted that at the 2016 Annual Meeting of the Evangelical Theological Society, Grudem publicly affirmed eternal generation. I do not know, however, if he has revised his position in print.

[13]See Wayne Grudem, "Christ Preaching Through Noah: 1 Peter 3:19-20 in the Light of Dominant Themes in Jewish Literature," *TrinJ* 7 (1986): 3-31; for similar arguments, see also John Feinberg, "1 Peter 3:18-20, Ancient Mythology, and the Intermediate State," *WTJ* 48 (1986): 303-36.

on at least three assumptions: (1) that in the early church, some doctrines were based on philosophical rather than biblical commitments; (2) that the modern tools of historical-grammatical exegesis, used on one or a few particular texts, are sufficient in order to arrive at doctrinal conclusions; and (3) that we can set aside our presuppositions in order to achieve the kind of exegetical clarity needed to evaluate earlier creeds and confessions and, perhaps, reject them in favor of new affirmations of our own making. In other words, this approach is thoroughly modern.[14] The end result of this kind of approach is to excise certain statements from the creeds. So, for instance, many evangelical churches simply leave out the Apostles' Creed's affirmation concerning Christ's descent to the dead (if they recite a creed at all).[15]

Postmodern approaches to authority—namely, their communal emphasis—only exacerbate this issue. On the one hand, a postmodern approach may lead to a "what it means to us" attitude, where creedal statements are authoritative in the way that a local church or denomination affirms them. In turn, this may or may not be connected to how they have been understood throughout Christian history. So creedal affirmations mean what a particular community says they mean, instead of having their meaning rooted in the biblical witness and the derivative tradition. On the other hand, a postmodern approach to creedal authority could only exacerbate the tendency to excise certain statements, since particular communities are free to affirm what they want. As Kevin Vanhoozer argues,

> In a postmodern climate, it is more difficult than ever to pretend that one's preferred formulation of Christian faith is immune to cultural conditioning.

---

[14]Gerald Bray summarizes the modern sentiment nicely: "Today we live in a world that prizes originality, rejects tradition, and lets people think that they can make up their own version of the truth." See his essay, "Whosoever Will Be Saved: The Athanasian Creed and the Modern Church," 45-57 in *Evangelicals and the Nicene Faith*, 50-51. For a historical overview of the shift from premodern to modern notions of authority and the philosophical, cultural, and theological underpinnings of those shifts, see Alister E. McGrath, *The Genesis of Doctrine: A Study in the Foundation of Doctrinal Criticism* (Grand Rapids: Eerdmans, 1997), 103-71.

[15]E.g., Grudem expressly calls for the excision of the descent clause in his essay, "He Did Not Descend."

This awareness contributes, at least indirectly, to an ethos of congregational consumerism and ultimately to a devaluation of doctrine.[16]

Again, for the descent doctrine, this has certain implications. Some have chosen to reject it completely, while others have made it mean something it never did in Christian history.

Interestingly, the last two decades have brought a renewed appreciation of "tradition" among postmodern approaches to church life, particularly in the Emergent Church movement and their emphasis on an "ancient/future faith."[17] This re-appropriation of the Christian tradition, though, is sometimes used as a rationale for a minimal, rather than a maximal, view of Christian doctrine. The phrase "Nicaea is enough" is typical in this model, and its connotation is that as long as someone affirms the Nicene Creed then they may be all over the map in other areas of Christian doctrine without abandoning the faith. Further, even affirmations of Nicaea are subject to individual and communal interpretations.[18] This is not a retrieval of the Christian tradition as much as it is an attempt to conceive of the Christian doctrinal tent as covering as much ground as possible.

Neither of these options captures the spirit of an evangelical view of tradition's derivative authority. While both approaches have positive contributions to make—modernism's emphasis on what the text says rather than a blind appropriation of all tradition,[19] and postmodernism's

---

[16]It is my understanding of Vanhoozer's point here that by "devaluation" he means not (merely) the lack of interest in doctrine as a whole but the rejection of particular creedal phrases and/or confessional beliefs. See Kevin J. Vanhoozer, *The Drama of Doctrine: A Canonical Linguistic Approach to Christian Theology* (Louisville, KY: Westminster John Knox, 2005), 445-46. For further discussion of what he means by "devaluation," see the rest of the chapter, 445-57.

[17]See Robert E. Webber, *Ancient-Future Faith: Rethinking Evangelicalism for a Postmodern World* (Grand Rapids: Baker Academic, 1999), esp. 174-204. Webber is admittedly much more careful in this regard than some of those in the Emergent Church who followed him. See also the discussion in John Jefferson Davis, *Worship and the Reality of God: An Evangelical Theology of Real Presence* (Downers Grove, IL: IVP Academic, 2010).

[18]On a cultural-linguistic understanding of authority, upon which many postmodern reflections about creedal authority are based, see George Lindbeck, *The Nature of Doctrine: Religion and Theology in a Postliberal Age* (Louisville, KY: Westminster John Knox, 1984).

[19]See George's comments about credalism in his "Introduction," xxi-xxii.

recognition of presuppositions, for instance[20]—neither provides the path for an evangelical understanding of the Christian tradition. What is needed is a more robust grasp on how tradition and the Bible relate to one another under the rubric of *sola Scriptura*.[21]

Others have recently attempted to articulate this relationship between Scripture and classic Christian doctrine. Kevin Vanhoozer, for instance, categorizes doctrine as scriptural performance, or the outworking of Scripture's teachings in contemporary contexts.[22] In this view, doctrine and tradition are derivative of Scripture but nevertheless essential to the Christian life. Scripture is not static or stale, but living and active through its divine author, the Holy Spirit. Thus reading Scripture demands a response, and tradition and doctrine are rational and linguistic responses to the Bible's content. In Vanhoozer's terms, the Spirit is the playwright, the Bible is his script, and tradition and doctrine are the faithful performances of that script. In this model, then, Scripture is ultimately authoritative via its divine inspiration, and doctrine and tradition are derivatively authoritative as long as they are worked out—performed—in according with the *norma normans non normata* of Scripture.[23] In this derivative and performative role,

---

[20]See, e.g., James K. A. Smith, *Who's Afraid of Postmodernism? Taking Derrida, Foucault, and Lyotard to Church*, The Church and Postmodern Culture (Grand Rapids: Baker Academic, 2006); Smith, *Who's Afraid of Relativism? Community, Contingency, and Creaturehood*, The Church and Postmodern Culture (Grand Rapids: Baker Academic, 2014); and Merold Westphal, *Whose Community? Which Interpretation? Philosophical Hermeneutics for the Church*, The Church and Postmodern Culture (Grand Rapids: Baker Academic, 2009).

[21]Here we should note that there are a number of retrieval projects afoot from within evangelicalism, including Michael Allen and Scott R. Swain, eds., *Christian Dogmatics: Reformed Theology for the Church Catholic* (Grand Rapids: Baker Academic, 2016); Allen and Swain, *Reformed Catholicity: The Promise of Retrieval for Theology and Biblical Interpretation* (Grand Rapids: Baker Academic, 2015); W. David Buschart and Kent D. Eilers, *Theology as Retrieval: Receiving the Past, Renewing the Church* (Downers Grove, IL: IVP Academic, 2015); and Kenneth J. Stewart, *In Search of Ancient Roots: The Christian Past and the Evangelical Identity Crisis* (Downers Grove, IL: IVP Academic, 2017). See also the discussion in Alister E. McGrath, "Faith and Tradition," 81-98 in Gerald R. McDermott, ed., *Oxford Handbook of Evangelical Theology* (Oxford: Oxford University Press, 2010), as well as his *The Genesis of Doctrine*.

[22]See Vanhoozer, *Drama*, esp. 151-210.

[23]George, "Introduction," xxi-xxii and Oliver Crisp, "Desiderata for Models of the Hypostatic Union," 19-41, in *Christology Ancient and Modern: Explorations in Constructive Dogmatics*, Los Angeles Theology Conference Series 1 (Grand Rapids: Zondervan Academic, 2013), esp. 22, 27,

doctrine is both subject to Scripture and, insofar as it is faithful to Scripture, a guide for reading Scripture. When we say that doctrine or tradition is derivatively authoritative, then, we mean that it aids in our grasp of Scripture's content insofar as it is faithful to Scripture's content.[24] In Vanhoozer's terms, it is a ministerial, not ultimate, authority. Its purpose is to minister the hermeneutical and doctrinal truth to us, not to serve as the arbiter or giver of truth.[25] Those latter categories belong to God alone, who communicates truth to us in the person of God the Son and the Scriptures that testify to him through the inspiration of God the Spirit.[26]

DERIVATIVE AUTHORITY AND THE DESCENT

Of course, the question at hand is whether or not the creeds, particularly the Apostles' and Athanasian, have accurately ministered biblical teaching on what happened to Jesus between his death and resurrection. Did Jesus in fact "descend into hell [to the dead]"? Is this clause saying something that reflects biblical teaching? Or is it—on the one hand and in the case of the Apostles' Creed—a needless repetition of the burial clause or—on the other hand—a mistaken notion about harrowing or torment that should be deleted? Wayne Grudem and the so-called

---

both use this terminology to refer to the supreme authority of Scripture while also acknowledging the derivative authority of tradition. See also on this relationship Allen and Swain, *Reformed Catholicity*, 49-94; and Heath A. Thomas, "The *Telos* (Goal) of Theological Interpretation," 197-217 in *A Manifesto for Theological Interpretation*, ed. Craig G. Bartholomew and Heath A. Thomas (Grand Rapids: Baker Academic, 2016), 214-15. Finally, for what may be the foundational use of the phrase in twentieth-century theology, see Karl Rahner, "Scripture and Theology," in *Theological Investigations* 6 (Baltimore: Helicon, 1969), 93 (89-97). Thanks to Heath Thomas for the latter reference.

[24]For more on the derivative relation of dogmatic formulations to the Bible, see John Webster, *Holy Scripture: A Dogmatic Sketch*, Current Issues in Theology (Cambridge: Cambridge University Press, 2003), 51-52, 122-23; and Webster, *Word and Church*, Essays in Church Dogmatics (London: T&T Clark, 2001), 84-86.

[25]For a description of the relation of creeds and confessions to Scripture in terms of speech-act theory, see Anthony C. Thiselton, *The Hermeneutics of Doctrine* (Grand Rapids: Eerdmans, 2007), 8-18.

[26]See Vanhoozer, *Drama*, 207-10. See also Scott R. Swain, *Trinity, Revelation, and Reading: A Theological Introduction to the Bible and its Interpretation*, T&T Clark Theology (London: T&T Clark, 2011), 100-118.

"neo-deletionists"[27] argue that the answer to both of these latter questions is "yes" and that, therefore, the phrase should be excised.

But it is at exactly this point that the derivative authority of the creeds should give us pause. If the creeds have stood the test of time, and if, in standing that test, their phrases have been proven, generation upon generation, to be an accurate summary of biblical content, those phrases that give us most trouble today should be seen not as hurdles to be jumped or chaff to be separated from the wheat but as challenges to our (post)modern imaginations. Acknowledging the derivative authority of the creeds means that, on the one hand, we confess them precisely because they are accurate summaries of Scripture. On the other hand, it also means that derivative creedal authority is a communal and ecclesial balance that acts as a check against any of our mistaken, individual interpretations. Understanding creedal authority this way is thus an exercise in seeing how the creeds ask us to return to Scripture rather than depart from it. At minimum, it says to the interpreter who questions a creedal phrase, "search the Scriptures again, and do so with the communion of the saints."[28]

SEARCHING THE BIBLICAL FIELDS

When we return to the field of Holy Scripture and search once again for creedal treasure, particularly as it relates to the descent clause, we find biblical warrant to understand "he descended to the dead" as an accurate summary of Christ's time between his death and resurrection. Of course, we should recognize that "biblical warrant" is more encompassing than just the common expression, "give me a chapter and verse." That phrase is a narrow, imprecise, and inaccurate view of what it means for a doctrine to

---

[27]This phrase is used by Jeffrey L. Hamm in his recent article on Grudem's interpretation of the descent clause, "*Descendit*: Delete or Declare? A Defense Against the Neo-Deletionists," *WTJ* 78.1 (2016): 93-116.

[28]See Allen and Swain's articulation of theology as the "school of Christ" in *Reformed Catholicity*, 17-48. See also Oberman's distinction between Tradition I (tradition subservient to Scripture) and Tradition II (tradition equal in authority to Scripture) in Heiko O. Oberman, *The Harvest of Medieval Theology* (1963; Grand Rapids: Baker Book House, 2000), 365-90.

be biblical. Rather than simply proof-texting,[29] a theological method that seeks to be biblical recognizes that, to use David Yeago's terms, a properly "biblical" doctrine is one in which the theologian's conceptual terms render accurate judgments about the patterns of biblical language.[30]

"Patterns" can be anything from a few explicit verses grouped together (the common means of "doing theology" among evangelicals[31]), to following intertextual threads,[32] to what are properly called "patterns." While we should not discount forming doctrinal conclusions via exegesis and interpretation of one verse or passage, it may come as a surprise to some to realize that some doctrines simply cannot be formed this way.[33] More often, doctrinal formulation requires, at the very least, the interpretation of a few passages together, giving attention to both their literary and canonical contexts. Regarding canonical context, the theologian ought to read and interpret the passage not only in its individual context but also with respect to its context in the entirety of Scripture. This means that the theologian should seek to understand the intertextual resonances of a particular passage,[34] as well as its place in the economy, or narrative,[35] of Scripture.

---

[29]Although see Allen and Swain, "In Defense of Proof-texting," in *Reformed Catholicity*, 117-42.

[30]See David Yeago, "The New Testament and Nicene Dogma," 87-100 in Stephen Fowl, ed. *The Theological Interpretation of Scripture: Classic and Contemporary Readings* (Oxford: Blackwell, 1997).

[31]Wayne Grudem describes (and follows) this method perfectly in his *Systematic Theology*, 21-46, esp. 35-37.

[32]For an example of an intertextual approach to biblical theology that has dogmatic implications (in this case, especially for the doctrine of eschatology), see G. K. Beale, *A New Testament Approach to Biblical Theology: The Unfolding of the Old Testament in the New* (Grand Rapids: Baker Academic, 2011).

[33]For example, it would be difficult to arrive at the doctrine of eternal generation simply through the exegesis of Prov 8:22-31. See my "The Role of Proverbs 8: Eternal Generation and Hermeneutics Ancient and Modern" in Fred Sanders and Scott R. Swain, eds., *Retrieving Eternal Generation* (Grand Rapids: Zondervan Academic, 2017), 44-66.

[34]For instance, with regard to Prov 8 and its referent, one must wrestle with the NT passages that identify Christ as God's Wisdom (esp. 1 Cor 1:24; cf. also Rev 3:14). The early church relied on these kinds of connections in identifying Christ as divine. See, for example, Justin Martyr, *Dial.* 61.1-5; 126.1; and 129.3; and Irenaeus, *Epid.* 43. On other early interpretations of Prov 8, see Manlio Simonetti, "Sull'interpretazione patristica di Proverbi 8, 22," in *Studi sull'Arianesimo* (Rome: Editrice Studium, 1965), 9-87.

[35]For an introduction to the idea of reading "economically" through the lens of Irenaeus's hermeneutic, see John O'Keefe and R. R. Reno, *Sanctified Vision: An Introduction to Early Christian Interpretation of the Bible* (Baltimore: Johns Hopkins University Press, 2005), 33-44.

Biblical patterns: "Son of Man" as an example. For instance, when
we attempt to understand the Son of Man passages in the Gospels, we
must understand those that clearly allude to Daniel 7 in relation to that
OT passage.[36] But intertextual resonances and the canonical context
they provide usually consist of a whole host of interconnected allusions.
So, with respect to Daniel 7, we also need to dig further into its relationship with Daniel 2, since both chapters share many of the same
phrases and serve as the beginning and end of a linguistic *inclusio* in the
book (they start and end the Aramaic section of Daniel).[37] And once we
have drawn the appropriate textual connections between Daniel 7 and
Daniel 2, we must dig even further into the host of allusions Daniel 2
makes to other OT passages and themes, particularly with respect to the
temple.[38] Thus understanding what "Son of Man" means for the purposes of formulating a Christology is not limited to exegeting those
Gospel passages alone, nor is it limited to noting the connection to
Daniel 7 and exegeting that passage as well. Rather, understanding "Son
of Man" entails understanding an entire intertextual matrix of OT allusions and echoes.

Additionally, the "Son of Man" language requires interpretation in
Scripture's narrative context. This is a key element in the pro-Nicenes'
formulation of what we now call Trinitarian orthodoxy. Rather than
"Son" in its various uses, including but not limited to "Son of Man," indicating some kind of ontological subordination, the narrative of
Scripture teaches that God the Son took on human flesh and only in that
act within the economy of redemption does he *become* a servant.

---

[36]For a thorough discussion of the Son of Man language and its meaning in the Gospels, and
specifically in Mk 13, see N. T. Wright, *Jesus and the Victory of God*, Christian Origins and the
Question of God 2 (Minneapolis: Fortress Press, 1996), 512-19.

[37]On the literary structure of Daniel, see James M. Hamilton, *With the Clouds of Heaven: The Book
of Daniel in Biblical Theology*, NSBT 32 (Downers Grove, IL: IVP Academic, 2014), 61-83.

[38]For a discussion of the relationship of Daniel 7's Son of Man to rest of Daniel, as well as
to the temple, see Hamilton, *With the Clouds of Heaven*, 135-54. I first encountered the
specific connections between Daniel 7 and Daniel 2 and their relationship to the temple,
however, in one of my seminary professor's OT notes. Robert L. Cole, unpublished class
notes on Daniel.

Philippians 2:5-11 is crucial in this regard, as it provides biblical support for bifurcating the life of the Son *ad intra* and *ad extra*.[39] Eternally, he exists in "the form of God," that is, as the second person of the Godhead; only in the incarnation does he take on "the form of a servant." Thus when we read titles like "Son of Man" or "Son of God," it is important that we apply this narratival, or economic, principle in understanding how the Son *became* obedient in the incarnation.[40]

Finally, with respect to actual patterns of biblical language, we move from "Son of Man" language to the broader pattern of Father/Son language from which the church fathers derived the doctrine of eternal generation.[41] While there are only a few passages that may link Father/Son language with the eternal generation of the Son (e.g., Prov 8:22-31;[42] Jn 5:26[43]), eternal generation arose out of reflection on the divine names. "Father" and "Son" imply a certain relationship, one in which the person of the Father generates, or communicates the divine essence to, the Son. And because the Son is eternal (as is the Father), this relationship does not have a starting or stopping point—thus *eternal* generation.[44] This lynchpin of Nicene orthodoxy was not formulated primarily via exegeting one or a few verses (although that certainly was included in the pro-Nicenes' theological reflection), but instead was forged through

---

[39]For an introduction to the hermeneutical strategies of the pro-Nicenes, including attention to the divine names, the economy of Scripture, and partitive exegesis, see Lewis Ayres, *Nicaea and Its Legacy: An Approach to Fourth-Century Trinitarian Theology* (Oxford: Oxford University Press, 2004), esp. 111-14.

[40]This is referred to as "partitive exegesis," on which see John Behr, *The Nicene Faith, Part I, Formation of Christian Theology* 2 (Crestwood, NY: St. Vladimir's Seminary Press, 2004), 208-15; and Matthew R. Crawford, *Cyril of Alexandria's Trinitarian Theology of Scripture*, Oxford Early Christian Studies (Oxford: Oxford University Press, 2014), 13-17. See also Ayres, *Nicaea and Its Legacy*, 106.

[41]For example, Athanasius, *C. Ar.* I.5.16; Basil, *Spir. Sanct.* 7.17, 8.19, 9.22, 17.43, 18.14. See Khaled Anatolios, *Retrieving Nicaea: The Development and Meaning of Trinitarian Doctrine* (Grand Rapids: Baker Academic, 2011), 110-14.

[42]On Prov 8:22-31, see my "The Role of Proverbs 8."

[43]On pro-Nicene interpretation of Jn 5:26, see Ayres, *Nicaea and Its Legacy*, 152.

[44]For a demonstration of these hermeneutical commitments (including the eternality of the divine processions) and their relevance for the development of the doctrine of eternal generation, see Anatolios, *Retrieving Nicaea*, 140-204.

noticing the patterns of language that occur throughout Scripture regarding the names of the first and second persons of the Triune God—Father and Son.

The biblical patterns for the descent. When we ask what biblical warrant exists for the descent, then, we must pay attention not only to the exegesis of particular verses, like 1 Peter 3:18-22 and 4:6,[45] but also to the patterns of biblical language related to Christ's time in the tomb. Examples include inner-biblical allusions between texts describing Christ's burial and OT descriptions of Sheol, Christ's own testimony of his time in the tomb as the "sign of Jonah," and reflections on biblical anthropology and its impact on how we view Christ's burial for three days (more on each of these and others in chapters two and three). Additionally, the history of biblical interpretation can aid us in our search for an accurate summary of biblical language, and in this respect the early church is replete with reflections on Christ's burial.[46] When we ask for the biblical warrant for the descent, then, it is important to consider how the communion of saints has answered that question, not only in terms of their exegesis of individual passages but also with respect to how they read the Bible as an intertextual, narratival, and canonical whole.

Attending to patterns across various doctrines. Another consideration regarding theological decision-making lies with properly dogmatic questions. That is, sometimes our conclusions about a particular doctrine rests on what impact our articulation of it will have on other doctrinal loci.[47] Further, we must ask whether the payoff for affirming a certain doctrine is worth the impact it will have on other, perhaps

---

[45]And as we will see in chapters two and three, these two verses were not even used for support of the descent until the beginning of the third century, at which point the descent had been ubiquitously affirmed for the first century of the postapostolic church's life via reflection on other texts of Scripture.

[46]For a summary, with citations for additional readings, see Bass, *Battle for the Keys*, 1-19.

[47]See, for example, the discussion of dyothelitism and prior theological commitments that bear on its articulation in R. Lucas Stamps, *"Thy Will Be Done": A Contemporary Defense of Two Wills Christology* (Minneapolis: Fortress Press, forthcoming).

more important, doctrines. So, for instance, regarding the question of kenotic Christologies and/or monothelitism, how would such articulations of the hypostatic union affect our Trinitarian formulations? If either of them, or both, imply trithelitism for the Trinity, is that modification of classic Trinitiarianism worth it for the sake of affirming, say, monothelitism?

These kinds of questions could be multiplied for a whole host of doctrinal formulations and their impact elsewhere in systematics. The point here is that, when we formulate our understanding of particular doctrines, we must ask what impact our understanding of biblical teaching on a particular subject has on other dogmatic loci. Christian theology is a fabric,[48] and when we pull on one thread—the descent, for instance—it impacts other doctrines and the way we formulate them.[49] For this reason, it is important that we ask how dismissing or significantly altering a particular doctrine will affect the entirety of Christian theology. And the more important and foundational the doctrine is, the more important it is to be cautious in our attempts to revise or excise that doctrine. So, while the descent may not be a primary question, it is an important one.

Patterns in practical theology. Finally, in asking what is biblical, we must pay attention not only to the dogmatic impact of our formulation but also to its pastoral and contextual implications. That is to say, doctrinal formulation is always performed in a particular sociohistorical context, and therefore it must be conversant with the issues of the day and the impact it will have on them.[50] For instance, in the chapter on anthropology, we will explore the mind-body problem, a question endemic not only to Christian theology but, more generally, to philosophy

---

[48]Richard Lints, *The Fabric of Theology: A Prolegomena to Evangelical Theology* (Grand Rapids: Eerdmans, 1993).

[49]See, for example, the way that Thiselton explores the intersection of hermeneutics and doctrinal loci, including how different loci impinge upon one another in Part III of his *The Hermeneutics of Doctrine*, 177-581.

[50]See the discussion about the audiences of theology in Cornelis van der Kooi and Gijsbert van den Brink, *Christian Dogmatics: An Introduction* (Grand Rapids: Eerdmans, 2017), 5-7.

and biology. We therefore must put our theological reflection on the descent in conversation with this pressing modern question. That is not to say that we should put the secular cart before the scriptural and dogmatic horse, allowing philosophy or biology to dictate the terms to Christian theology. Rather, our contemporary context at least means that as we speak about God, we must speak also to and with our world.

The above methodological considerations, then, will guide us as we work through the biblical, historical, and theological rationale for affirming the descent doctrine. Chapters two and three will be crucial in this regard, as they attempt to provide a biblical and historical defense of the descent. And the rest of the book demonstrates the theological and practical implications of this largely overlooked doctrine.

PURPOSE AND STRUCTURE

This book is therefore an attempt to recapture a doctrine neglected in many evangelical circles today—Christ's descent to the dead—via biblical, historical, dogmatic, and practical reflection. In chapters two and three, we will survey the biblical and historical evidence for the descent clause and provide a working definition of the phrase "he descended to the dead" based on that evidence. These historical and biblical arguments are intertwined, and so I will begin by demonstrating the common biblical arguments for the descent as they are found throughout church history. This will answer the objection about a lack of biblical warrant and also address 1 Peter 3:18-22. Then, in the next chapter, we will map the various ways that Christians have confessed the descent throughout church history, demonstrating particularly in analysis of patristic writings that the Harrowing of Hell concept, which relies on an extrapolated cosmology of hell and holds that Christ emptied the first level of hell (the so-called *limbus patrum*, or Limbo of the Fathers) of at least virtuous Jews and pagans via the *preparatio evangelicum*, is not necessary to or found among the earliest or most universally accepted understandings of the confession that Jesus descended to the dead.[51] This will bring us to an exploration of the insertion of the phrase into the Apostles' Creed. After these biblical and historical explorations, we will again and with support define the phrase "he descended to the dead" as the confession that Jesus experienced human death as all humans do—his body buried and his soul departing to the place of the dead—and in so doing, by virtue of his divinity, he defeated death and the grave.[52] While this is perhaps where many evangelicals falter, and while this book was originally conceived as simply a biblical-historical defense of the descent, there has been good work done in this area over the last few years, and it would not be appropriate to retread well-covered ground.[53] Instead, much of the remainder of the book will consist of a biblical-theological reflection on Christ's descent and its impact on other dogmatic loci. In chapter four, we will reflect on the descent's impact on our Trinitarian formulations, especially with respect to the relations of origin and inseparable operations. Chapter five will explore the relationship of the descent to the doctrine of creation, including questions of cosmology, the Promised Land, and the importance of physical burial. Because creation is tied

---

[51]This appears to have been a common objection to the doctrine as a whole in the post-Reformation period; see the discussion in Catherine Ella Laufer, *Hell's Destruction: An Exploration of Christ's Descent to the Dead* (Surrey: Ashgate, 2013).

[52]Interestingly, Grudem makes the following qualifying remark in his article on excising the creedal clause:

> These texts indicate, then, that Christ in his death experienced the same things believers in this present age experience when they die: His dead body remained on earth and was buried (as ours will be), but his spirit (or soul) passed immediately into the presence of God in heaven (as ours will). Then on the first Easter morning Christ's spirit was reunited with his body and he was raised from the dead, just as Christians who have died will (when Christ returns) be reunited to their bodies and raised in their perfect resurrection bodies to new life.
>
> That fact has pastoral encouragement for us. We need not fear death, not only because eternal life lies on the other side but also because we know that our Savior himself has gone through exactly the same experience we will go through. He has prepared (even sanctified) the way, and we follow him with confidence each step of the way. This is much greater comfort regarding death than could ever be given by any view of a descent into hell.

Grudem, "He Did Not Descend," 113. What Grudem fails to mention (or, perhaps, to realize) is that this is exactly the basic affirmation of the clause throughout the patristic and medieval periods until Jud, Bucer, and Calvin.

[53]See especially Bass, *Battle for the Keys*. If the reader desires an in-depth, historical and exegetical study of the descent, I refer them enthusiastically to this excellent treatment.

closely to the doctrine of humanity, chapter six will narrow our focus to christological anthropology and ask how the descent impacts our understanding of the unity of the human person, the intermediate state, and the nature of the body-soul relation.

Chapters seven and eight ask how the descent impacts soteriology and ecclesiology. For the former, the descent has perennial issues regarding what exactly happens in it, as well as who it affects. Here, then, we will explore the nature of paradise, Christ's work on Holy Saturday, and the relationship between penal substitution and *Christus victor* in light of the descent. Regarding ecclesiology, or soteriology applied, we will explore the Sabbatarian nature of the descent, its relationship to baptism, and its relation to the doctrine of the communion of the saints. To end our biblical-theological reflection, the descent's relationship with eschatology will be examined in chapter nine, with particular focus on the intermediate state, the resurrection of the dead, and the timing of the millennium. A final chapter will explore the practical implications of our understanding of the descent, including for hermeneutics, liturgy, creedal recitation, pastoral care, and mission.

A few caveats are necessary before we begin our exploration of the descent. First, the descent is not a major note in Scripture, nor is it ever portrayed narratively. It happens "off-stage," so to speak.[54] Of course, the actual resurrection also occurs "off-stage," but then the resurrected Jesus strides into the scene as the resurrected Lord. We cannot say the same thing about the descent. But this does not mean it is not taught in Scripture (it is), that it is not important in church history (it is, especially in the patristic and medieval periods), or that it is not creedal (it is).[55] While we should keep in mind that the descent is not as explicit as other doctrines, we will argue that it remains important for Christians today because it is biblically taught and creedally confessed.

---

[54]I am grateful to Fred Sanders for making this observation in his review of an earlier draft of the book.

[55]These points will be argued in chapters two and three.

Second, it is important to remember that, throughout these individual chapters, our aim is not to provide an exhaustive treatment of either the descent or its relation to the topics under consideration, but rather to demonstrate how this particular doctrine fits into and impinges upon other Christian beliefs, and particularly how so for evangelicals.[56] As the reader will see in the footnotes and the main text of some of the chapters, there has been sustained reflection on the descent in other traditions, particularly Roman Catholicism and Eastern Orthodoxy. I do not wish to suggest or to give the impression that this book is the only recent reflection on this topic or that it covers the descent exhaustively. There is still work to be done with respect to an updated and extensive study of the history of the doctrine, especially during the medieval period; an exploration of the descent's place in Christian liturgies, both historically and prescriptively for today; and more extensive and focused studies on the many of the topics explored in this book (e.g., the descent and the *extra Calvinisticum*, or the descent and the millennium).

I also recognize that, while I consider this a retrieval project, not all Christians will agree with all of my conclusions. Again, my goal is not to provide either a definitive or an exhaustive treatment of the descent but to recover its confession and importance, and particularly for evangelicals. This qualification is especially important in the second half of the book, beginning in chapter four. There are a host of issues I touch on in chapters four and following, such as universalism, purgatory, the extent of the atonement, the millennium, and the like, that have a wide variety of understandings both within evangelicalism and outside of it. I do not pretend to have a last word on any of those issues, although I have done my best to speak clearly to them from consideration of the descent and, most importantly, from the teaching of Scripture. Readers

---

[56]In this regard, it is important to point out that the majority of "scholarly conversation" in the book occurs in chapters two and three, and in the chapters that deal with topics typically covered in discussions of the descent by other traditions (namely, soteriology).

should not feel as though they have to follow me on our conclusions about any of those issues to see the larger point of the book, which is that the descent is an important piece in the fabric of Christian theology and impinges upon our understanding of various other dogmatic issues.

Thus my goal in this biblical-theological exploration is simple: to recover the doctrine of the descent for evangelicals today. I hope that this book serves as a motivation for further reflection on the descent, not as some kind of final word either in scope or in argument. It is therefore my desire that the following will assist the reader in seeing the biblical rationale for the descent, its importance in relation to the other loci of Christian theology, and its practical implications for Christians today. The descent is, in my opinion, a beautiful doctrine that not only fits into the fabric of Christian theology but is also integral to that fabric. While some may believe we can simply discard the descent, it is my conviction that this doctrine, held ubiquitously for the first 1500 years of the church's life, is an integral one for the health of Christian theology and practice.

"HE DESCENDED
TO THE DEAD"

A Biblical Defense of the Descent

The most common criticism of the descent clause is that it is unbiblical. And while there are other criticisms of the doctrine, to identify
a doctrine as "unbiblical" among evangelicals is, if substantiated, a
death knell for a particular belief. Charges that the descent doctrine
lacks biblical support usually take one of two forms,[1] although these
are not mutually exclusive. Some theologians posit that the descent
rests on 1 Peter 3:18-22, a passage that, in their opinion, upon careful
exegesis, does not yield support for the descent.[2] Another argument
is that the descent teaches that Jesus entered (and in some articulations, was tormented in) and then emptied hell, a teaching not

---

[1]There are others besides these. Perhaps the most common besides the two main ones
discussed in this chapter is that "he descended to the dead" is redundant with "he
was buried." According to Justin W. Bass, "Zwingli's Zurich colleague Leo Jud (AD
1482–1542) in a 1534 catechism and Martin Bucer (AD 1491–1551) were the first to
argue that the *Descensus* meant merely that Christ descended to the grave (burial)."
See his *The Battle for the Keys: Revelation 1:18 and Christ's Descent into the Underworld*, Paternoster Biblical Monographs (Eugene, OR: Wipf and Stock, 2014), 18.
For further discussion of the historic meaning of the descent, see chapter three
of this book.

[2]Wayne A. Grudem, "Christ Preaching Through Noah: 1 Peter 3:19-20 in the Light
of Dominant Themes in Jewish Literature," *TrinJ* 7 (1986): 3-31; see also John S.
Feinberg, "1 Peter 3:18-20, Ancient Mythology, and the Intermediate State," *WTJ*
48 (1986): 303-36.

found in Scripture.[3] A defense of the descent, then, must deal with these two charges.[4]

But these attempts to discredit the doctrine can be answered on two levels, both of which are important in defending the descent. First, one must ask if these objections arise from an accurate reading of the church's confession about the descent's meaning. If these objections to the descent arise from a faulty understanding of how it has been believed throughout church history—if they arise from some doctrinal opponent of our own making—then it is not the descent that is unbiblical but a recently constructed straw man. And indeed, this is what we find, at least in part, when we survey church history in light of both of these objections. 1 Peter 3:18-22 is certainly not the only biblical passage or exegetical argument used to support the descent, nor is it in many cases the crux of a theologian's argument for the doctrine.[5] Second, with respect to the objection that the descent means Jesus entered into the place of torment and released those in it, we need to make clear that this concept is not necessary, universal, nor earliest (at least with respect to entering the place of torment) in confessions about the descent.[6]

This chapter explores the evidence that these modern objections are unfounded given a close reading of Scripture. To put it positively, the *descensus* is a thoroughly biblical doctrine, which teaches that Jesus experienced human death as all humans do—his body was buried,[7] and

---

[3]This is also discussed repeatedly in Wayne A. Grudem, "He Did Not Descend into Hell: A Plea for Following Scripture Instead of the Apostles' Creed," *JETS* 34.1 (1991): 103-13.

[4]For an introduction to a biblical case for the descent and one that is similar to the basic contours of my argument here, see Michael F. Bird, *What Christians Ought to Believe: An Introduction to Christian Doctrine Through the Apostles' Creed* (Grand Rapids: Zondervan, 2016), 143-46.

[5]No one cited 1 Pet 3:18-22 in discussions of the descent until Clement of Alexandria in AD 200, but the doctrine was already regularly discussed in the first century. See Justin W. Bass, *The Battle for the Keys: Revelation 1:18 and Christ's Descent into the Underworld*, Paternoster Biblical Monographs (Eugene, OR: Wipf and Stock, 2014), 85.

[6]See on this both chapters three and seven.

[7]I am not ruling out cremation or other means of taking care of a dead body. I use *buried* both because of its normalcy in ancient Jewish life and because it is what happens to Jesus' body. In other words, Jesus experiencing "death as all humans do" does not mean that all humans are

his soul departed to the place of the dead[8]—and, in so doing, by virtue of his divinity, he defeated death and the grave. This core confession is biblically supported and historically warranted, given the way the church has confessed that Jesus "descended to the dead" for the last two millennia. These scriptural arguments form the foundation for the chapters that follow, which evaluate the history of the doctrine and explore both the doctrine itself and its connections to the whole of Christian theology and practice.

THE DESCENT'S BIBLICAL CRUX

Contrary to some modern detractors, 1 Peter 3:18-22 is not the only passage upon which the doctrine of the descent is based.[9] In fact, the biblical support for the descent, when surveyed throughout church history, consists of a tapestry made of inner-biblical allusions, Jesus' own and the apostles' testimony to the work of redemption, and patterns of biblical language. Additionally, the Bible's historical background, including ancient Near Eastern (ANE) concepts of death, Second Temple Judaism, and Greco-Roman thought, points to at least the core understanding of the descent outlined above. In what follows, we will argue that a variety of NT texts teach the descent, and also that

---

buried, only that all humans upon death have dead bodies that need to be cared for and interred in some manner.

[8]Specifically, he departs to the place of the righteous dead, otherwise known as paradise or Abraham's bosom. In many Second Temple Jewish cosmographies the place of the dead contained all the dead but was compartmentalized between the righteous, unrighteous, and fallen angels. This means that while all the dead went to the same place, so to speak, they also were separated from the other dead and the fallen angels. Thus the New Testament can speak of the dead being able to communicate across compartments but also separated from one another (e.g., Lk 16:19-31; and, as I will argue later, 1 Pet 3:18-22). As we will argue below, this means that Jesus' descent is a referent to him descending to the place of the dead, and specifically to the place of the righteous dead (paradise), but also in such a way that he proclaims victory to all the dead by virtue of the commonality of the place of the dead. This will be argued in detail below and in chapter six.

[9]"Clement of Alexandria was the first to directly cite 1 Peter 3:18-22 in support of the descent in AD 200. The doctrine of the *Descensus* arose independently of 1 Peter 3:18-22; 4:6 as early as Ignatius as a result of such texts as Matthew 12:40; 27:52-53; Acts 2:27, 31; and Ephesians 4:8-10." Bass, *Battle for the Keys*, 85. See similar comments in 11n46.

1 Peter 3:18-22 can be plausibly read as referring to the descent. Again, though, the doctrine does not stand or fall on any single one of these texts, including 1 Peter 3.

BIBLICAL AND HISTORICAL BACKGROUNDS REGARDING THE PLACE OF THE DEAD

Before we turn to specific NT texts that teach the descent, it is important to understand their context in ANE, Greco-Roman, and OT thought about death and the afterlife.

The afterlife according the Old Testament. Philip S. Johnston in his *Shades of Sheol* exemplifies a common contemporary portrayal of ancient Jewish beliefs about the afterlife as expressed in the Old Testament.[10] Johnston argues that the Old Testament does not explicitly teach a conscious intermediate state, but instead "death and its aftermath were of little concern."[11] Sheol is "predominately associated with the wicked in the Hebrew Bible" and "there is no clearly articulated alternative to Sheol, no other destiny whose location is named, no other fate whose situation is described, however briefly. So the majority of Israelites may well have envisaged no alternative."[12] This argument that the Old Testament is relatively uninterested in the afterlife due to its focus on life in the Promised Land, and therefore also gives scant attention to the intermediate state (if any at all), is common in biblical studies today.[13] But at least two recent monographs have demonstrated that this scholarly edifice should at least be reexamined, if not torn down.[14]

---

[10]Philip S. Johnston, *Shades of Sheol: Death and Afterlife in the Old Testament* (Downers Grove, IL: IVP Academic, 2002).

[11]Johnston, *Shades of Sheol*, 70.

[12]Johnston, *Shades of Sheol*, 199.

[13]This kind of argument has also many times come laden with the Hellenization thesis, i.e. the idea that Israel only began to care about an afterlife when it encountered Greek thought. An example of this comes in William A. Irwin, "The Hebrews," in *The Intellectual Adventure of Ancient Man: An Essay on Speculative Thought in the Ancient Near East*, ed. Henri Frankfort et al. (1946; Chicago: The University of Chicago Press, 1977), 263-65 (223-362).

[14]In addition to the two recent monographs discussed in the following paragraphs, see also the comments of Friedman and Overton:

First, Richard Steiner has argued that there is evidence that *nephesh* does not only mean "life" (a common piece of data used to argue for the above view about the Old Testament and the afterlife) but can in some instances legitimately refer to "soul" as distinct from a person's body. He also argues that there are other meanings to Sheol besides the ones Johnston and others marshal as evidence for their view of the OT conception of death and the afterlife (or lack thereof).[15]

Second, Christopher B. Hays's recent book *A Covenant with Death* argues that ancient Egyptian, Mesopotamian, and Ugaritic cultures had conceptions of death and the afterlife that included conscious existence, interaction with the living, and certain levels of comfort or blessedness that could be achieved. He also demonstrates that these cultures had various means of interacting with and influencing ancient Israel (specifically eighth-century Israel), and that there are at least some texts in the Old Testament that imply that kind of cultural context. While Hays is careful not to press the evidence too far, his book ably demonstrates that the texts in the Old Testament that speak

---

We have few unquestionable references to life after death in the Hebrew Bible. . . . This whisper is faint enough to make people, especially nonspecialists, imagine that there is virtually no belief in afterlife in constitutive biblical religion or in early biblical Israel thereafter. . . . But we *know* that there was belief in an afterlife in Israel. The combination of the archaeological record and the references that we do have in the text leave little room for doubt.

Richard Elliott Friedman and Shawna Dolansky Overton, "Death and Afterlife: The Biblical Silence," in *Judaism in Late Antiquity*, vol. 4: *Death, Life-After-Death, Resurrection and the World-to-Come in the Judaisms of Late Antiquity*, ed. Alan J. Avery-Peck and Jacob Neusner (Leiden: Brill, 2000), 35-36 (35-59).

Friedman and Overton in the remainder of the chapter survey the relevant archaeological and textual evidence, including—with respect to the latter—some pieces of data that are not usually considered in this discussion. In addition to Friedman and Overton's essay, see also the remaining essays in the book for discussion of death in the Judaisms of late antiquity, including explorations of specific biblical corpora. See also Roland de Vaux, *Ancient Israel: Its Life and Institutions*, trans. John McHugh (1961; London: Darton, Longman, and Todd, 1998), 56-61; and Philip J. King and Lawrence E. Stager, *Life in Biblical Israel*, Library of Ancient Israel (Louisville, KY: Westminster John Knox, 2001), 363-382, esp. 374-75, for a careful discussion of Sheol in the Old Testament, its relation to the surrounding ANE cultures, its context within Israel's practices surrounding death and burial, and its relation to Israel's affirmation of an afterlife.

[15]Richard C. Steiner, *Disembodied Souls: The Nefesh in Israel and Kindred Spirits in the Ancient Near East, with an Appendix on the Katumura Inscription*, Ancient Near Eastern Monographs (Atlanta: SBL Press, 2015).

about the dead and the afterlife in a negative fashion may not be carte blanche statements about those elements but rather, polemical reactions to the surrounding cultures' misconceptions about or misapplications of the truths about what happens to a person at death. Further, in that kind of cultural climate, texts like Isaiah 14 stand out as more in line with cultural expectations than out of step with them.[16] In addition to these two monographs, we could also point to more positive statements, like Abraham and Jacob being "gathered to their fathers," the latter *before* his bodily burial (i.e., the two are not equivalent), as evidence for some kind of assumed conscious intermediate state.[17] It should not be assumed, then, that the Old Testament does not teach a conscious afterlife or that the afterlife could not be anything other than a shadowy, miserable existence.[18]

Second Temple Judaism and the place of the dead. Regarding Greco-Roman understandings of the afterlife, the New Testament differs significantly at points[19] but also shares some crucial elements in common, namely, viewing the world with three tiers—the lowest being the place of the dead—and portraying salvific descents to the place of

---

[16]Christopher B. Hays, *A Covenant with Death: Death in the Iron Age II and Its Rhetorical Uses in Proto-Isaiah* (Grand Rapids: Eerdmans, 2011). The portraits given of the ANE background (see especially 55-56, 89-91, 131-32) demonstrate that, e.g., Is 14 actually has much in common with other ANE cultures, particularly Mesopotamian and Syrian-Palestinian, in terms of the focus on kingship in the underworld and some kind of conscious existence.

[17]See, for instance, Paul R. Williamson, *Death and the Afterlife: Biblical Perspectives on Ultimate Questions*, NSBT 44 (Downers Grove, IL: IVP Academic, 2018), 39-40.

[18]For an argument similar to Hays but abbreviated and more generally concerned with the entire Old Testament rather than just the prophet Isaiah's eighth-century context, see Williamson, *Death and the Afterlife*, 7-14, 38-40. Williamson deals not only with Isaiah 14 but also with other important texts related to the Old Testament's acknowledgement of some kind of conscious intermediate state and in relation to other ANE beliefs and practices (e.g., 1 Sam 28 in relation to necromancy, a common practice in ANE cultures). See also the older study of Robert Martin-Achard, *From Death to Life: A Study of the Development of the Doctrine of the Resurrection in the Old Testament*, trans. John Penney Smith (Edinburgh: Oliver and Boyd, 1960), esp. 17-47 for conceptions of the dead and the place of the dead in relation to Israel's ANE context.

[19]For a comparison of beliefs about the afterlife in Greco-Roman thought and Second Temple Judaism, as well as their relation to the New Testament, see N. T. Wright, *The Resurrection of the Son of God* (Christian Origins and the Question of God 3; Minneapolis: Fortress Press, 2003), 1-206.

the dead.[20] Of course, even those common elements differ with both Second Temple Judaism and the New Testament. On the other hand, the New Testament's conception of the place of the dead is not all that different from Second Temple Judaism. The concept of the afterlife in Jewish thought progressed from simply reflecting on the commonality of death and the fact that the dead remain dead to expressing explicit hope in a general resurrection of Israel (e.g., Ezek 36–37)[21] that included a resurrection of individual bodies (Dan 12:1-2).[22] This kind of progression continued in the Second Temple literature, where we see the dead compartmentalized, or separated, between the righteous and unrighteous and experiencing a foretaste of their eternal fate, whether punishment or reward. These ideas are found mostly in apocalyptic literature, although there are some nonapocalyptic works that discuss these issues. The subgenre that developed out of Jewish reflection on the afterlife is the "Tours of Hell," and in texts that contain a tour we see that these Second Temple Jewish works affirmed an intermediate state, compartmentalization of the righteous and unrighteous, proleptic punishments and rewards, and a hope for the general resurrection of the dead.[23]

---

[20]On Greco-Roman descents to the dead, see Richard Bauckham, *The Fate of the Dead: Studies on the Jewish and Christian Apocalypses*, NovTSup 93 (Atlanta: SBL Press, 1998), 19-32.

[21]Of course, the pattern of death and resurrection existed seemingly from early on in Jewish thought, since stories of near-death experiences followed by God restoring those persons to life happen throughout the Old Testament; e.g., John D. Levenson, *The Death and Resurrection of the Beloved Son: Transformation of Child Sacrifice in Judaism and Christianity* (New Haven, CT: Yale University Press, 1995); and Williamson, *Death and the Afterlife*, 74-83. We want to insist, therefore, that while we note the progression of Israel's thought concerning the afterlife in various places, it is a *coherent* progression. That is, Israel's later thought does not contradict her earlier thought and vice versa, but rather they are both pieces of a whole cloth (along with the New Testament) that together provide a full and coherent picture.

[22]On this progression and the theological rationales for them, see, for example, Terrence Nichols, *Death and Afterlife: A Theological Introduction* (Grand Rapids: Brazos, 2010), 19-27; and Joseph Ratzinger, *Eschatology: Death and Eternal Life*, 2nd ed. (Washington, DC: Catholic University of America Press, 1988), 78-84, 113-14.

[23]On the development of this type of literature, especially in the genre of apocalypse, see Martha Himmelfarb, *Tours of Hell: An Apocalyptic Form in Jewish and Christian Literature* (Philadelphia: Fortress Press, 1983). See also Bauckham, *Fate of the Dead*, 33-38, 49-96.

The compartments are particularly important for our purposes, since they will impact how we understand Jesus' descent. Bass lists three: paradise, or Abraham's bosom;[24] the abyss, or Tartarus;[25] and Gehenna, or the lake of fire.[26] The former is the place where righteous saints dwell, both in the intermediate state (Abraham's bosom, "paradise" in Lk 23:43[27] and 2 Cor 12:3) and in the new heavens and new earth (Rev 2:7), while the latter is used to refer to the place where the unrighteous experience final judgment (Dan 7:9-10; Mt 25:41; Rev 20:10, 13-15; 21:8). The middle term can be used as a reference to the general realm of the dead ("abyss," see Rom 10:7) or for the prison that holds fallen angels. This latter use, aside from Romans 10:7, is its exclusive usage in the New Testament (Lk 8:31; Rev 9:1, 2, 11; 11:7; 17:8; 20:1, 3). And, according to Bass, "The Abyss is also predominately understood as the dwelling place of fallen angels (demons) in the underworld throughout the intertestamental literature."[28] Here, these demons await final judgment, in which they will be thrown into the third compartment, the lake of fire (Rev 20:13-15).

This provides background for NT texts like Luke 16:19-31, which, when seen against the above Second Temple Jewish backdrop,[29] appears

---

[24]Bass, *Battle for the Keys*, 47-56; as well as Justin W. Bass, "Paradise," in *The Lexham Bible Diction-ary*, ed. John D. Barry (Bellingham, WA: Lexham Press, 2016). On compartmentalization of the underworld, see also Williamson, *Death and the Afterlife*, 48.

[25]Bass, *Battle for the Keys*, 56-59.

[26]Bass, *Battle for the Keys*, 59-61.

[27]Not everyone agrees that this text contains Jesus affirming the common Second Temple Jewish view of the afterlife. For a recent example of arguments against this view, see Kim Papaioannou, *The Geography of Hell in the Teaching of Jesus: Gehena, Hades, the Abyss, the Outer Darkness Where There is Weeping and Gnashing of Teeth* (Eugene, OR: Pickwick, 2013).

[28]Bass, *Battle for the Keys*, 56-57.

[29]So Bass:

> During the Second Temple period, paradise was one of the primary locales for the righteous in the afterlife. The Testament of Levi presents the Messiah opening the "gates of paradise" for the saints (*T. Levi* 18.10-11). This is the earliest example of a religious use of "paradise" outside of the Old Testament (Jeremias, *TDNT*, 5.765). Paradise is the dwelling place of the righteous dead in the afterlife. Paradise may have been:
> - The Underworld (*1 En.* 22; *4 Ezra* 4:7-8; 7:37, 38; compare Josephus, *Antiquities* 18.14-15).
> - In the earth (*Jub.* 3.12; 4.26; 8.16, 19; compare Origen, *First Principles* 2.11.6).
> - In heaven (*1 En.* 60.8; 65.2; 70.3; 89.52; *Pss. Sol.* 14.2-3; *2 En.* 8-9; *L.A.E.* 37.5).
> The word *paradise* only occurs in the New Testament three times (Lk 23:43; 2 Cor 12:3; Rev 2:7). In Paul's writings, paradise is presented as synonymous with the third heaven

to be a clear NT case of a "tour of heaven and hell."[30] It also should affect how we understand 1 Peter 3:19 and its reference to "spirits in prison."[31] In other words, when the New Testament speaks about "the dead," it has a specific background, one that affirms "the [place of the] dead" as a location containing the disembodied souls of both the righteous and unrighteous (albeit in separate compartments).[32] This lends credence to the idea that when the NT writers and later the creeds speak about Christ's resurrection "from the dead," they mean not only from the state of being dead but from the place of the dead and from among the dead ones (disembodied souls).

Particularly important in this regard is 1 Corinthians 15. This chapter, in which Paul explicates the importance of Jesus' bodily resurrection, contains many references to "the dead." Especially pertinent to our discussion are verses 20 and 27. In 1 Corinthians 15:20, Paul speaks of Christ being raised "from the dead" (ἐκ νεκρῶν), a phrase that typically

---

(2 Cor 12:2, 4). In Revelation, it is synonymous with the New Jerusalem (Rev 2:7; 21:2). This shows the transferable nature of the term παράδεισος (*paradeisos*) in the New Testament. Paradise is clearly distinguished from "heaven" (τοῦ οὐρανοῦ, *tou ouranou*) in Rev 21:2, but Paul equates paradise and heaven (2 Cor 12:2, 4).

The book of Luke presents Jesus stating that he will see the man crucified next to Him in paradise, that day (Lk 23:43), but it also includes Peter's statement that Christ's soul dwelt in Hades between His death and resurrection (Acts 2:27, 31). This may suggest that Luke considered paradise to be the abode of the righteous in the Underworld (compare *1 En.* 22; *4 Ezra* 4:7-8; 7:37, 38; Josephus, *Antiquities* 18.14-15). Paradise could also be a transferable locale in the New Testament because the presence of Christ is what makes the reality paradise.

• The criminal was with Christ in paradise in the Underworld on Good Friday.
• Paul visited paradise in the third heaven where Christ currently dwells (2 Cor 12:2, 4; Phil 1:21-26; 3:20).
• The saints enter paradise in the New Jerusalem because the Lamb (Christ) will dwell there forever and ever (Rev 2:7; 21:22; 22:1-5, 14).

Bass, "Paradise." Thanks to Steve Stanley for pointing me to this reference.
[30]See Matthew Ryan Hauge, *The Biblical Tour of Hell*, LNTS 485 (London: Bloomsbury, 2013), esp. 99-154; also Williamson, *Death and the Afterlife*, 52-55.
[31]Bass, *Battle for the Keys*, 59.
[32]I mean this and all other spatial references to the place of the dead and its compartments metaphorically. There is good reason to think the ancient world also viewed their language about cosmography to be flexible and thus not necessarily indicative of a literalistic meaning. In other words, just because the NT writers use the concept of a three-tiered universe doesn't mean they believe that the underworld is physically below the earth. They could simply be using spatial language for nonspatial realities. I argue thus in chapter six.

indicates the location of the place of the dead. Further, Paul goes on to speak about Christ's subjection of all rulers and authorities through his death and resurrection, a subjection that appears both to have already happened (1 Cor 15:27) and to happen consummately at his return (1 Cor 15:24-28). Here Paul appears to be saying that through Christ's death, burial, and resurrection (1 Cor 15:3-5), he has put death under his feet. We see this again in 1 Corinthians 15:54-57, where death is defeated because of the work of Christ. This will be important later when we ask what happened at the descent, but for now it is important to note that Christ's victory is accomplished through his death, burial, and resurrection, a resurrection that brings Christ up from the place of the dead (ἐκ νεκρῶν).

While the cosmography assumed by the New Testament and the descent's relation to it will be discussed in detail in chapter five, here we can summarize the conceptual background for the NT texts related to Christ's descent in the following way. First, Sheol in the Old Testament and Hades in the LXX and in Greco-Roman thought can be used to refer to both a general place for all the dead as well as a place of torment or consignment for the unrighteous. Second, this place was normally located under the earth, although it could also be referred to as "beyond the sea" or, in the case of the righteous dead, in the "third heaven." Third, over time, and especially during Second Temple Judaism, this general place of the dead was increasingly discussed in terms of its compartments, namely one for the righteous and another for the unrighteous. The former is often referred to as "paradise" and "Abraham's bosom" in Second Temple literature, while the latter is referred to using terms like "Hades" and "Gehenna." Tartarus, the prison for evil spirits, was also generally conceptualized as a lower portion of the unrighteous compartment of the dead.

Third, these compartments, while separated, are nevertheless in the same place, the place of the dead, and thus there can be communication between them (as illustrated in Jesus' parable of the rich man and

Figure 2.1. Hebrew view of the universe

Lazarus in Lk 16:19-31). Finally, these compartments in the New Testament and in Second Temple Judaism are related to faith in YHWH, as the righteous compartment is filled with those who await the vindication by the Messiah on the last day and the unrighteous compartment, those who await final judgment and eternal torment. These compartments are thus proleptic judgments on their inhabitants.[33]

---

[33]For a summary of the Second Temple and NT conceptions of the afterlife, including the compartmentalization discussed here and the argument that Jesus only descended to Abraham's bosom, or paradise, see Donald G. Bloesch, "Descent into Hell (Hades)," in *Evangelical Dictionary of Theology*, 2nd ed., ed. Walter E. Elwell (Grand Rapids: Baker Academic, 2001), 338-40. Bloesch's essay summarizes well many of the arguments employed in this book, including the

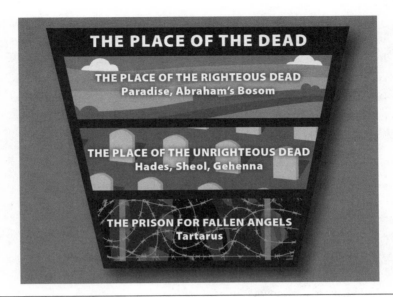

Figure 2.2. The Place of the Dead (Hades, Sheol)

When the New Testament talks about Jesus' descent and all that is accomplished in it, we need to keep this conceptual background in mind. It is to those particular NT texts that we now turn. In sum, these texts teach that when Christ died, he experienced death as all humans do: his body was buried, and his human soul went ("descended") to the place of the dead. He descended to the righteous compartment of the dead ("paradise," Lk 23:43), but he could also communicate with *all* the dead. In this way, he proclaims his victory to those "under the earth" (Phil 2:10).

ACTS 2:25-28 AND PSALM 16:8-11

For proponents of the descent, perhaps the most popular text to which they make an appeal is Acts 2:25-28 and its quotation of Psalm 16:8-11.[34] For the sake of context, Acts 2:22-28 reads:

---

historical background for the descent, the NT data, the theological and creedal development of the descent throughout church history, and the doctrine's theological import.

[34]On this passage, see, for example, Nancy deClaissé-Walford, Rolf A. Jacobson, and Beth LaNeel Tanner, *The Book of Psalms*, NICOT (Grand Rapids: Eerdmans, 2014), 181-82; and John Goldingay,

Men of Israel, hear these words: Jesus of Nazareth, a man attested to you by God with mighty works and wonders and signs that God did through him in your midst, as you yourselves know—this Jesus, delivered up according to the definite plan and foreknowledge of God, you crucified and killed by the hands of lawless men. God raised him up, loosing the pangs of death, because it was not possible for him to be held by it. For David says concerning him,

"I saw the Lord always before me,

for he is at my right hand that I may not be shaken;

therefore my heart was glad, and my tongue rejoiced;

my flesh also will dwell in hope.

For you will not abandon my soul to Hades,

or let your Holy One see corruption.

You have made known to me the paths of life;

you will make me full of gladness with your presence."

Here, in Acts 2:25-28, Peter reads Psalm 16 as a prophecy that points to Christ, a prophecy that speaks of the Messiah's soul in Hades and his body in the grave.[35] In the psalm's original contexts, both historical and literary, the writer is speaking about the same thing as Peter in Acts— that the Messiah's human body will be raised and rejoined with his human soul, previously in Hades.[36] "Corruption" is a reference to bodily

---

Psalms, vol. I: *Psalms 1–41*, BCOTWP (Grand Rapids: Baker Academic, 2006), 233-34. Modern scholars, including those cited, seem reticent to deal with the references to "soul" and "Sheol" here, preferring instead to affirm the unity of the human person and speak in general and holistic terms about the hope of the resurrection.

[35]While Barrett's interpretation of the character of the afterlife is one with which we will disagree in the latter portion of this chapter and in chapter six, he nevertheless notes that Peter seems to be expressing "confidence that God will not allow [his Messiah's] destiny to be that of the inferior, unhappy, existence which was all that men looked forward to after death." In other words, Barrett interprets "soul in Hades" as a reference to a conscious afterlife. C. K. Barrett, *Acts 1–14*, ICC (London: T&T Clark, 1994), 145-46.

[36]Some commentators limit the scope of Ps 16:8-11 to merely saving the psalmist from death. See, for example, the brief comments in the IVP Bible Background Commentary: "In the context this refers to not allowing someone to be put to death at the hand of malicious enemies. The psalmist will not be consigned to Sheol; he will not see decay because his life will

decay,[37] while the phrase "will not abandon my soul to Hades" indicates that God will not allow the Messiah's human soul to remain in Hades.[38] As Augustine says, "Thou wilt neither give My soul for a possession to those parts below."[39]

Because in the Old Testament the Messiah stands with and for Israel,[40] his hope of resurrection is also her hope. There is, in other words, hope of resurrection for the human person in both body and soul. And in Acts, Peter says that Jesus has been raised in just that fashion as Israel's Messiah. At minimum, then, this text affirms that Jesus experienced human death as all humans experience human death, in body and soul. His body was buried, and his soul went to the place of the (righteous) dead.[41]

JESUS AND JONAH

We see this in Jesus' own testimony about his death as well. In conversation with the Pharisees, who challenge Jesus to give them a sign that

---

be spared (see Ps 30:2-3)." John H. Walton, Victor H. Matthews, and Mark W. Chavalas, *The IVP Bible Background Commentary: Old Testament* (Downers Grove, IL: InterVarsity Press, 2000), electronic ed., Ps 16:10. But, as Cyril notes, "He said not, neither wilt Thou suffer Thine Holy One to see death, since then He would not have died; but corruption, saith He, I see not, and shall not abide in death." Cyril of Jerusalem, "The Catechetical Lectures of S. Cyril, Archbishop of Jerusalem" (*NPNF*² 7:95). In other words, if the Psalm were merely about saving life in the face of death, the reference to corruption would make little sense.

[37]See Goldingay, *Psalms*, 233, for a discussion of the lexical issues involved.

[38]This fits with common Jewish conceptions of the afterlife, both in the Psalm's historical and literary contexts, and in Acts. Further, one should not assume that "Hades" means "place of torment"; rather, in this instance, it is probably a reference to the common fate of all people, the place of the dead, which is further compartmentalized between (at least) the righteous and the unrighteous. See the discussion of compartments in the previous section of this chapter. On Acts 2:27, see Williamson, *Death and the Afterlife*, 120n108.

[39]Augustine, "Exposition of the Book of Psalms" (*NPNF*¹ 8:49).

[40]On this aspect of Peter's speech, see William H. Willimon, *Acts*, Interpretation (Louisville, KY: Westminster John Knox, 2010), 34-37.

[41]While the Bible and the Christian tradition use spatial references to refer to the fate of the dead (i.e. of souls separated from their bodies by death), we do not mean by using them that there is an accessible location beyond the sea or under the earth where the dead dwell. These terms are figurative, but nevertheless communicate truths about reality, namely that the souls of the dead are conscious and experience a foretaste of their eternal state in the afterlife. On the anthropological and cosmological aspects of the afterlife, particularly as they relate to the descent, see chapters five, six, and nine.

he is the Messiah, Jesus tells them that the only sign he will give them is the sign of Jonah.[42] Jesus says somewhat cryptically, "For just as Jonah was three days and three nights in the belly of the great fish, so will the Son of Man be three days and three nights in the heart of the earth" (Mt 12:40).[43] For those who deny the descent clause, particularly by saying it is redundant with the confession, "he was buried," this passage teaches merely that Jesus was buried for three days.[44] But if we look at the intertextual connections of this passage with its source, Jonah 2, we find that there is more here than mere bodily burial.

In Jonah 2, Jonah prays to YHWH for deliverance from the depths of the ocean. Then, after the fish is sent to rescue him, he prays again, thanking YHWH for saving him from the depths of the ocean. In both of these prayers, Jonah describes the depths of the ocean as Sheol, the abyss, the place of the dead.[45] While "heart of the sea" and "belly of Sheol" differ

---

[42]For an overview of the interpretive options of this passage, see John Nolland, *The Gospel of Matthew: A Commentary on the Greek Text* (Grand Rapids: Eerdmans, 2005), 511. Nolland also correctly notes that this sign is primarily one of judgment:

> The time in the belly of the sea monster functioned to confirm Jonah (ahead of the actual exercise of his ministry) in his role as a preacher of judgment; the three days in the earth will function to confirm Jesus (at the end of his ministry) as one who has had to declare judgment, inasmuch as his ministry met with rejection, a rejection which culminated in his death.

[43]Some would argue this is a reference to Jesus' resurrection. The context, however, would seem to exclude this as the *exclusive* interpretation, since Jesus is refusing to give them a sign and the resurrection would in fact be a sign. See John Woodhouse, "Jesus and Jonah," *RTR* 43.2 (1984): 35.

[44]While Luz is cautious here, he still maintains this position, saying, "The Son of Man Jesus is 'in the heart of the earth,' that is, probably in the grave; Jesus' descent into hell, important in the church's interpretation, would be singular in the synoptic tradition and is therefore more improbable, although we cannot rule it out." Ulrich Luz, *Matthew: A Commentary*, Hermeneia (Minneapolis: Augsburg, 2001), 217. Others simply do not adjudicate the issue; Morris, for example, focuses on the temporal period of the sign (3 days) and its meaning, rather than on what exactly it means for Jesus to be "in the heart of the earth." He finishes his comments on the verse thus: "However we understand it in detail, the expression indicates that after the crucifixion Jesus will be three days in the tomb." Leon Morris, *The Gospel According to Matthew*, PNTC (Grand Rapids: Eerdmans, 1992), 326. See similar comments, focus, and neglect of what "heart of the earth" means in Craig Blomberg, *Matthew*, NAC 22 (Nashville: Broadman & Holman, 1992), 206.

[45]Billy K. Smith is worth quoting at length here:

> The term "Sheol" was used in various ways. It may be said with certainty that in Hebrew thought the term referred to a place of the dead. It was spoken of as located under the earth (Amos 9:2). Normally those who were in Sheol were seen as separated from God (Ps 88:3; Isa 38:18), yet God was shown to have access to Sheol (Ps 139:8). Sheol was used as an expression for being in the grave (Ps 18:6; 30:3; 49:14; Isa 28:15). With this imagery Jonah here described

with respect to the exact terms used, they are still used here as metaphorical synonyms.[46] In fact, the phrases that are repeated in Matthew 12:40 occur in Jonah 2:4 (LXX) and 2:7 (LXX), both of which make reference or are parallel to Hades/Sheol (Jon 2:2; 2:3 LXX).[47] Consider the following: Matthew 12:40 reads, ὥσπερ γὰρ ἦν Ἰωνᾶς ἐν τῇ κοιλίᾳ τοῦ κήτους τρεῖς ἡμέρας καὶ τρεῖς νύκτας, οὕτως ἔσται ὁ υἱὸς τοῦ ἀνθρώπου ἐν τῇ καρδίᾳ τῆς γῆς τρεῖς ἡμέρας καὶ τρεῖς νύκτας.[48] The quotation is from Jonah 1:17 (2:1 LXX), but the other phrases in Matthew 12:40 also parallel portions of Jonah 2.[49] First, while Jesus says he will go into the heart (καρδίᾳ) of the earth, Jonah is, in Jonah 2:3 (2:4 LXX), cast by the LORD into the heart (καρδίας) of the sea. Further, this reference in Jonah 2:3 (2:4 LXX) is parallel to "the belly of Sheol" in Jonah 2:2 (Jon 2:3 LXX; ἐκ κοιλίας ᾅδου, literally "belly of Hades"). Notice how this phrasing thus lexically connects "belly of the fish" (Jon 1:17; 2:1 LXX), "belly of Sheol" (Jon 2:2; 2:3 LXX), and "heart of the sea" (Jon 2:3; 2:4 LXX).[50] Finally, and perhaps most importantly, Jesus' statement that he will be three days and three nights "in the heart of the earth" (καρδίᾳ τῆς γῆς) finds a clear parallel in Jonah 2:6 (2:7 LXX) with the phrase κατέβην εἰς γῆν ("I went down to the land").[51] Both Jesus (literally) and Jonah (figuratively and symbolically)

---

his experience of being "at the very brink of death." Fretheim agrees that the language used here goes beyond the literal sense, especially regarding Sheol: "Inasmuch as Sheol was believed to be under the floor of the ocean, Jonah was spatially near the place." It also helps to understand at this point that in the Old Testament, death is understood to be more a process than an event. As for Jonah's place in that death process, life had ebbed so much that he could have been reckoned more among the dead than among the living.

Billy K. Smith and Frank S. Page, *Amos, Obadiah, Jonah*, NAC 19B (Nashville: Broadman & Holman, 1995), 245-46.

[46]Marvin A. Sweeney, *The Twelve Prophets*, vol. 1: *Hosea, Joel, Amos, Obadiah, Jonah*, Berit Olam: Studies in Hebrew Narrative and Poetry (Collegeville: Liturgical Press, 2000), 320.

[47]Woodhouse, "Jesus and Jonah," 36.

[48]"For just as Jonah was three days and three nights in the belly of the great fish, so will the Son of Man be three days and three nights in the heart of the earth" (ESV).

[49]On the exegetical points that follow, see Woodhouse, "Jesus and Jonah," 36.

[50]We should also note the later parallels with chaos (Gen 1:2) in Jonah 2:5 (2:6 LXX), on which see Sweeney, *Twelve Prophets*, 321-22.

[51]"[I]n the heart of the earth' [is] a reference to Sheol, the Hebrew underworld." Dominic Rudman, "The Sign of Jonah," *ExpTim* 115.10 (2004): 325. See also Sweeney, who says that, "Verse 7 [NRSV: 6] employs the imagery of descent to Sheol or the netherworld, i.e., he is going down

descend to the depths of the pit, Hades, Sheol, the abyss. These are all synonymous terms in Jonah 2,[52] and the lexical similarities between that chapter and Matthew 12:40 indicate that, "The primary meaning of the 'sign of Jonah' . . . is . . . the correspondence between Jonah's experience in the belly of the sea creature, and Jesus' experience in death, *his* descent to Hades."[53] For these reasons, we could accurately say that Jonah's descent into the belly of the sea, and, derivatively, into the belly of the fish, is figuratively portrayed as his descent to the place of the dead.

This puts Jesus' statement in clearer context. Jesus does not merely compare the timeframe of his death to the timeframe of Jonah's time in the fish, nor is the comparison merely one between Jonah's prophetic ministry and that of Jesus. Rather, Jesus compares himself to Jonah because what happens to them—the former literally and the latter figuratively—is the same. Or, as Nolland puts it, "Both [the belly of the sea monster and the heart of the earth] represent liminal states connected with death."[54] They descend to the place of the dead.[55] Jonah's body is in the fish (grave) while his soul, metaphorically, is in Sheol; Jesus' body is in the heart of the earth (grave) while his soul, literally, is in the place of the dead.[56] And again, it is Jesus himself who affirms this. While we do not want to bifurcate between different parts of Scripture and their levels of inspiration, we also want to

---

to the world of the dead who are barred from reentering the world of the living." Sweeney, *Twelve Prophets,* 321.

[52]As indicated by the intertextual parallels noted in the exegesis above. See also Rudman, "The Sign of Jonah," 326: "it is clear that Jonah's psalm [2:3-10] links imagery of being engulfed by water and of being imprisoned in Sheol."

[53]Woodhouse, "Jesus and Jonah," 36.

[54]Nolland, *Gospel of Matthew,* 511.

[55]The comparison between the sea (as represented by the fish) and death is made in various other places throughout the Old Testament. As Rudman explains, this is because "the Deep and Sheol could therefore be seen by Israelite writers as comparable in the sense that both were places of chaos and non-creation." Rudman, "The Sign of Jonah," 327.

[56]We will discuss the anthropological assertion that humans possess both a body and a soul, the latter of which remains conscious after bodily death, in chapter six. Here it is simply worth noting that it would have been a logical absurdity for Jonah to believe he could have cried out from the pit (Jon 2:6) if his body (even figuratively speaking) was dead. In other words, while his body is in a grave (metaphorically portrayed through the fish's belly), his soul is still able to cry out to God for salvation.

affirm that the words and teachings of Jesus in the Gospels carry a particular weight to them. And one such teaching is that Jesus, the true and better Jonah, will spend three days and nights in the place of the dead, his body in the grave, his soul in the righteous compartment of Hades.

PAULINE STATEMENTS ABOUT THE DESCENT

Paul also teaches that, upon death, Jesus descended to the place of the dead, his body to the grave and his soul to the place of the (righteous) dead. Two passages in particular demand our attention.

Ephesians 4:9. First, Ephesians 4:7-10 says,

> But grace was given to each one of us according to the measure of Christ's gift. Therefore it says,
>
> > "When he ascended on high he led a host of captives,
> > and he gave gifts to men."
>
> (In saying, "He ascended," what does it mean but that he had also descended into the lower regions, the earth? He who descended is the one who also ascended far above all the heavens, that he might fill all things).

As many have noted,[57] there are three options for interpreting this passage and its reference to "descending": that it refers to Christ's incarnation,[58] his descent to the dead,[59] or his descent at Pentecost via

---

[57]In this section I am largely dependent on William Bales, "The Descent of Christ in Ephesians 4:9," *CBQ* 72 (2010): 84-100. I am mostly summarizing his argument and am reliant upon his footnotes for the footnotes below regarding secondary literature and the history of interpretation. Where I have departed from Bales's argument or relied on another commentator, I have noted it in the main text.

[58]See, e.g., Markus Barth, *Ephesians: Introduction, Translation, and Commentary*, 2 vols., AB 34 and 34A (Garden City, NY: Doubleday, 1974), 432-34; Ernest Best, *A Critical and Exegetical Commentary on Ephesians*, ICC (Edinburgh: Clark, 1998), 383-88; F. F. Bruce, *The Epistles to the Colossians, to Philemon, and to the Ephesians*, NICNT (Grand Rapids: Eerdmans, 1984), 343-45; Harold W. Hoehner, *Ephesians: An Exegetical Commentary* (Grand Rapids: Baker, 2002), 533-36; Richard N. Longenecker, *The Christology of Early Jewish Christianity*, SBT 2/17 (London: SCM, 1970), 60; Pheme Perkins, *Ephesians*, Abingdon New Testament Commentaries (Nashville: Abingdon, 1997), 97-99; and Rudolf Schnackenburg, *Ephesians: A Commentary*, trans. Helen Heron (Edinburgh: Clark, 1991), 177-80.

[59]While certainly not the predominate view in modern scholarship, it still has its proponents. See, e.g., Clinton E. Arnold, *Power and Magic: The Concept of Power in Ephesians* (1989; Grand

sending the Spirit.[60] There are exegetical arguments that give warrant to each of them, but here I wish to defend the view that Paul references Christ's descent to the dead. This interpretation hinges on the OT passage(s) to which Paul alludes here,[61] although there are also arguments to make that arise from within Ephesians itself.

Regarding OT allusions in Ephesians 4:9, William Bales notes three classes of possible LXX backgrounds for the phrase κατέβη εἰς τὰ κατώτερα τῆς γῆς (translated in the ESV as "descended into the lower regions, the earth"). First are those LXX texts that are highly similar at the lexical level to Ephesians 4:9. According to Bales, two LXX verses fit this description: Psalm 62:10 (Ps 63:9)[62] and Psalm 138:15 (Ps 139:15).[63]

Rapids: Baker, 1992), 56-58; Robert G. Bratcher and Eugene A. Nida, *A Translator's Handbook on Paul's Letter to the Ephesians*, Helps for Translators (New York: United Bible Societies, 1982), 99-100; Friedrich Büchsel, "κατώτερος," in *TDNT* (1965; Grand Rapids: Eerdmans, 1995) 3:640-42; James D. G. Dunn, *Christology in the Making: A New Testament Inquiry into the Origins of the Doctrine of the Incarnation* (London: SCM, 1980) 186-87; Anthony Tyrrell Hanson, *The New Testament Interpretation of Scripture* (London: SPCK, 1980) 136-41; and Larry J. Kreitzer, "'The Plutonium of Hierapolis and the Descent of Christ into the 'Lowermost Parts of the Earth' (Ephesians 4,9)," *Bib* 79 (1998): 381-93.

[60]See, for instance, G. B. Caird, *Paul's Letters from Prison: Ephesians, Philippians, Colossians, Philemon, in the Revised Standard Version*, New Clarendon Bible (Oxford: Oxford University Press, 1976), 73-75; David E. Garland, "A Life Worthy of the Calling: Unity and Holiness. Ephesians 4:1-24," *RevExp* 76 (1979): 517-27; W. Hall Harris, *The Descent of Christ: Ephesians 4:7-11 and Traditional Hebrew Imagery*, AGJU 32 (Leiden: Brill, 1996); and Andrew T. Lincoln, *Ephesians*, WBC 42 (Dallas: Word, 1990) 244-48.

[61]Contrary to much current scholarship, I take it that Paul wrote Ephesians. The question of authorship does not bear on the interpretation of this text, though, because, as Bales notes,

> If Paul is the author of Ephesians, then the underlying cosmology of the letter is almost certainly three-tiered. To assert otherwise would be to say that Paul's cosmology had changed since he wrote Philippians [as evidenced in, e.g., Phil. 2:10], something very unlikely. If Paul is not the author, the underlying cosmology is likely three-tiered, as it is unlikely that a prominent leader from the Pauline school would hold to a cosmology different from that of Paul, the revered master and mentor. Finally, if Ephesians espouses a two-tiered cosmology, it would represent a departure not only from OT traditions but from other NT writings as well.

Bales, "Descent of Christ," 99-100.

[62]αὐτοὶ δὲ εἰς μάτην ἐζήτησαν τὴν ψυχήν μου· εἰσελεύσονται εἰς τὰ κατώτατα τῆς γῆς. Emphasis mine. As Bales notes, the only change aside from the verb is a minor variation from τὰ κατώτατα in Ps 62:10 LXX (Ps 63:9) to τὰ κατώτερα in Eph 4:9. Further, again noted by Bales, this change is explainable via the shift from away from using superlatives in favor of comparatives in Koine Greek. Bales, "Descent of Christ," 92.

[63]οὐκ ἐκρύβη τὸ ὀστοῦν μου ἀπὸ σοῦ, ὃ ἐποίησας ἐν κρυφῇ. καὶ ἡ ὑπόστασίς μου ἐν τοῖς κατωτάτοις τῆς γῆς. Emphasis mine. Again, other than the verb change, the only difference

In both of these passages, the Psalmist makes reference to "the lowest regions of the earth." And while they each use a slightly different prepositional phrase (see the two previous footnotes), the difference of which is negligible, the MT of both texts is also nearly the same.[64] As Bales notes, this phrase in the MT, when used in this construction, "indicates 'the lowest regions of the earth,' one of the many phrases and terms that OT authors use to refer to the underworld."[65] The important point to make here is that the two verses in the LXX that most closely resemble Ephesians 4:9 both make clear references to the underworld.[66] Paul does not allude to passages that speak of a descent from heaven to earth, as the incarnation and Pentecost interpretive options would demand. Rather, he alludes to two passages that speak clearly of a descent to the lowest regions of the earth, a phrase that is synonymous with the underworld, or place of the dead, in the OT and ANE cognate literature.[67]

A second class of texts that Bales examines includes verses that use τῆς γῆς in a similar manner to Ephesians 4:9; that is, they use it in reference to a descent. Here, Bales lists Psalm 70:20 LXX (Ps 71:20); Isaiah 14:15; Ezekiel 26:20, and 32:18 as examples,[68] but Isaiah 14:15[69]

---

between this text and Eph 4:9 is the shift from a superlative form to a comparative form with respect to τοῖς κατωτάτοις. As with Ps 62:10 (LXX), this change is "probably inconsequential." Bales, "Descent of Christ," 93.

[64]Ps 63:10 (MT): בתחתיות הארץ.

Ps 139:15 (MT): בתחתיות ארץ.

The only difference between these two phrases, a negligible one, is the lack of definite article before ארץ in Ps 139:15.

[65]Bales, "Descent of Christ," 92.

[66]Bales includes a third, Pr Man 13. This is indeed an important verse conceptually speaking, as it demonstrates one view within Second Temple Judaism regarding judgment and the afterlife. For our purposes, however, we are trying to ascertain what allusions Paul may have been making to Holy Scripture, not OT pseudipigrapha. On the lexical connections between Eph 4:9 and Pr Man 13, see Bales, "Descent of Christ," 93-94. On what books were considered Scripture at the time of the writing of the New Testament, see Roger Beckwith, *The Old Testament Canon of the New Testament Church and its Background in Early Judaism* (1985; Eugene, OR: Wipf and Stock, 2008).

[67]On the ancient Near Eastern and Greco-Roman cosmographies that provide the conceptual background for the New Testament, see Bauckham, *Fate of the Dead*, 9-48.

[68]For an exposition of each of these texts and their relation to Eph 4:9, see William A. Bales, "The Meaning and Function of Ephesians 4:9-10 in Both its Immediate and More General Context," PhD dissertation (Washington, DC: The Catholic University of America, 2002), 201-203.

[69]νῦν δὲ εἰς ἄδου καταβήσῃ, καὶ *εἰς τὰ θεμέλια τῆς γῆς*. Emphasis mine.

stands as exemplary in this class for him and for us. It is worth quoting Bales at length here to see just how important this text is for understanding Paul's language in Ephesians 4:9.

> After death [the tyrant in Isa. 14:4-21] will join other tyrants in Hades (vv. 9—11, 15). In Isa. 14:15, τὰ θεμέλια τῆς γῆς is parallel to ᾅδου, the LXX rendering of the Hebrew שְׁאוֹל. The verb καταβήσῃ does double duty, operating with the prepositional phrase εἰς τὰ θεμέλια τῆς γῆς in v. 15b as well as with εἰς ᾅδου in v. 15a. Contextually, both ᾅδου and τὰ θεμέλια τῆς γῆς are places to which one descends (καταβήσῃ) upon death. The tyrant will be brought to the place of the dead, the underworld.
>
> For purposes of comparison with κατέβη εἰς τὰ κατώτερα τῆς γῆς in Eph. 4:9, it is worth noting that Isa. 14:15 uses a form of καταβαίνω in describing a descent to the underworld. Further, it is significant that the tyrant's descent strikes an ironic contrast with his presumed "ascent" (using a form of ἀναβαίνω) in the previous verse. . . . The mention of an "ascent" (using a form of ἀναβαίνω) followed by a "descent" to the underworld" (using a form of καταβαίνω) finds a striking parallel in Eph. 4:9.[70]

Here, then, we have another text that clearly refers to descending to the underworld and that clearly has lexical and conceptual parallels to Ephesians 4:9. Not only in this instance do we find lexical similarities, as in the first class of texts, but we also find a conceptual parallel in the ascent/descent pattern utilized in both texts.[71]

The final class of texts to which Bales compares Ephesians 4:9 contains passages that use καταβαίνω similarly. Again, Bales lists several texts in this regard,[72] but three are particularly instructive: Numbers 16:30,

---

[70]Bales, "Descent of Christ," 94. On the conceptual and sociohistorical background for the nominal cognate of καταβαίνω, see Alberto Bernabé, "What Is *Katábasis*? The Descent into the Netherworld in Greece and the Ancient Near East," *Les Études Classiques* 83 (2015): 15-34.

[71]The other texts listed by Bales in this category do not share this conceptual similarity, but they are still important because they use τῆς γῆς in a similar manner to Is 14:15 and to Eph 4:9, i.e. as a reference to the underworld.

[72]Gen 37:35; Job 17:16; Ps 27:1; 29:4, 10; 54:16; 62:10; 70:20; 87:5; 113:15; 142:7; Is 14:15, 19; Ezek 26:20; 31:14, 15, 16, 17, 18; 32:18, 24, 27, 29, 30; Jon 2:7 (all verses listed are LXX). Bales also lists, from the OT Apocrypha and Pseudipigrapha, Tob 13:2 (א); Bar 3:19; and Pr Man 13. He groups these into three sets: those that refer to dying or death metaphorically; those that refer to a

33 (LXX); Psalm 138:8 LXX (Ps 139:8); and Isaiah 14:11 (LXX). And the use of "descend" (καταβαίνω) alone is not the only important feature of these texts; they also "display a striking formal similarity to κατέβη εἰς τὰ κατώτερα τῆς γῆς in Eph. 4:9: (a form of) καταβαίνω + the preposition εἰς + a word or phrase designating the underworld."[73] The last piece of that equation is particularly important for our purposes; in each of these texts, the descent that occurs is clearly to the underworld. In Numbers 16:30, 33,[74] Moses warns the people that those who have provoked the Lord will descend alive into Hades (ᾄδου). In Psalm 138:8 LXX (Ps 139:8),[75] the Psalmist speaks of the Lord's omnipresence by declaring, "If I ascend to heaven, you are there! If I make my bed in Sheol [lit., "descend to Hades," καταβῶ εἰς τὸν ᾄδην], you are there!" Again, the combination of καταβαίνω ("descend") with the preposition εἰς ("to," "into") is followed in this instance by the word *Hades* (τόν ᾄδην), which we have already seen is used in parallel to τῆς γῆς ("the earth") in Isaiah 14:15. And perhaps more importantly, we have here again in Psalm 138:8 LXX (Ps 139:8) another conceptual parallel to Paul's ascent/descent pattern in Ephesians 4:11. Finally, in this class of texts, Bales mentions Isaiah 14:11,[76] which refers to the Babylonian tyrant's glory and happiness descending to Hades.

Again, this is crucial for our understanding of Ephesians 4:9. The OT texts with the most similar structure and verb usage are ones that refer to death, the underworld, and/or afflictions that are portrayed metaphorically using the language of death and the underworld (see previous note, Bales' list of texts that use καταβαίνω). To summarize Bales's thoroughly persuasive case, the most likely LXX texts to which Paul

---

descent into the actual underworld, or place of the dead; and those that refer metaphorically to various trials or afflictions. For these groupings, see Bales, "Descent of Christ," 96n39-41. For an exposition of these texts, see Bales, "Meaning and Function in Ephesians 4:9-10," 204-20.

[73]Bales, "Descent of Christ," 95.

[74]Num 16:30: καταβήσονται ζῶντες εἰς ᾄδου.

Num 16:33: κατέβησαν αὐτοὶ καὶ ὅσα ἐστὶν αὐτῶν ζῶντα εἰς ᾄδου.

[75]ἐὰν καταβῶ εἰς τὸν ᾄδην πάρει.

[76]κατέβη δὲ εἰς ᾄδου ἡ δόξα σου, ἡ πολλή σου εὐφροσύνη.

alludes in Eph 4:9, i.e., the texts with the clearest lexical, conceptual, verbal, and structural parallels, are those which refer to a descent to the underworld, the place of the dead. For this reason I believe it is most likely that Paul is referring to Christ descending to the "lower regions of the earth," that is the underworld, Hades, the place of the dead.

Given these arguments, I am convinced that Paul refers to Christ's descent to the dead in Ephesians 4:9. Others, however, do not understand the passage that way. The other two views, which purport that Paul is referring either to the incarnation or to Pentecost, are strongly advocated by most exegetes today. It is worth briefly examining those positions and answering them given our exposition above. Perhaps the most consistent objection to this reading comes with respect to how one understands Paul's allusion to Psalm 68:18 in Ephesians 4:8. For those who argue for a reference to Pentecost, Paul is alluding not to Psalm 68:18 directly but rather to *Tg.* Psalm 68.[77] This makes some sense of the differences between LXX Psalm 67 and Ephesians 4:8, but it does not make sense of the Ephesians' context. Why would Paul assume that his readers, situated in Asia Minor in what appears to be a predominately Gentile context (e.g., Eph 2:11-22), were familiar with an Aramaic gloss of the MT?[78] And, as Bass notes, this makes little sense of the conjunction in Ephesians 4:9, which presumes that the descent occurs prior to the ascent. Nor does it consider the fact that the gifts appear to be given in the ascent, not the descent. On the Pentecost interpretation, both of these orders should be reversed: the ascent should occur first and the gifts should be given upon descent, but neither appears to be the case in this passage.[79]

---

[77]On the textual history of *Tg.* Psalms and whether or not it should be seen as one work or a compilation of many different targums, see Harris, *Descent of Christ*, 66n6.

[78]We should note, though, that Paul could make reference to both biblical and extrabiblical sources without assuming his audience would catch all his allusions. On both the arguments for Paul's use of *Tg.* Psalm 68 and whether or not this makes sense given Paul's Gentile context in Ephesians, see Best, *A Critical and Exegetical Commentary on Ephesians*, 379-80.

[79]See Bass, *Battle for the Keys*, 79. For a much more extensive discussion, upon which Bass relies, see Harris, *Descent of Christ*, 64-142.

Regarding the incarnation interpretation of the passage, the adjudication between it and the descent interpretation mainly hinges on how one understands "the lower parts of the earth" in Ephesians 4:9.[80] We have already made an argument above for how to understand this phrase, but it is worth noting here that the incarnation interpretation appears to rely on assuming Paul in Ephesians has a two-tiered, not three-tiered, cosmology. But while Paul certainly contrasts heaven and earth elsewhere in the letter,[81] his cosmology in other letters certainly evinces a three-tiered universe (e.g., Rom 10:6-7; Phil 2:10).[82] This option does not appear to give enough credit to the ANE and Greco-Roman cosmologies that provide background for Paul's thought,[83] or to the evidence that he holds to a three-tiered cosmology in his other letters. As MacCulloch summarizes it,

> No part of the universe—Hades, Earth, Heaven—was to be unvisited by Him. This is implied in Phil. ii. 10: Christ's obedience even to death is the cause of His exaltation and His universal sovereignty not only over the heavenly and the earthly, but over τὰ καταθόνια ["those under the earth," Phil. 2:10], the usual classical expression for those in Hades.[84]

The other possible means by which one could read the passage as a reference to the incarnation is to argue that Paul did not use the typical words for the underworld: "Hades" and "abyss."[85] But, as Frank Thielman points out, the phrase "the lower regions of the earth," would be "an odd way of referring to the surface of the earth."[86] Furthermore, again, given

---

[80]Bass, *Battle for the Keys*, 79.

[81]For a discussion of the comparative and superlative aspects of this passage, especially as they relate to "above the heavens" and "lower regions of the earth," see E. Bröse, "Der Descensus ad Inferos Eph. 4, 8-10," *NKZ* 9 (1898): 447-55.

[82]For a balanced discussion of this objection, see Lincoln, *Ephesians*, 244-45.

[83]In this respect, in addition to the broad background noted above, we could also point to the explicit interpretation of Ps 68:18 as a reference to a descent to Hades in *T. Dan* 5:10-11. See Bauckham, *Fate of the Dead*, 38.

[84]J. A. MacCulloch, *The Harrowing of Hell: A Comparative Study of an Early Christian Doctrine* (Edinburgh: T & T Clark, 1930), 46.

[85]See Hoehner, *Ephesians*, 535.

[86]Frank S. Thielman, *Ephesians*, BECNT (Grand Rapids: Baker Academic, 2010), 270.

the fact that, "Greco-Roman culture was awash with stories of descent to the underworld," it is much more likely that "everyone [in Paul's context] knew that one went 'down' to get to the underworld, and various words beginning with the preposition κατά (*kata*, down) were frequently associated with the realm of the dead."[87] In addition to Greco-Roman descents, Thielman notes that, in Paul's context,

> One was brought 'down' (κατάγω, *katago*; e.g. Gen. 37:35; 42:38; 44:29, 31; 1 Sam. 2:6; 1 Kings 2:6, 9; 1 Clem. 4.12; Lucian, *Men*. 1, 6) or simply 'went down' (κατάβαινω, *katabaino*; Gen. 37:35 LXX; Num 16:30, 33 LXX; Aristides of Athens, *Apol*. 11.3; Diodorus Siculus, *Biblio. Hist*. 4.25.4; Artemidorus Daldianus, *Oneir*. 2.55; cf. BDAG 514) to hades (cf. Rom 10:6-7), and the path to hades went 'downward' (κάτω, *kato*), below the earth's surface (e.g., Aristophanes, *Ran*. 70; Plato, *Resp*. 10.614c; Deut. 32:22 LXX). Not surprisingly, then, the place of the dead could be referred to simply as τὰ κάτω (*ta kato*, the [parts] below; Lucian, *Men*. 2).[88]

For these reasons, I conclude with Thielman, then, that, "It seems extremely unlikely that Paul would use the phrase κατέβη εἰς τὰ κατώτερα τῆς γῆς in such a cultural environment and expect his readers to understand by it anything other than a descent to the realm of the dead."[89]

Again, the descent does not stand or fall on Ephesians 4:9-10 (or on 1 Pet 3:18-22). One could plausibly interpret this passage as a reference to the incarnation or to Pentecost and still arrive at a doctrine of the

---

[87]Thielman, *Ephesians*, 270-71.

[88]Thielman, *Ephesians*, 271. In a footnote after this passage, Thielman also argues that,

> Paul did not need to use the term "hades," therefore, to make a reference to the realm of the dead understood (*pace*, e.g., Eadie 1883: 292; cf. Best 1998: 384), nor did he need to use the superlative form κατώτατα (Pss. 62:10 LXX [63:10 MT; 63:9 Eng.]; 138:15 LXX [139:15 MT, Eng.]) to draw a contrast with the phrase ὑπεράνω πάντων τῶν οὐρανῶν (far above all the heavens) in 4:10 (*pace*, e.g., Lincoln 1990: 245).

[89]Thielman, *Ephesians*, 271. Clinton Arnold makes similar comments about the comparative and about the Hellenistic context of κατώτερα τῆς γῆς in his *Power and Magic*, 57. See also Kreitzer, for the argument that the phrase "the lowermost parts of the earth" is "a veiled reference to the Plutonium of Hierapolis, a small subterranean cavern situated next to the temple of Apollo in the centre of the city and commonly regarded as a passageway to the underworld" (Kreitzer, "Plutonium of Hierapolis," 381).

descent via other passages of Scripture, even via other Pauline passages.[90] While I argue that it is such a descent reference, others need not agree to affirm the descent doctrine. One can affirm it from other passages in both the New Testament as a whole (like Acts 2) and in Paul's other letters. To just such a Pauline passage that we now turn our attention.

Romans 10:7. The other Pauline passage worth considering is Romans 10:6-9. Here Paul says,

> But the righteousness based on faith says, "Do not say in your heart, 'Who will ascend into heaven?' (that is, to bring Christ down) or, 'Who will descend into the abyss?' (that is, to bring Christ up from the dead)." But what does it say? "The word is near you, in your mouth and in your heart" (that is, the word of faith that we proclaim); because, if you confess with your mouth that Jesus is Lord and believe in your heart that God raised him from the dead, you will be saved.

The phrase particularly relevant for our purposes is in Romans 10:6-7, where Paul asks who will ascend into heaven to bring Christ down or descend into the abyss to bring Christ up from the dead. The latter phrase in Greek is Τίς καταβήσεται εἰς τὴν ἄβυσσον; τοῦτ᾽ ἔστιν Χριστὸν ἐκ νεκρῶν ἀναγαγεῖν. There are a number of relevant exegetical features of this passage related to the descent. First, as Bales notes, "The word ἄβυσσος is used in parallel with νεκρῶν, 'the dead,' here as a synecdoche for Hades."[91] In other words, Paul equates the abyss with the place of the dead,[92] from which Christ cannot be brought up by human capacities (Rom 10:7). Second and relatedly, ἐκ νεκρῶν ("the dead") is participially plural, meaning that the emphasis of the phrase lies with those dead persons from among whom Christ was raised. It is not, in other words, a phrase that just means bodily resurrection

---

[90]Of course, the presence of the descent in other Pauline passages may lend even more weight to interpreting Eph 4:9-10 as a reference to the descent.

[91]Bales, "Descent of Christ," 98.

[92]On the synonymous relationship of the sea and the underworld in this passage, as well as their equivalency in Jewish thought, see James D. G. Dunn, *Romans 9-16*, WBC 38B (Dallas: Word, 1988), 606.

(although it certainly entails that); rather, the meaning of the phrase is that Christ was raised *from among the dead ones*.[93] This emphasis on the place of the dead, and particularly its inhabitants, is contrasted by Paul with "heaven" (τὸν οὐρανόν) in Romans 10:6, and this indicates, at the very least, the spatial contrast between these two realms.[94]

This spatial contrast between "heaven"[95] and "the dead" is confirmed by the OT background of the passage. Paul quotes here Deuteronomy 30:12-14, a text that refers to the extreme limits of God's creation that are inaccessible to human beings. While the LXX of Deuteronomy 30:13-14 refers to going "beyond the sea" (πέραν τῆς θαλάσσης), this should not deter us from thinking Paul has retained the proper sense of the passage in Romans 10:7. "Beyond the sea" can be plausibly read as a reference to the place of the dead, given that this was a common spatial metaphor for the realm of those who have passed from the land of the living in both ancient Judaism and the ancient Near East.[96]

In any case, Paul in Romans 10:6-7 makes a clear reference to going down to the abyss to bring Christ up from among the dead ones (ἐκ νεκρῶν) and does so in such a way that "abyss" is clearly parallel to "from the dead." This brings us to a last exegetical point: "abyss" is synonymous with both "the sea" and terms used for the place of the dead in the Old Testament (e.g., Sheol, Hades, etc.).[97] The word is used

---

[93]See again Dunn: "The language echoes that of Ps 71 [LXX 70]:20—ἐζωοποίησάς με καὶ ἐκ τῶν ἀβύσσων τῆς γῆς ἀνήγαγές με; Wisd Sol 16:13—'you have power of life and death, and you lead down to the gates of hell and back again (ἀνάγεις).'" Dunn, *Romans 9–16*, 606.

[94]On the concept of the three-tiered universe in the ancient Near East, Second Temple Judaism, and Greco-Roman culture, see Bauckham, *Fate of the Dead*, 9-48.

[95]Schreiner cogently argues that the first half of the clause is a reference to the incarnation and the second clause a reference to the place of the dead. Thomas R. Schreiner, *Romans*, BECNT 6 (Grand Rapids: Baker Academic, 1998), 558. Mounce glosses these as references to "incarnation and resurrection." Robert H. Mounce, *Romans*, NAC 27 (Nashville: Broadman & Holman, 1995), 208.

[96]See Bauckham, *Fate of the Dead*, 9-48; as well as the discussion in Bass, *Battle for the Keys*, 45-61.

[97]On the relationship between "abyss," "sea," and "place of the dead," see my *Christ and the New Creation: A Canonical Approach to the Theology of the New Testament* (Eugene, OR: Wipf and Stock, 2013), 159-60, although I now disagree with my conclusion that John uses it differently in Revelation than Paul does in Rom 10:7.

thirty-two times in the LXX,[98] and in twenty-nine of those it is parallel to "the sea." The three instances in which it is not parallel to "the sea" are verses where it is parallel to the place of the dead (Ps 35:7; 71:20;[99] 135:6). Again, though, it is important that we not make a stark contrast between "the sea," "abyss," and "the Pit" (or other synonymous terms with the place of the dead). While these are certainly not always synonymous in every instance they are used, they do bear a close relationship with one another in the Old Testament, and they also appear to have a similar synonymous relationship here in Romans 10:6-7.[100]

Given these considerations, it is, in my estimation, plausible that Paul in Romans 10:7 refers to Christ in the realm of, or his descent to, the dead. This should prompt revisiting Ephesians 4:9, since these two texts are textually and conceptually parallel. Regarding the latter, they both have an ascent/descent pattern. They also share much of the same OT background. But most importantly, they are syntactically and lexically similar, as noted by Bales.[101] Consider:

| Ephesians 4:9 | κατέβη | εἰς | τὰ κατώτερα τῆς γῆς |
| Romans 10:7 (Τὶς) | καταβήσεται | εἰς | τὴν ἄβυσσον |

The parallels here are striking: same verb, same εἰς + prepositional phrase construction. The only difference is the content of that prepositional phrase, with Ephesians 4:9 referring to "the lower regions of the earth" and Romans 10:7 referring to "the abyss." Given our analysis above, it is highly plausible that Paul means these two terms to be synonymous, especially given the syntactical, conceptual, and lexical

---

[98]Gen 1:2; 7:11; 8:2; Deut 8:7; 33:13; Job 28:14; 36:16; 38:16, 30; 41:31, 32 (41:23, 24 LXX; 2x v. 24); Ps 33:7 (32:7 LXX); 35:7; 42:7 (41:8 LXX, 2x); 71:20 (70:20 LXX); 78:15 (77:15 LXX); 103:4; 106:9 (105:9 LXX); 107:26 (106:26 LXX); 135:6 (134:6 LXX); Prov 8:24; Is 44:27; 51:10; 63:13; Ezek 26:19; 31:4, 15; Jon 2:5 (2:6 LXX); Hab 3:10 Amos 7:4.

[99]For the inner biblical and Second Temple allusions in this passage, including Ps 71:20 but also Ps 107:26 (Ps 106:26 LXX) and Wis 16:13, see Schreiner, *Romans*, 558-59.

[100]So Schreiner: "Perhaps the alternation from 'sea' to 'abyss' would not have been considered that significant since the sea and the abyss were closely identified in Jewish thought." Schreiner, *Romans*, 559. Schreiner cites both Bietenhard and Moo in support. He also lists around twenty texts in support.

[101]Bales, "Descent of Christ," 98.

similarities between these two passages. Thus Paul refers to Christ's descent to the dead in both Ephesians 4:9 and Romans 10:7.

REVELATION 1:18

I will return to the General Epistles at the end of our biblical-theological survey when considering 1 Peter 3:18-22. First, however, I will marshal evidence from the last section of the NT canon—Revelation—as well as from other patterns of descent in the Bible. Regarding Revelation, the pertinent text is Revelation 1:18: "I died, and behold I am alive forevermore, and I have the keys of Death and Hades." As David Aune notes, "the possessive genitive is often understood as implying the tradition of the *descensus ad inferos*, '[Christ's] descent to Hell,' for if the keys formerly belonged to the personified Death and Hades, they must have been forcibly taken from them."[102] Likewise, G. K. Beale says of this passage that,

> [The keys imagery] is utilized to indicate that through the victory of the resurrection Christ became king even over the realm of the dead in which he was formerly imprisoned. Now, not only is no he longer held in death's bonds but he also holds sway over who is released and retained in that realm.[103]

As Bass notes, Death and Hades are personified throughout Revelation and are always mentioned in that order, and, following Aune, he suggests that Death should therefore be seen as the ruler of the realm, Hades.[104] He goes on to note that, "The primary interpretive crux of

---

[102]David F. Aune, *Revelation 1-5*, WBC 52A (Dallas: Word, 1997), 104.

[103]G. K. Beale, *The Book of Revelation*, NICGT (Grand Rapids: Eerdmans, 1999), 215. Bauckham also sees a battle between Christ and Death and Hades as the background here, as do many others. For Bauckham, see *Fate of the Dead*, 39. For an extensive list of other commentators who see a battle background for this text, see Bass, *Battle for the Keys*, 108.

[104]Bass, *Battle for the Keys*, 106. In what follows I rely extensively on Bass, *Battle for the Keys*. As previously noted, he has done the most extensive work from an evangelical context on the biblical and historical background of the descent. And, for the purposes of this section, he is among the very few who have engaged in an extended study and discussion of the descent background of Rev 1:18.

this passage is whether Death and Hades are places or personified entities."[105] The key to determining that issue is whether or not the phrase τὰς κλεῖς τοῦ θανάτου καὶ τοῦ ᾅδου should be taken with a possessive or objective genitive. The former ("the keys belonging to Death and Hades") would imply that Jesus holds the keys belonging to Death and Hades, and that, therefore, there was a battle between them in the underworld in which Christ was victorious. The latter ("the keys of [that open] Death and Hades") would imply that Jesus owns the keys to the realms of Death and Hades and may not necessarily indicate anything about Christ's descent.[106]

Bass argues that the genitive is possessive. He relies on three main points: that most commentators have taken it and still do take it as possessive;[107] that Death and Hades, although used with locative references elsewhere in Revelation, are personified throughout the book;[108] and that "keys" has a clear background in ANE, Second Temple Jewish, and Greco-Roman literature, as well as in the Old Testament and New Testament, namely, via references to the "gates of Death/Sheol/Hades."[109] With respect to the personification of Death and Hades in this passage, Bass admits that Revelation 1:18 is somewhat ambiguous. The other two personifications of Death and Hades in Revelation, Revelation 6:8 and 20:13-14, do not shed any light, since the former is obviously a personification. The latter reference in chapter twenty includes both a locative sense (Rev 20:13) and a personified sense (Rev 20:14). In other words, Death and Hades can be used both locatively and in a personified manner in Revelation.

Is this, then, an exegetical impasse? Perhaps it is not, and for two reasons. First, the plundering of the locations of Death and Hades in Revelation 20:13 immediately precedes the personification of Death and Hades in Revelation 20:14. Additionally, Revelation 6:8 pictures Death as

---

[105]Bass, *Battle for the Keys*, 106-7.
[106]Bass, *Battle for the Keys*, 107.
[107]For a list of these, see Bass, *Battle for the Keys*, 110n67.
[108]Bass, *Battle for the Keys*, 107-10.
[109]Bass, *Battle of the Keys*, 110.

a figure that has been beaten and is fleeing. In other words, both of the clear "personification" senses of Death and Hades include an implication of Christ's victory over them. Further, the only clearly locative reference—Revelation 20:13—is found in the context of Christ's own victory over Death and Hades, his plundering of their inhabitants, and his destruction of both of them. In other words, while the syntax of Revelation 1:18 may be ambiguous, John elsewhere in Revelation clearly presents them as personified enemies of Jesus who are plundered. Since Revelation 1–3 and 20–22 are so conceptually and lexically similar,[110] it is not hard to imagine that John intends Revelation 1:18 and Revelation 20:13-14 to parallel one another. In Revelation 1:18, Christ has already descended to the realm of the dead and thereby defeated Death and Hades, taking the keys to their kingdom, and rises from them in his resurrection and ascension; whereas in Revelation 20:13-14 Christ descends to the earth for the final judgment, uses his keys to raise the dead up from the realm of Death and Hades, and triumphantly throws Death and Hades personified into the lake of fire. At the very least, then, it is in our judgment probable that John uses "Death and Hades" with both a locative and personified sense in Revelation 1:18, with the emphasis on the latter.[111]

The reference to "the keys" in Revelation 1:18 may point to second reason to understand a personified sense for Death and Hades. As Bauckham notes, "Revelation 1:18 . . . presupposes that the gates of Hades, which release none who has entered them, have been for the first time opened for a man to leave. The divine prerogative of releasing from the realm of death . . . now belongs to Christ."[112] The "gates of hell" (cf. Mt 16:18), as well as Death and Hades, were often personified in ANE, Greco-Roman, and Second Temple Jewish literature, not allowing any dead person to escape their grasp.[113] This figurative understanding

---

[110]G. K. Beale, *John's Use of the Old Testament in Revelation*, JSNTSup 166 (Sheffield: Sheffield Academic Press, 1998), 300.
[111]See Bass, *Battle for the Keys*, 107; and Beale, *Revelation*, 214.
[112]Bauckham, *Fate of the Dead*, 39.
[113]See Bass, *Battle for the Keys*, 20-30.

is found also in the early church, where Christ's descent and resurrection are portrayed as defeating a personified Death and/or Hades.[114] Further, key holders in ANE, Second Temple Jewish, and Greco-Roman literature were often associated with the realm of the dead.[115] And in Revelation (Rev 3:7; 9:1-2; 20:1-3), keys are associated with the person who grants access to a particular location and not just with the location itself.[116] All of this evidence points to Death and Hades as personified in Revelation 1:18 and the genitive as one of possession. Jesus is the one who has died and now lives and therefore owns the keys that belong to Death and Hades. And, as Bass argues, the most likely timeframe for this to occur was "his three day interval in the realm of the dead between his death and resurrection," since this "makes the most sense with Christ['s and the New Testament's other references] to Death and Hades" (cf. Mt 12:40; Acts 2:27, 31; Rom 10:7; Eph 4:9; 1 Pet 3:19)."[117]

Revelation 1:18, then, should be seen as another passage that teaches or implies the descent in the New Testament. We now have evidence from the Gospels, Acts, the Pauline Epistles, and the Apocalypse for the descent doctrine. All that is missing from the NT canon's various corpora is the General Epistles. Before we turn to them, and specifically to 1 Peter 3:18-22, it will assist our exegesis of that particularly thorny text if we first examine some other patterns of descent and ascent in Scripture and in its various historical backgrounds.

OTHER BIBLICAL PATTERNS OF DESCENT

In addition to particular NT texts, there are also patterns of biblical language that point to Christ's descending to the dead in both body and soul. These can be as simple as the repetition in the Psalms and

---

[114]Among the earliest of such portrays is Melito of Sardis, *Peri Pascha* 70-71 and 101-2. For an introduction to *Peri Pascha* including critical issues, thematic and theological issues, and a translation, see Melito of Sardis, *On Pascha and Fragments*, rev. ed., trans. and ed. Stuart George Hall, Oxford Early Christian Texts (1979; Oxford: Clarendon, 2012).

[115]Bass, *Battle for the Keys*, 31-35.

[116]Bass, *Battle for the Keys*, 41-43.

[117]Bass, *Battle for the Keys*, 110.

elsewhere in the Old Testament of YHWH's people expressing faith that he will snatch them out of Sheol's grasp.[118] We also find images in the Old Testament of YHWH doing just that, from Genesis 22 to Jonah 2. In these cases, God's servant/people are as good as dead, and yet God does not abandon them to death but draws them out of it. And while these examples rely on metaphor—no one actually dies—they still express the hope that God will draw his people out of death. This comes to fruition more fully in the hope of bodily resurrection (e.g., Dan 12:1-2) but the precursor and corollary to this is the hope that God will descend to Sheol to draw his people out of it.[119]

Michael Heiser's recent monograph has made an important contribution to our understanding of this descent/ascent pattern in the Old Testament, specifically its supernatural elements. Heiser argues that the Old Testament should be read as the struggle between YHWH and the serpent, the latter of whom leads and represents the members of the divine council (angels) who rebelled against YHWH at the beginning of creation. This battle is not only spiritual but also geographical, according to Heiser. When the serpent, Satan, rebelled, he was cast down to the realm of the dead, represented geographically in the Old Testament by the area of Bashan. When reading the flood, exodus, and conquest narratives of the Old Testament, Heiser argues that we should see the "descents" (my terminology) of the people of God into and out of the flood waters, the Red Sea, and then Bashan and also the Jordan, as entries into and victorious exits out of the "realm of the serpent." And while Bashan and, specifically, Mt. Hermon are not literally the realm

---

[118]Of course, these are by and large statements referring to near-death experiences in which the Psalm writer was in mortal danger, not actually in the intermediate state. Still, the Jewish people, or at the very least, their songwriters, saw fit to compare near-death (living) experiences with the state of death. See on this issue Ratzinger, *Eschatology*, 81-83. Contrast Ratzinger's approach with the more dichotomized articulation of Johnston, *Shades of Sheol*, e.g., 23-46, 86-98. I will discuss the intermediate state and Israel's understanding of it extensively in chapter six.

[119]On the relation between the *threat* of death (e.g., sickness, violence, etc.) and the actual state of death in the Old Testament, see Ratzinger, *Eschatology*, 81-83.

of the dead, they are the geographical representations of the "land of the serpent," which in a spiritual sense is the underworld, or Sheol. Thus Israel's military battles against Sihon and Og, the Canaanites, and the Philistines are not just battles between Israel and ANE peoples but ultimately between YHWH and the serpent. In order to gain complete victory over the serpent, YHWH must go into his realm, the realm of the dead, and vanquish him.[120] Israel doesn't do this, and, as Heiser points out, this means that YHWH comes himself to do what Adam and Israel could not. Interestingly, though, Heiser proverbially punts on the descent, which should be a natural affirmation given his telling of the OT narrative. In any case, Heiser's work gives biblical rationale for why Jesus descending to the place of the dead to achieve victory over death is a natural culmination of the OT narrative, a narrative that focuses on the battle between YHWH and the serpent as seen in the conflict between their respective peoples in their respective places. YHWH's place is Canaan, while the serpent's place is the realm of the dead. To vanquish the serpent, YHWH's Messiah needs to enter the serpent's realm, the underworld, and vanquish him. This happens in Christ's descent.[121]

A second pattern we see beginning in the Old Testament and stretching into the New is that of vicarious work. Again in Genesis 22, as well as in the atonement laws in Leviticus and the Servant Songs in Isaiah, we find that YHWH provides a substitute, one who will take Israel's suffering in her place.[122] Regarding the relation of the church to

---

[120]Interestingly, the *glossa ordinaria* for Gen 22:17, where in Latin it reads, "possidebit semen tum portas inimicorum suorum" has "Quia descendet Christus infernum spoliatutus." Thanks to Todd Hains for this reference.

[121]This paragraph is an attempt to summarize much of Heiser's book. See Michael S. Heiser, *The Unseen Realm: Recovering the Supernatural Worldview of the Bible* (Bellingham: Lexham, 2015). See also his brief blog post about Jesus' reference to the "gates of hell," which is in many ways a summary of the one of the book's main theses. Heiser, "What Did Jesus Mean by 'Gates of Hell'?" *LogosTalk* (blog), April 10, 2018, https://blog.logos.com/2018/04/jesus-mean-gates-hell/.

[122]On YHWH's Servant and the substitutionary language related to him, see Stephen G. Dempster, "The Servant of the Lord," in *Central Themes in Biblical Theology: Mapping Unity in Diversity*, ed. Scott J. Hafemann and Paul R. House (Downers Grove, IL: InterVarsity Press, 2007), 128-78. See also Andrew T. Abernethy, *The Book of Isaiah and God's Kingdom: A Thematic-Theological*

Christ's work in the New Testament, the apostles describe that relation as one of union. In Romans 6, in particular, we hear Paul saying,

> Do you not know that all of us who have been baptized into Christ Jesus were baptized into his death? We were buried therefore with him by baptism into death, in order that, just as Christ was raised from the dead by the glory of the Father, we too might walk in newness of life.
>
> For if we have been united with him in a death like his, we shall certainly be united with him in a resurrection like his. (Rom 6:3-5)

Believers are united to Christ's work, or, to say it differently, Christ's work is enacted on behalf of and in continuity with his people. It is vicarious.[123] If this can be ascribed to all of his work, then that includes the descent.

This matters for our purposes in two ways: first, it means that, in the chapter on soteriology, we must ask if the descent is part of the atonement—that is, his vicarious suffering on behalf of his people's sins—or of Christ's exaltation, his ascent to glory. In the Old Testament, vicarious work is most often related to atonement. Is, then, Christ's descent a vicarious work in the sense that it is suffering experienced on behalf of God's people? In more common theological terms, we must ask whether Christ's descent to the dead is part of his humiliation or his exaltation.[124] The second question is whether or not Christ's descent is

---

Approach, NSBT 40 (Downers Grove, IL: IVP Academic, 2016), 137-59. On atonement in the Old Testament more broadly, see Jay Sklar, *Sin, Impurity, Sacrifice, Atonement: The Priestly Conceptions*, HBM 2 (Sheffield: Sheffield Phoenix, 2015); as well as his *Leviticus*, TOTC 3 (Downers Grove, IL: IVP Academic, 2014).

[123]I mean by this that Christ experiences it both with us and for us. What the "for us" means will be covered in chapter seven.

[124]Jeremy Treat has rightly critiqued a strict separation between these two states in the life of Christ, arguing instead for what he calls exaltation in and through humiliation. See Jeremy Treat, *The Crucified King: Atonement and Kingdom in Biblical and Systematic Theology* (Grand Rapids: Zondervan, 2014), 156-65. Still, I think that, in accordance with Phil 2:7-8, the climactic moment of Christ's humiliation occurs on the cross, even if, as Treat (rightly) argues, we also see Jesus as king from his cross. Beginning with the descent, as will be argued below, Christ's exaltation is in primary view, even if as Treat (rightly) notes, "he remains humble after the cross." Treat, *Crucified King*, 158. Treat's more nuanced articulation of the states, in addition to my previous comment that humiliation and exaltation are the *primary* state prior to/during

vicarious in more general terms unrelated (or at least tangential) to penal substitution; that is, is his descent an act on behalf of and in continuity with his people? Given the NT pattern of union with Christ discussed above, it appears that we can say that it is.

For now, the important point to note is that this vicarious pattern provides us with a rationale for talking about and confessing Christ's descent to the dead. If Christ's whole course of obedience[125] from incarnation to ascension is vicariously for his people, sharing in their humanity and redeeming it, this (sharing in their humanity, e.g., Phil 2:8) would include what every human experiences: death. This seems to be the way that the early church understood Christ's life and death; the incarnation, from conception to death and resurrection, was *pro nobis* ("for us") not just in the sense that Christ's life prepared him for his atoning death but also in the sense that Christ's human experience was both one in which he identified with our plight, experiencing all we do (including death) and also redeeming humanity from that plight. Christ's descent, then, is part of what Christ experiences for us in the incarnation. Death, both the moment of dying and the state of being dead, is a universal human experience, and Christ experiences it with us and for us.[126]

---

the cross and after the cross, respectively, may help assuage debates about whether the descent in particular should be seen as humiliation or exaltation. Balthasar, whose view I will discuss in the next chapter, wrongly in my estimation portrays Christ's descent as experiencing torment, or humiliation. It is for Balthasar the proper continuation of the cross; the penalty not only of dying but also the state of death is experienced by Christ. The common distinction between the states of Christ says that his humiliation ends at the cross. Still, Treat's nuanced articulation of the relationship between the states may allow us to appreciate Balthasar's acknowledgement that, in the descent, Christ experiences the very depths of sin's effects—namely, being dead. So we might say that, yes, Christ is still humble, in the sense that he experiences human death like all humans do, but the *primary* state is that of exaltation, as the intent of the descent is to provide and proclaim victory over Death and Hades.

[125]This phrase is from Thomas F. Torrance, *Incarnation: The Person and Life of Christ*, ed. Robert T. Walker (Downers Grove, IL: IVP Academic, 2007), 79-82. Torrance is reliant on Calvin for it.

[126]This is one of the most commonly cited meanings of the descent today. See, for example, Steffen Lösel, "A Plain Account of Salvation? Balthasar on Sacrifice, Solidarity, and Substitution," *Pro Ecclesia* 13.2 (2004): 141-71. I do not agree that solidarity need be contrasted with substitution, as Lösel does (more on this in chapter seven). Nevertheless, the essay's articulation of solidarity is helpful. For further reflection on the theme of solidarity in the descent in

This *pro nobis* pattern also fits within a third pattern related to Christ's descent, that of the larger pattern of ascent and descent in Scripture. From Abraham and Israel going down into Egypt and coming up again, to the same descent happening in the exile, Israel's history is filled with ascents and descents. Adam and Israel consistently descend into sin and darkness; they need a Messiah to bring them up again. Thus Jesus' own descent in the incarnation, and later in his baptism and descent to the dead, as well as his ascent in the resurrection and ascension, are fulfillments of this patterned hope.[127]

A fourth pattern related to Christ's descent is that of the phrase "from the dead" (ἀπό/ἔκ νεκρῶν).[128] When this phrase occurs in the New Testament, it does so in reference to the place of the dead.[129] Additionally, even when it is not this exact phrase that is used, the participial usage still typically denotes the place of the dead.[130] Notice the plural form of the participle, which could be accurately translated "[from/among/out of] the dead ones." This is further supported by the historical milieu of the New Testament, in which both the Jewish and Greco-Roman religious cultures affirmed a "place of the dead" to which everyone who died went. Of course, the New Testament's definition of this place may be different than that of ancient Israel, the Old Testament, Second

---

conversation with Balthasar, see Jonathan Cahill, "The Descent into Solidarity: Christ's Descent into Hell as Stimulus for Justice," *JRT* 9 (2015): 237-48.

[127]On this ascent/descent pattern of Christ's work, see Metropolitan Hilarion Alfeyev, *Christ the Conqueror of Hell: The Descent into Hades from an Orthodox Perspective* (Crestwood, NY: St. Vladimir's Seminary Press, 2009), 217. On the ascent/descent pattern of Scripture, see Douglas Farrow, *Ascension and Ecclesia: On the Significance of the Doctrine of the Ascension for Ecclesiology and Christian Cosmology* (Grand Rapids: Eerdmans, 2009), 278.

[128]On this term, see Bass, *Battle for the Keys*, e.g., 94n149.

[129]Particularly important in this regard are Lk 16:30-31; Rom 10:7; and Heb 13:20. Walter Bauer and Frederick William Danker, *BDAG: A Greek-English Lexicon of the New Testament and Other Early Christian Literature*, 3rd ed. (Chicago: The University of Chicago Press, 2000), 668.

[130]But note also the abundance of instances where this phrase or a similar one occurs in such a way that it appears to refer to the place of the dead in the NT. Mt 11:5; 14:2; 17:9; 22:31; 23:27; 27:64; 28:7; Mk 12:26; Lk 7:22; 20:37; 24:5; Jn 5:21; Acts 17:32; 23:6; 24:21; 26:8, 23; Rom 1:4; 1 Cor 15:12b, 13, 15f, 21, 28, 29a, 32, 35, 42, 52; Col 1:18; 1 Thess 1:10; 1 Pet 1:3; Rev 1:5. See Bass, *Battle for the Keys*, 94n149. Bass also lists, Rom 4:17, 2 Cor 1:9, and Rev 16:3, although the former two appear to refer simply to the dead as persons and not also to a place, and the latter equates the second bowl judgment to "the blood of a corpse."

Temple Judaism, and the Greco-Roman culture, but the point here is that, given the New Testament's historical context, the phrase "from the dead" probably carried with it specific connotations about location and the afterlife. We have discussed the conceptual milieu of these NT patterns earlier in the chapter and will discuss them in more detail in chapter five. For now it is sufficient to note that "from among the dead ones" probably carried with it particular connotations about the nature of the afterlife.

BACK TO 1 PETER 3:18-22

Given these explicit texts and implicit patterns, what then do we make of 1 Peter 3:18-22 (and perhaps of 1 Pet 4:6)? The passage reads,

> For Christ also suffered once for sins, the righteous for the unrighteous, that he might bring us to God, being put to death in the flesh but made alive in the spirit, in which he went and proclaimed to the spirits in prison, because they formerly did not obey, when God's patience waited in the days of Noah, while the ark was being prepared, in which a few, that is, eight persons, were brought safely through water. Baptism, which corresponds to this, now saves you, not as a removal of dirt from the body but as an appeal to God for a good conscience, through the resurrection of Jesus Christ, who has gone into heaven and is at the right hand of God, with angels, authorities, and powers having been subjected to him.

Is it plausible to read this passage as referring to anything but Christ's descent to the dead? Further, even if it not, is the claim warranted that biblical support for the descent is negligible? With respect to the second question, it appears from the exegetical and biblical-theological arguments above that the answer is "no." Support for Christ's descent to the place of the dead does not hinge on 1 Peter 3:18-22 any more than, say, eternal generation hinges on an exegetical analysis of Proverbs 8:22-31. Most doctrines do not rise or fall with one text, and even in the early church, theologians differed with respect to whether particular texts supported particular doctrines.[131] Regarding the descent, Augustine offers one of the earliest exegeses of 1 Peter 3:18-22 that does not see it as supporting this particular doctrine. He instead offers the interpretation that it is referring to the time of Noah, where Christ preached through Noah in spirit.[132] But again, given the New Testament's testimony to the descent elsewhere—as well as 1 Peter's Second Temple and Greco-Roman backgrounds—is it likely that this text is not referring to the descent? Further, is it exegetically warranted to read this text as referring to anything except Christ's descent?

When and where. The answer to that question depends, for the most part, on one's interpretation of ἐν ᾧ ("in which"). There are plausible arguments made for all the options, which need not detain us here.[133] I agree with Bass that ἐν ᾧ "should be translated as a conjunction ('during which time') because this is how Peter uses this grammatical

---

[131]For example, Augustine affirmed the doctrine of the descent but did not see 1 Pet 3:18-22 as a supporting text for it, while Athanasius and Basil of Caesarea both affirmed the doctrine of eternal generation but disagreed as to how Prov 8:22-31 fit into that discussion.

[132]Augustine, *Letters of St Augustin* CLXIV, "To Evodius" 515-21 (*NPNF*[1] 1:515). Augustine addresses a number of different questions in this letter, including when, where, and why Christ descended. His comments are laden with references to their speculative nature and to the difficulty of 1 Pet 3:18-22, so we should be careful in using it as endemic of the early Christian view. In many ways, Augustine's speculations in this particular letter veer away from the early Christian view rather than demonstrate continuity with it. Nevertheless, he affirms some core aspects of the descent, namely that it was on Saturday in his human soul and that it was victorious, not a continuation of the torment of the cross.

[133]For instance, I. Howard Marshall argues that these verses do refer to a victorious proclamation by Christ over the powers and principalities and evil angels, but according to him it occurs after his resurrection in the heavens. While I do not agree with Marshall about the timing or location of 1 Pet 3:18-19, he does state clearly the options involved in the interpretation of this passage; the ANE, Second Temple, and Greco-Roman backgrounds to the passage; and the victorious proclamatory purpose of this act in the context of Christ's redemptive work. In other words, I am in agreement with Marshall about Christ's victorious proclamation to evil angels and about the conceptual background of the passage, but I remain unconvinced of his argument of the timing and location of that victorious proclamation. See I. Howard Marshall, *1 Peter*, IVPNTC 17 (Downers Grove, IL: InterVarsity Press, 1991), 120-32. See also the similar comments in Peter H. Davids, *The First Epistle of Peter*, NICNT (Grand Rapids: Eerdmans, 1990), 138-40; Karen H. Jobes, *1 Peter*, BECNT (Grand Rapids: Baker Academic, 2005), 238-40; J. Ramsey Michaels, *1 Peter*, WBC 49 (Waco, TX: Word, 1988), 206-10. Jobes and Michaels also both make explicit mention of Feinberg's and Grudem's interpretation of the clause and reject it, although they also adopt Marshall's solution to the meaning of it (post-resurrection proclamation to evil angels).

construction four other times in this letter (1 Pet. 1:6; 2:12; 3:16 [temporal]; 4:4)."[134] Regarding the objection raised by, among others, France[135] and Grudem[136] that elsewhere in 1 Peter there is no preceding masculine or neuter noun that could serve as the clause's antecedent, Selwyn notes that both σαρκὶ and πνεύματι are adverbial datives, and "there is no example in the NT of a dative being the antecedent to a relative sentence."[137] Further, this sentence is narratively structured, beginning with his suffering and death (1 Pet 3:18a) and ending with his resurrection (1 Pet 3:21) and ascension (1 Pet 3:22). To speak of 1 Pet 3:18b-19 as a reference to his pre-incarnate state would interrupt this storied organization[138] and leads us further down the trail of this reading's implausibility. In other words, the phrase's usage within 1 Peter, the fact that datives do not serve as antecedents, and the passage's narratival structure each point to the phrase being used as a temporal conjunction ("during which time").

Because of Peter's reference to Christ's "being made alive in the spirit" in 1 Peter 3:18, the subsequent question becomes whether Christ preached to the spirits in prison between his crucifixion and resurrection or between his resurrection and ascension. There are a few issues related to answering this question, including the reference of "spirits" in verse 19.[139] But here I wish to focus on the phrase "in prison" (ἐν φυλακῇ). As Bass notes, in the New Testament, it is typically used with reference to earthly places of punishment, like dungeons, but in Revelation it is used synonymously with "Abyss" (Rev 20:3 NIV). Further, the only other time in the New Testament that φυλακή and

---

[134]Bass, *Battle for the Keys*, 89.

[135]R. T. France, "Exegesis in Practice: Two Examples," 252-81 in *New Testament Interpretation: Essays on Principles and Methods*, ed. I. Howard Marshall (Grand Rapids: Eerdmans, 1977), 269.

[136]Grudem, "He Did Not Descend."

[137]E. G. Selwyn, *The First Epistle of St. Peter: The Greek Text with Introduction, Notes, and Essays*, 2nd ed. (Grand Rapids: Baker, 1981), 315. This point follows Bass, 89n120.

[138]Bass, *Battle for the Keys*, 87.

[139]Bass convincingly argues that it is in reference to the disobedient angels in Gen 6:1-4. Bass, *Battle for the Keys*, 89-91.

πνεύματος are used together is in Revelation 18:2, in reference to evil spirits in prison. While this could be a prison in the heavenlies, both 2 Peter's use of Tartarus (2 Pet 2:4; cf. Jude 1:6) and 1 Peter's reliance on *1 Enoch* (a book in which the evil spirits are housed in the underworld) point to 1 Peter 3:19 using "in prison" with reference to the compartmentalized portion of the place of the dead in which evil spirits reside.[140]

Christ's actions. Given this interpretation that, in his death, Christ in human body remained in the grave and in his human spirit remained in the place of the dead, the question now arises as to what exactly Christ did or accomplished during this time. Bass notes three options borne out in the history of the *descensus* doctrine: a preaching tour, releasing the saints of the Old Testament, and victory over Death and Hades.[141] Regarding the first, this is dependent upon our interpretation of 1 Peter 3:18-20. If, as we have argued, ἐν ᾧ is a temporal conjunction that places Christ's preaching in the spirit between his death and resurrection, and if this preaching is to the spirits in prison, what is the nature of this preaching?

The verb Peter uses here is ἐκήρυξεν, and it is a generic word that simply indicates proclamation, good or bad, in both the Old Testament (LXX Gen 41:43; Ex 32:5; 36:6; 2 Kings 10:20; Esther 6:9; Jon 1:2) and the New Testament (Lk 4:19; 8:39; 12:3; Rom 2:21; Rev 5:2). Elsewhere in 1 Peter, εὐαγγελίζω is used for the specific proclamation of the gospel (1 Pet 1:12, 25; 4:6). In other words, there is nothing in 1 Peter 3:18-20 or in the rest of the canon of Scripture that demands or even implies that this preaching is a postmortem gospel proclamation that can be responded to in faith, resulting in the salvation of those who believe.[142] Rather, given that Peter specifies this proclamation's audience as "spirits in prison," or disobedient angels, the more

---

[140]See Bass, *Battle for the Keys*, 56-59.

[141]Bass, *Battle for the Keys*, 2.

[142]Bass, *Battle for the Keys*, 92-93.

likely—and lexically and contextually consistent—the proclamation by Christ is one of victory. Jesus descends to the place of the dead, and while there, he proclaims his victory over the evil spirits as well as over death itself through his death, remaining dead, and awaiting resurrection from the dead.[143]

1 Peter 4:6. What then do we do with 1 Peter 4:6, which states, "For this is why the gospel was preached even to those who are dead, that though judged in the flesh the way people are, they might live in the spirit the way God does"? It seems unlikely that Peter here shifts from the physically dead in 1 Peter 4:5 ("him who is ready to judge the living and the dead") to the spiritually dead in verse 6, given that he uses the same Greek word (νεκρός) in both verses and given that the phrases are joined to one another, at least in terms of immediate context. Does this mean that, while there is no postmortem gospel proclamation in 1 Peter 3:18-20, there is here in 1 Peter 4:6? I would say no, for at least two reasons. First, canonically, it seems clear that whatever decisions one makes in this life determine one's eternal fate. We see this in Luke 16:30-31; Hebrews 9:27; and Revelation's depiction of the righteous dead, among other places.

Further, as Bass notes, the possibility of a postmortem salvation would make little sense in the context of 1 Peter, given its strong emphasis on persevering in the faith unto death. If the audience is going to get another chance, why does Peter give such strong exhortations to

---

[143]One wonders if the modern evangelical notion of "gospel," focused almost exclusively on the salvation of individual souls rather than on Christ's holistic work in his death and resurrection, is to blame for this consternation over 1 Pet 3:19. If we define the gospel first and foremost as what Christ did, namely that he died, remained dead, and rose in such a way that he atoned for the sins of those who believe *and* achieved victory over all earthly and heavenly powers, then it is not such a problem that Christ "preached the gospel" to the spirits. In fact, he did preach the gospel—the good news that he has atoned for sin and thereby vanquished the powers of evil in his work. See on this, e.g., Scot McKnight, *The King Jesus Gospel: The Original Good News Revisited*, rev. ed. (Grand Rapids: Zondervan, 2016), although I think McKnight swings the pendulum the other direction and continues to bifurcate individual salvation and Christ's victory. A more balanced approach comes from Treat's *Crucified King*, in which Treat keeps together the atoning function of Christ's death and the victory it and his resurrection achieve over all rulers and authorities.

persevere now?[144] The other option, if we read νεκρός consistently in both verses as referring to those who have physically died, is that the latter half of the verse, "though judged in the flesh in the way people are, they might live in the spirit as God does," is a reference to all those who have believed from Noah's time to Peter's present.[145] This means that the preaching that occurred was, again, not a proclamation that could result in a postmortem salvation, but, as in 1 Peter 3:19, a proclamation of Christ's victory. This is what the righteous dead would have been waiting for, to see what they had trusted in come to tangible fruition. So, once again, we see that what is taught in both passages in 1 Peter is not a postmortem call to salvation but, rather, "a preaching tour in the underworld even to those who had died before Christ's incarnation (all true believers since the beginning of the world),"[146] as well as to those who did not believe and to the disobedient spirits.

CONCLUSION

I am choosing to suspend judgment about the release of OT saints until the chapters on creation, soteriology, and eschatology. For now, all that remains to be summarily said is that, based on Matthew 12:40 and the rest of the biblical witness regarding death, Christ between his death and resurrection experienced death as all humans do: his human body buried in a tomb and his human soul departing to the place of the dead. Further, based on Romans 10:7; Ephesians 4:9; Philippians 2:10; and Revelation 1:18, Christ achieved victory over Death and Hades in his descent to the dead. Finally, based on 1 Peter 3:18-20 and 4:6, Christ, in his descent, proclaimed this victory, achieved through his death, descent, and impending resurrection, to all the dead, righteous and unrighteous, and to the disobedient angels. Christ's descent, in other

---

[144]Bass, Battle for the Keys, 94-95.

[145]There is (potentially) a third option, that ἐκήρυξεν is a reference to a salvific proclamation that occurred before those who are now dead had yet died. In any case, I find Bass's explanation below entirely convincing.

[146]Bass, Battle for the Keys, 95.

words, is *primarily* part of his exaltation, not his humiliation.[147] We might say that, while it is one sense the *dénouement* of his humiliation in that he remains dead, it is *primarily* the beginning of his exaltation, as, having descended to the lowest part of human existence, he begins his ascent by proclaiming to those in those lower regions the news that he is their victorious king. What, then, do we make of the history of this doctrine and the different ways that various Christians have thought about the descent? This question will be explored in the following chapter.

---

[147] Again, though, see Treat's nuanced articulation between the relationship between the states and also my comments about how exaltation is *primary* in the descent, not exclusive, in the above note on the humiliation and exaltation.

"ON THE THIRD DAY HE ROSE FROM THE DEAD, AND HE ASCENDED INTO HEAVEN"

A Historical Defense of the Descent

> Christ lay in death's bonds
> given over for our sins,
> He has risen again
> and brought us life . . .
> It was a strange battle,
> that death and life waged,
> life claimed the victory,
> it devoured death.
> The scripture had prophesied this,
> how one death gobbled up the other,
> a mockery has been made out of death.
> Hallelujah!

MARTIN LUTHER, "CHRIST LAG IN TODESBANDEN"

This chapter explores the evidence that modern objections to the descent are straw men for more reasons than the misinterpretation of Scripture. Objectors either misread early church literature, conflate historical modifications with the doctrine itself, or both—failing to treat the descent doctrine's dogmatic history in light of the biblical evidence.

THE CREEDAL PHRASE IN RECENT EVANGELICAL LITERATURE

Before surveying the ways in which various groups of Christians have understood the descent, it is important to review how the phrase "he descended to the dead" came to be included in the Apostles' Creed (as well as the Athanasian Creed). Some have objected that the descent clause should not be included both for biblical-theological reasons (discussed in the previous chapter and below) and also because of the supposed murky history of the creedal phrase.[1] On the contrary, this chapter demonstrates that the belief in Christ's descent, as defined in the previous chapter, was ubiquitous throughout the patristic and medieval periods,[2] and that this is the historical sense of the creedal phrase. Not until the time of the Reformation, and particularly with Calvin, did the phrase begin to mean something markedly different, but that departure from the original sense has led to a proliferation of other options since the Reformation. This in turn has led some evangelicals to call for excision of the clause, a call I do not believe is justified based on the biblical and historical data.

One such evangelical is Wayne Grudem. Following Schaff, Grudem asserts that the creedal clause has a checkered past and that there should be no reason to avoid excluding it. In his view, in fact, there is compelling reason to exclude it since, according to him,

> some have argued that the phrase means just what it appears to mean on its reading: That Christ actually did descend into hell after his death on

---

[1] As Grudem calls it. He also refers to the phrase as a "late intruder" into the Apostles' Creed. Wayne A. Grudem, "He Did Not Descend into Hell: A Plea for Following Scripture Instead of the Apostles' Creed," *JETS* 34.1 (1991): 103.

[2] So J. A. MacCulloch: "From at least the second century there was no more well-known or popular belief . . . and its popularity steadily increased." MacCulloch, *The Harrowing of Hell: A Comparative Study of an Early Christian Doctrine* (Edinburgh: T & T Clark, 1930), 45.

the cross. It is easy to understand the Apostles' Creed to mean just this (indeed, this is certainly the natural sense). But then another question arises: Can this idea be supported from Scripture?[3]

Aside from the fact that Grudem cites no examples of those who believe Jesus descended into *hell*, and that he derives much of his argument from the fact that the English word *hell* does not mean "place of the dead" but "place of torment,"[4] there are a number of other issues with Grudem's historical and exegetical work that need to be addressed.

First, as Jeffery L. Hamm has forcefully argued, "Grudem has unwittingly placed himself in the awkward situation of quoting an error and mistakenly, though honestly, disseminating it."[5] The error to which Hamm refers is that of Philip Schaff, who asserts that the clause is not uniformly attested and was only included by Rufinus in 390 AD. According to Schaff, other versions of the Creed did not contain it between 200 and 650 AD. Further, argues Schaff, Rufinus only included it as another way to say that Christ was buried.[6] Hamm demonstrates in his

---

[3] Grudem, "He Did Not Descend," 107.

[4] Grudem, "He Did Not Descend," 107. This is a poor argument. Those who study the history of the creedal phrase will realize that, as Laufer notes,

> The Latin varies: *descendit ad inferna, descendit ad inferos, descendit ad infernum* and *ab inferis resurrectionis* all occur in different documents [here she cites Badcock, *History of the Creeds*, 145-6]. The two root words of the expression, *infernum* and *inferus*, are synonyms for the underworld or "lower parts of the earth," the place of the dead, as indicated by the Greek καταχθόνιος, subterranean parts [as used in the Formula of Sirmium in 359], or ἅδης, Hades, the realm of the dead. *Descendit ad inferna* became the standard form; more recently, *descendit ad inferos* has been preferred as, in later ecclesiastical Latin, *infernus* indicates the place of the damned while *inferos* has the more general meaning, the place of the dead. Similarly, the English translation "he descended into hell" and the German "abgestiegen zu der Hölle" both carry the implication of descent to the place of eternal punishment although the root of the English word at least held no meaning. The recent translation "he descended to the dead" is a more accurate rendering of the sense of the Latin and its Greek precursor.

See Catherine Ella Laufer, *Hell's Destruction: An Exploration of Christ's Descent to the Dead* (Surrey: Ashgate, 2013), 30. Further the idea that we should make an argument based on our own English language when we are dealing with a Latin Creed trying to summarize a Hebrew, Aramaic, and Greek Bible is certainly not a preferred historical or exegetical method.

[5] Jeffrey L. Hamm, "*Descendit*: Delete or Declare? A Defense Against the Neo-Deletionists," *WTJ* (2016): 95.

[6] See Philip Schaff, *The Creeds of Christendom*, 3 vols., ed. Philip Schaff, rev. David S. Schaff (1931; Grand Rapids: Baker, 2007), 1:14-23; 1:21n6; 2:46n2; and 2:52-55; and Philip Schaff, *History of the Christian Church* (1858; Peabody, MA: Hendrickson, 1996), 2:532n3.

essay that neither Schaff nor Grudem has understood Rufinus correctly. This is mostly due to the fact that both Schaff and Grudem attempt to interpret Rufinus's comment about the descent clause without reference to Rufinus's wider body of work.

The comment to which Schaff and Grudem refer comes in Rufinus's commentary on the Apostles' Creed, where he says, "'He descended into Hell,' is not added in the Creed of the Roman Church, neither is it that of the Oriental Churches. It seems to be implied however, when it is said that 'He was buried.'"[7] They take Rufinus to mean that (a) the clause is not attested elsewhere and (b) the clause is redundant with "he was buried" (i.e., it simply means Christ's body was in the grave). But Hamm demonstrates that this is clearly not what Rufinus meant by his comment. Through Hamm's thorough analysis of the Aquilean bishop's other writings, it is evident that Rufinus believes that Christ descended qua human to the realm of the dead, that his descent was victorious by virtue of the hypostatic union, that while in the realm of the dead he proclaimed his victory to the dead, and that by virtue of the presence of Christ the nature of the righteous compartment for the dead was thereby changed. Rufinus's view was, in other words, the commonly held view of the early church.[8]

Further, Hamm shows that Rufinus's comment regarding the clause's absence in the Roman and Eastern Churches is not due to the fact that they don't confess that Christ descended to the dead, but because in those churches it was seen as already being confessed in the clause "he was buried." In other words, the Roman and Eastern Churches meant by "he was buried" what Rufinus means by "he descended to the dead"— namely, Christ's victorious descent to the realm of the dead.[9] This is why they did not include the line in their creeds, not because they didn't believe in the descent but because they already felt it was communicated

---

[7]Rufinus, "A Commentary on the Apostles' Creed," (*NPNF*[2] 3:18, 550, 541-63).

[8]For such a thorough reading of Rufinus in light of other early church writings about the descent, see Hamm, "*Descendit*: Delete or Declare?" 96-99.

[9]Hamm, "*Descendit*: Delete or Declare?" 96.

by "he was buried." Or, as Michael Bird puts it, "The reason for the elasticity of wording is that a burial implies a descent, and the descent presupposes a burial."[10] Rufinus, on the other hand, seems to think it needs explicit inclusion among the other lines so as not to be overlooked or forgotten.[11]

In light of this evidence regarding Rufinus's own beliefs and Schaff's and Grudem's misunderstanding of them, what are we to do with the fact that so many earlier versions of the Apostles' Creed leave out the descent? Given the evidence cited above regarding Rufinus's actual comments, and given the very clear and virtually irrefutable claim that the descent was ubiquitously believed in the early church,[12] it seems unlikely that the evidence presented by Schaff and repeated and misinterpreted by Grudem regarding the fluctuation in the descent clause should be interpreted as he suggests. Rather than seeing it as evidence for the descent's ambiguous place in early Christian thought, we should rather see that fluctuation as geographically and ecclesially rooted in how particular churches viewed the clause "he was buried."[13] If, as Rufinus notes, particular churches view the burial clause as including the descent, they do not include a further and more explicit descent clause. If, however, certain churches do not view the burial clause as containing the descent, they include a descent clause explicitly.[14]

---

[10]Michael F. Bird, *What Christians Ought to Believe: An Introduction to Christian Doctrine Through the Apostles' Creed* (Grand Rapids: Zondervan, 2016), 148.

[11]See on this Rufinus, "Commentary" 2 (*NPNF*[2] 3:542-43), where he explains that the Creed was not written down until later because it was used as code when Christians were under persecution from the Roman Empire. On this point see also Hamm, "*Descendit*: Delete or Declare?" 99.

[12]Hamm, "*Descendit*: Delete or Declare?" 99-100; see also Justin W. Bass, *Battle for the Keys: Revelation 1:18 and Christ's Descent into the Underworld*, Paternoster Biblical Monographs (Wipf and Stock, 2014), 7, 11, 19.

[13]For an overview of how the early church referred to the descent in creeds and church orders, see MacCulloch, *Harrowing of Hell*, 67-82. For information on the clause in the Apostles' Creed, including its inclusion, phrasing, and geographical and ecclesial issues related to those shifts, see Liuwe H. Westra, *The Apostles' Creed; Origin, History, and Some Early Commentaries*, IPM 43 (Turnhout: Brepols, 2002), 539-62.

[14]As Hamm notes,

Rufinus' view of *descendit* is unambiguous. The Aquilean theologian explains that in different regions, from Rome to his own locale, various versions of the Creed were recited. Some

This makes much more historical sense of the descent clause than the solution posited by Grudem, especially when we consider how creeds were used in the early church. As Hamm notes, many churches prior to Constantine used creeds not only for catechesis but also as a sort of password, so that churches could know if someone was a true believer and not just trying to infiltrate the church for the purpose of persecution.[15] This in part explains some of the earlier fluctuation in the descent's explicit inclusion in local creeds.

A further salient point regarding creedal formation is that the three ecumenical creeds—Nicene-Constantinopolitan, Apostles,' and Athanasian—were all written in response to false teaching regarding particular doctrines. Given the descent's ubiquitous affirmation in the early church, there was no reason to ever have a uniform and explicit affirmation of it, especially if many churches believed it was already affirmed in the burial clause. Notice that when it is clearly attested, first by Rufinus in AD 390 and then again by the Sacramentarium Gallicanum in AD 650, it is precisely when the church is dealing with the threat of Apollinarianism. This heresy argues that in the incarnation the Logos assumes a human body but not a human soul, as the Logos is the mind (or soul) of Christ.[16] Athanasius deals with that christological heresy in his writing in the earlier part of the fourth century,[17] but it

---

formulas used "descended," others "buried." The clauses were interchangeable since "buried" implied "descent." In no way, though, does this mean that the location to which Christ descended is confined to a grave plot.

Hamm, "*Descendit*: Delete or Declare?" 98; see Rufinus, "Commentary" 17 (*NPNF*[2] 3:550).

[15]Hamm, "*Descendit*: Delete or Declare?" 99.

[16]On Apollinarius and Apollinarianism, see Aloys Grillmeier, SJ, *Christ in Christian Tradition: Volume One—From the Apostolic Age to Chalcedon (451)*, 2nd ed., trans. John Bowden (Atlanta: John Knox, 1975), 329-40.

[17]So MacCulloch:

Athanasius uses the Descent of Christ's Soul to Hades as an argument against the Apollinarian denial of a human soul in Christ. The soul of Christ was thought to be that of a mere man by Death, but Christ came with a soul which could not be kept in bonds, in order to burst the bonds of those kept in bonds and to give them freedom.

MacCulloch, *Harrowing of Hell*, 109. Here MacCulloch also notes that Athanasius cites the creeds of Sirmium, Nike, and Constantinople in support of the descent. On Athanasius's view of the descent, see *Apoll.* i. 13, ii. 8; *C. Ar.* iii. 29, 56; and *Ep. Epict.* lix, 5.

remains an issue after Constantinople I (381 AD) until the Council of Chalcedon (451 AD). It then becomes an issue once again between Constantinople II (553 AD) and Constantinople III (680–81 AD), the latter of which had to again explicitly condemn Apollinarianism, and especially its offspring, monothelitism.[18]

In other words, the two periods in which we find an explicit descent clause in Grudem's list are the two periods in which the church had to confront Apollinarianism most directly. And the descent is the perfect doctrine for which to combat that heresy, because it most clearly affirms that Christ possessed not only a human body but also a human soul, since it is in his human soul that Christ descends to the realm of the dead ones. While one could posit that the doctrine of the incarnation in general combats Apollinarianism, the reason the descent is uniquely important with respect to that particular heresy is because it necessitates that Christ have a human soul, which Apollinarianism denies. Apollinarians do not deny the incarnation; instead, they agree that a human being consists of body and soul, and that in the incarnation "the Logos joins himself to a human, fleshly nature [a body] to form a substantial unity and through this union constitutes a human being, i.e. a body [human nature] and a spirit [the Logos]."[19]

Finally, what Grudem fails to mention when reprinting Schaff's list is that Schaff[20] and the other persons mentioned in his list clearly and unequivocally affirm Christ's descent to the dead.[21] Even Augustine, who Grudem cites as an example of rejecting the descent in 1 Peter 3:18-22,[22] clearly affirms the doctrine based on other biblical

---

[18]On the potential anti-Apollinarian purpose of the descent clause, see Bass, *Battle for the Keys*, 7; Hamm, "*Descendit*: Delete or Declare?" 106; and Laufer, *Hell's Destruction*, 28, 199.

[19]Grillmeier, *Christ in Christian Tradition* I:331.

[20]Hamm, "*Descendit*: Delete or Declare?" 95.

[21]On the ubiquity of the descent doctrine in the early church, see Bass, *Battle for the Keys*, 1-19; and Hamm, *Descendit*: Delete or Declare?" 99-100. See also the discussion below of the early Christian view, as well as numerous citations throughout this book of early Christian writings about the descent.

[22]Grudem, "He Did Not Descend," 110.

passages.[23] In other words, the fact that the other versions of the Apostles' Creed besides Rufinus's and the Sacramentarium's do not contain the descent clause requires an alternative explanation. Contrary to Grudem's assertion that it indicates an ambiguity regarding its affirmation, the descent was ubiquitously affirmed among the early church, including by those who recorded alternative versions of the Apostles' Creed. This means that another explanation—that it is related to geographical and ecclesial emphases and the relative importance of combatting Apollinarianism at any particular time—is required.

While Grudem made a mistake that any scholar can in repeating as fact a faulty argument from a reliable source (i.e., Schaff's interpretation of Rufinus), what is perhaps more concerning is the incorrect way that Grudem describes the history of the doctrine and the early church's understanding of it. It is concerning not only as a matter of accuracy but also because Grudem's view of the clause has been widely influential among evangelicals. In short, both he and those who have adopted his argument reject the descent based on a straw man. In order to correct this error and demonstrate the early church's actual view of the descent, as well as the ways in which various Christian traditions have departed from that early view, a historical overview of the clause is given below.[24]

---

[23]For instance,

> It is established beyond question that the Lord, after He had been put to death in the flesh, "descended into hell;" for it is impossible to gainsay either that utterance of prophecy, "Thou wilt not leave my soul in hell," [Ps. 16:10]—an utterance which Peter himself expounds in the Acts of the Apostles, lest any one should venture to put upon it another interpretation,—or the words of the same apostle, in which it he affirms that the Lord "loosed the pains of hell, in which it was not possible for Him to be holden" [Acts 2:27]. Who, therefore, except an infidel, will deny that Christ was in hell?

Augustine, *Letters of St. Augustin* CLXIV, "To Evodius" (*NPNF*[1] 1:515-16). See the discussion of Augustine's position in Hamm, "*Descendit*: Delete or Declare?" 100.

[24]See also the historical summary of Friedrich Loofs, "Descent to Hades (Christ's)," in *Encyclopedia of Religion and Ethics*, vol. 4, *Confirmation–Drama*, ed. James Hastings (1912; Edinburgh: T&T Clark, 1981), 648-54, 654-63. The contours of Loofs's historical overview are similar to mine, including the fact that Loofs notes repeatedly that the descent is among the earliest of Christian theological views (e.g., Loofs, "Descent," 662). I differ, however, with Loofs with respect to his treatment of the biblical material (he does not find biblical support for the doctrine). And while he is correct to point out that the early Christian view of the descent was reliant upon the cosmology of Jewish-Christian beliefs in the first century AD, I do not agree with

THE EARLY CHRISTIAN VIEW(S)[25]

There are a number of possible interpretive options found in the history of the doctrine.[26] First, there is the early Christian view of the descent; it is indisputable that "by the second century the descent of Christ into Sheol is a well-attested belief, referred to, among others, by Ignatius of Antioch . . . , Polycarp, and Justin, Irenaeus . . . , Tertullian."[27] The early Christian view of the descent is primarily understood as Jesus' journey to the place of the dead, his body in the grave and his soul in the place of the (righteous) dead, where he proclaims his victory over death and Hades. Regarding the place to which Christ descended, Tertullian gives an explanation that accords well with both the biblical data and the commonly held early Christian view in *De anima* 7, 55, 58; and *Adversus Marcionem*, iv. 34. MacCulloch summarizes Tertullian's position in these sections as follows:

> Hades is a subterranean region, and in it all souls are enclosed. Christ, at his death, descended to Hades, to the souls of the patriarchs. Abraham's Bosom, though not a heavenly region, is yet a higher part of Hades, which offers meanwhile a place of refreshment to the souls of the

---

his subsequent conclusion that both that cosmology and the descent should be abandoned. I will say more about cosmology in chapter five.

[25]I use the term *view(s)* here and below in order to recognize the diversity of views in any of these periods and/or traditions while also acknowledging the task at hand—namely, to summarize these periods and/or traditions even given all their diversity. I do not believe that one has to limit the task of systematic theology to particularity. Or, to put it differently, even given the diversity of thought in these periods and/or traditions, I still think we can generalize in a way that is faithful to those particularities while also acknowledging what they have in common.

[26]A version of the following historical overview was previously published in Matthew Y. Emerson, "'He Descended to the Dead': The Burial of Christ and the Eschatological Character of the Atonement," *SBJT* 19.1 (Spring 2015): 115-31. Used with permission. I have adapted it in light of further research on the issue; especially noteworthy are the changes to the description of the Eastern Orthodox and Roman Catholic views.

[27]Killian McDonnell, "The Baptism of Jesus in the Jordan and the Descent into Hell," *Worship* 69.2 (1995): 100. See also Justin Bass, who says, "Even among modern scholars who deny that the doctrine of the *Descensus* is found in Scripture, there is virtual unanimity that from Ignatius to the medieval period, this doctrine was believed and affirmed by the church." *Battle for the Keys*, 7; and again: "All in all, the historical argument for the doctrine of Christ's *Descensus* is one of the most primitive and most agreed upon teachings of the ancient church. . . . The doctrine of the *Descensus* is very ancient beginning in the early second century, geographically widespread, and is unanimously assumed by the church for fifteen centuries." Bass, *Battle*, 19.

righteous. . . . Christ complied with the law of death, remaining *apud inferos* in the form and condition of a dead man. His purpose in going thither was to make the patriarchs and prophets partakers of Himself (*compotes sui faceret*)."[28]

Another important aspect of the early church's view is that Christ's victory in his descent implies that he releases the first Adam and all others who have awaited him by faith through his role as the second Adam.[29]

A related common feature of the early Christian belief about Christ's descent is that, in doing so, he liberates all those held captive who await him in faith.[30] For example, in his discussion of the early church's view on the descent, Jared Wicks summarizes Origen's view thus: "Christ broke death's oppressive power once and for all, for the benefit of all humankind, including death's prisoners, and so Paul rightly says in the passage being explained, 'death no longer has dominion over him' (Rom. 6:9)."[31] There is here a strong sense of Christ as victor, but victory is combined with liberation. Cyril of Alexandria, for example,

---

[28]MacCulloch, *Harrowing of Hell*, 93-94. I would only take issue with Tertullian's distinction elsewhere between paradise ("not a heavenly region") and Abraham's bosom; as we saw in the previous chapter, these could be considered synonyms in Second Temple Jewish thought.

[29]The most wide-ranging discussing of the descent in early Christian theological and apocryphal literature remains MacCulloch's treatment in *The Harrowing of Hell*, 83-152. Bass summarizes the same data well in *The Battle for the Keys*, 1-19. See also Metropolitan Hilarion Alfeyev, *Christ the Conqueror of Hell: The Descent into Hades from an Orthodox Perspective* (Crestwood, NY: St. Vladimir's Seminary Press, 2009), 43-104, for patristic and medieval texts, and 105-202 for liturgical texts used in the Orthodox Church, although I find Alfeyev's theological conclusions throughout his historical survey to be tendentious. I discuss this more in chapter seven. Finally, in German scholarship, see Aloys Grillmeier, "Der Gottesohn im Totenreich: soteriologische und christologische Motivierung der Descensuslehre in der alteren christlichen Überlieferung," *ZKT* 71 (1949): 1-53, 184-203; Markwart Herzog, *"Descensus Ad Inferos": Eine religionphilosophische Untersuchung der Motive und Interpretationen mit besonderer Berücksichtigung der monographischen Literatur seit dem 16. Jahrundert*, Frankfurter Theologische Studien 53 (Frankfurt: Knecht, 1997); and Josef Kroll, *Gott ünd Hölle: Der Mythos vom Descensuskampfe* (1932; Darmstadt: Wissenschaftliche Buchgesellschaft, 1963).

[30]See, for example, Malcolm L. Peel, "The 'Descensus Ad Inferos' in 'The Teachings of Silvanus' (CG VII, 4)," *Numen* 26.1 (1979): 39-49. See also John A. McGuckin, "Eschatological Horizons in the Cappadocian Fathers," in *Apocalyptic Thought in Early Christianity*, ed. Robert J. Daly, SJ, Holy Cross Studies in Patristic Theology and History (Grand Rapids: Baker Academic, 2009), 193-210.

[31]Jared Wicks, SJ, "Christ's Saving Descent to the Dead: Early Witnesses from Ignatius of Antioch to Origen," *Pro Ecclesia* 17.3 (2008): 306.

combines these two motifs in his understanding of the descent, arguing that Christ defeats both Hades *and* Adam's sin and its effects, which thereby liberates Adam's race from its captivity to Satan and death.[32] Similarly, Syrian theology, represented most notably by Ephrem, affirmed that "Christ, through his saving work, has undone the consequences of the fall and removed the curse from humanity [see, e.g., *Nisbene Hymn* 36:1]."[33]

One of the more common ways that the early church theologians discussed (and visually represented in iconography) Christ's victory in the descent is through tying it to his baptism,[34] and sometimes also to his incarnation. In both of these other descents, the God-man descends to a watery locale and, as a result, crushes Satan's head.[35] In doing so, Christ is victorious over Adam's jailer and thus liberates him

---

[32]Daniel Keating, "Christ's Despoiling of Hades: According to Cyril of Alexandria," *St. Vladimir's Theological Quarterly* 55.3 (2011): 253-69.

[33]Irina Kukota, "Christ, the Medicine of Life: The Syriac Fathers on the Lord's Descent into Hell," *Road to Emmaus* 6.1 (2005): 47. Another example comes from one of Ephrem's poems:

Jesus, bend down to us thy love, for us to grasp!
This is the branch which he bent down its fruit to the thankless;
they ate and were filled, but turned and insulted it; yet it bent down
    even to Adam in the midst of Sheol.
It ascended and brought him up and with him returned to Eden.
Blessed be he who bent it down to us
    for us to grasp and ascend by it!

The translation is from Robert Murray, *Symbols of Church and Kingdom: A Study in Early Syriac Tradition*, rev. ed. (London: T&T Clark, 2006), 109. Thanks to Andrew Tucker for this reference. On Ephrem's view of the descent, see Thomas Buchan, *"Blessed is He Who Has Brought Adam from Sheol": Christ's Descent to the Dead in the Theology of Saint Ephrem the Syrian* (Gorgias Dissertation 13; Early Christian Studies 2; Piscataway: Gorgias Press, 2004). Buchan traces Ephrem's theology of the descent in relation to the Syrian's view on other major Christian doctrines, much as this book attempts to trace an evangelical theology of the descent in relation to the whole fabric of Christian theology.

[34]See, for example, MacCulloch's comments on Gregory Thaumaturgos's connection of the descent to baptism in *The Harrowing of Hell*, 108.

[35]Here, the abode of the dragon is in the waters of chaos, and thus Christ's step into the waters means that he is stepping onto Satan's head, crushing it. On parallels between the descent and the incarnation, see, for example, Kukota, "Christ, the Medicine of Life," 19-20; Peel, "The 'Descensus ad Inferos,'" 35-36. On parallels between baptism and the descent, see, for example, Georgia Frank, "Christ's Descent to the Underworld in Ancient Ritual and Legend," in Daly, *Apocalyptic Thought*, 217, 224-25 (211-26); and especially McDonnell, "The Baptism of Jesus in the Jordan and the Descent into Hell," 98-109.

and his progeny from bondage. In the patristic sources, then, Christ defeats the universal enemies of Death, hell, and Satan and liberates those formerly bound by Death.[36] That is, Christ's descent liberates those of Adam's race who awaited the Messiah in faith from the effects of his sin.[37]

While this latter affirmation concerning the liberation of Adam's race may sound close to universalism, it is important here to note that, except for Origen and perhaps Clement of Alexandria,[38] Christians in the first four centuries of the church were careful to clarify that Christ's descent is only liberating for the faithful.[39] They did not affirm a postmortem second chance for salvation upon Christ's descent, and they explicitly denied that Christ's descent saved all those in Hades. For example, Hippolytus of Rome, speaking about John the Baptist as a forerunner to Christ's descent, says, "He also first preached to those in Hades . . . so

---

[36]Cyril of Alexandria explicitly ties the descent to the "binding of the strong man" in the Gospels. See his comments on Is 49:24 in Cyril of Alexandria, *Commentary on Isaiah*, vol. 3, trans. Robert Charles Hill (Brookline, MA: Holy Cross Orthodox Press, 2008), 220-22; see also Keating's comments on the victorious portrayal of the descent in Cyril in "Christ's Despoiling of Hades," 256-57.

[37]Although we should note here that many of the patristic theologians were careful about how they articulated this universal significance. Both Cyril of Alexandria and Augustine saw universal significance in Christ's descent but not necessarily universal salvation. See, respectively, Keating, "Christ's Despoiling of Hades," and Martin F. Connell, "*Descensus Christi Ad Inferos*: Christ's Descent to the Dead," *TS* 62 (2001): 262-82.

[38]See the discussion in Bass, *Battle for the Keys*, 11-14. One might also ask about Gregory of Nyssa's views here, on which see his *The Soul and the Resurrection*, Popular Patristics 12, trans. Catherine P. Roth, ed. John Behr (Crestwood, NY: St. Vladimir's Seminary Press, 1993); and Morwenna Ludlow, *Universal Salvation: Eschatology in the Thought of Gregory of Nyssa and Karl Rahner*, Oxford Theology and Religion Monographs (2001; Oxford: Oxford University Press, 2009).

[39]See, for instance, Augustine, *Haer.*, 79; and Gregory the Great, *Ep.* 15. See also Bede the Venerable, *The Commentary on the Seven Catholic Churches of Bede the Venerable* (Kalamazoo: Cistercian, 1985), 104; Boniface, *Ep.* 57; and the Council of Toledo (AD 625), which declared that Christ only liberated the righteous dead from Hades. MacCulloch, *Harrowing of Hell*, 242, also notes that many of the earliest witnesses to the descent limited the liberating effects of Christ's Preaching in the descent to the OT saints. Presumably this is because, for them, Preaching implied the good news of the liberation from Hades that was about to occur, and the earliest witnesses (MacCulloch lists Hippolytus, Cyprian, Irenaeus, Justin, and Tertullian) did not want to affirm universal salvation. This view of the liberating element of Christ's work is not ubiquitous, as we will see; others took the Preaching to be to all in Hades, but this did not imply universalism since for them it was a proclamation of victory and not of a call to repent and believe or a proclamation that all who heard it had been freed from Death and Hades.

Figure 3.1. Orthodox icon of the Resurrection depicting Christ removing Adam and Eve from the grave

that there too he might intimate that the Savior would descend to ransom the souls of the saints from the hand of Death."[40]

Another important example in this regard is Cyril of Alexandria. Given Cyril's prominence in pro-Nicene thought and in the christological controversies leading up to the Council of Chalcedon (451 AD),[41] his thoughts on this particular aspect of the work of Christ are especially relevant. He is also relevant not just to our discussion of the descent but also more particularly to whether the descent was seen as universally salvific in the early Christian period and into the medieval period. Many times Cyril is "portrayed as a universalist or quasi-universalist," and, "It is easy to locate short, punchy quotes from Cyril that make it sound as if he believes Christ simply liberated all the dead and brought them *en masse* to heaven."[42] But, as Daniel Keating, argues, this is not actually what Cyril teaches; instead, when we read Cyril closely on the descent, we find that he affirms Christ's descent is effective only for those who previously awaited him in faith.[43] Especially pertinent in this regard are Cyril's comments on John 10:11-18 and Jesus' role as the Good Shepherd.[44] Here, Cyril connects the Good Shepherd imagery with Death and Hades, commenting on John 10:12-13 that

---

[40]Hippolytus, *Antichr.* 45 (*ANF* 5: 213).

[41]For an introduction to Cyril, see the summary of scholarship on Cyril's life and thought in Matthew R. Crawford, *Cyril of Alexandria's Trinitarian Theology of Scripture* (Oxford Early Christian Studies; Oxford: Oxford University Press, 2014), 4-5; and the accessible introduction by John Anthony McGuckin, "Introduction," 9-48 in St. Cyril of Alexandria, *On the Unity of Christ*, trans. and ed. John Anthony McGuckin (Crestwood, NY: St. Vladimir's Seminary Press, 1995).

[42]Keating, "Christ's Despoiling of Hades," 268.

[43]There is some conjecture that Cyril taught that Jesus gave a postmortem gospel offer to the dead, but the evidence is not clear on this. The point here is that, for Cyril, Christ's descent is not universally effective or salvific for everyone, but only those who have responded to Christ in faith. On the issue of a postmortem offer, see Keating, "Christ's Despoiling of Hades," 262-66. As Keating notes, even if Cyril allows for a postmortem offer to those already in Hades upon Christ's descent, Cyril does not expect a positive response from those who had not been awaiting the Messiah's coming in faith. Keating, "Christ's Despoiling of Hades," 255-56.

[44]See Cyril of Alexandria, *Commentary on the Gospel According to St John by S Cyril, Archbishop of Alexandria*, vol. 2, trans. Thomas Randel (London: Walter Smith, 1885), 73-77.

The father of sin [Satan] used to put us *in Hades like sheep*, delivering us over to *death* as our *shepherd*, according to what is said in the Psalms: but the really Good Shepherd died for our sakes, that he might take us from the dark pit of death and prepare to enfold us among the companies of heaven, and give unto us mansions above, even with the Father.[45]

As Keating notes, while this may sound as though Jesus empties Hades and thus provides universal salvation, this is not actually what Cyril is arguing. In an earlier comment on John 10:10, Cyril makes clear that while the descent and resurrection of Jesus provide the basis for the general resurrection of the dead, it does not result in universal salvation. All will be raised, but not all will be raised to eternal life. Thus, "For Cyril there is a restoration to life that can also end in final punishment. . . . The resurrection of everyone from the dead is a universal effect of Christ's own resurrection [and descent], but it does not guarantee universal *salvation*."[46] We will return to the question of universalism and the descent in chapter seven, and the general resurrection will again be discussed in chapter nine. For now it is sufficient to agree with Keating that Cyril's, and virtually all of the rest of the early Christian witnesses', emphasis is on "the glorious victory that Christ won over death and Satan, such that Hades as the place of the dead *ruled by Satan* is completely undone."[47] Nevertheless, this does not imply universalism for the prevailing strain of thought regarding the descent in early Christian and medieval thought.[48]

The early Christian theologians thus emphasized that Jesus descends to the dead as any human does at death: his human body is placed in the grave while his human soul departs to the place of the dead, as all human souls do. And since Jesus is righteous, his descent is only to the compartment of Hades that houses the righteous dead (paradise,

---

[45]Cyril of Alexandria, *Commentary on the Gospel of John*, vol. 2, 77.

[46]Keating, "Christ's Despoiling of Hades," 259.

[47]Keating, "Christ's Despoiling of Hades," 259.

[48]Augustine explicitly and repeatedly denies this understanding of the descent. See, for example, *Letters* 164.4.16 (*NPNF*[1] 1:519-520).

Abraham's bosom), not the unrighteous. The clearest statement concerning this comes early, in *Ascen. Isa.* 10:7-11; 11:19:[49]

> And I heard the voice of the Most High, the Father of my Lord, saying to
> my Lord Christ who will be called Jesus: "Go forth and descend through all
> the heavens, and thou wilt descend to the firmament and that world: to the
> angel in Sheol thou wilt descend, but to Haguel thou wilt not go. And thou
> wilt become like unto the likeness of all who are in the five heavens. And
> thou wilt be careful to become like the form of the angels of the firmament
> [and the angels also who are in Sheol]. And none of the angels of that world
> shall know that Thou art with Me of the seven heavens and of their
> angels. . . ." And after this the adversary envied Him and roused the children
> of Israel against Him, not knowing who He was, and they delivered Him to
> the king, and crucified Him, and He descended to the angel (of Sheol).[50]

Notice that the author explicitly states that Christ did not descend into Haguel, what we might call "hell" or, in the second century, Tartarus or Gehenna. Jesus did not descend to the place of torment. This kind of clarification—that Jesus only descends to the place of the righteous dead—continues throughout the early Christian and medieval periods.[51]

Further, because Jesus is the God-Man, his death is a victorious one,[52] in the sense that he descends to the dead not only qua human but also

---

[49]For an introduction to *Ascen. Isa.*, including critical issues; thematic and theological issues; and a translation, see P. Bettiolo et al, eds., *Ascensio Isaiae: Textus*, CCSA 7 (Turnhout: Brepols, 1995); and E. Norelli, *L'Ascensione di Isaia: Studi su un apocrifo al crocevia dei cristianesimi*, Origini NS 1 (Bologna: Centro editorial dehoniano, 1994).

[50]See similar, if truncated, statements about the descent in *Ascen. Isa.* 4:21; and 9:12-17.

[51]For early examples, see e.g., Tertullian, *An.* 55 (*ANF* 3: 231); and an anonymous homily, previously associated with Chrysostom, in *Homélies Paschales*, I, *Une Homélie inspire du traité su la Paque d'Hippolyte*, ed. Pierre Nautin, Homily 55-56 (SC 27).

[52]Melito of Sardis is one of the earliest to speak of the descent in robust military terms. See his *Peri Pascha* 70-71 and 101-2. For an introduction to *Peri Pascha* including critical issues, thematic and theological issues, and a translation, see Melito of Sardis, *On Pascha and Fragments*, rev. ed., trans. and ed. Stuart George Hall, Oxford Early Christian Texts (1979; Oxford: Clarendon, 2012). For another accessible translation, see Melito of Sardis, *On Pascha*, trans. Alistair Stewart-Sykes, Popular Patristics 20 (Crestwood, NY: St. Vladimir's Seminary Press, 2001). For analysis of Melito's thoughts on the descent, see Bass, *Battle for the Keys*, 11; and Wicks, "Christ's Saving Descent," 291-93. For more on the earliest Christian views of the descent, see my "'The One Who Trampled Hades Underfoot': A Comparative Analysis of Christ's Descent to the

with the hypostatic union still intact and thereby defeats Death and Hades as God the Son incarnate.[53] This victory also brings release to those who awaited the Messiah by faith. As Bass says,

> Regardless of how imaginative the understanding of the *Descensus* becomes in the later centuries, the historical core of threefold purpose of Christ's descent: preaching, releasing the saints of the Old Testament, and triumphant defeat of Death and Hades is one of the best attested Christian doctrines from the second century.[54]

And this geographically widespread, virtually universally believed doctrine remains nearly ubiquitous through the medieval period,[55] retaining the main elements listed by Bass in the previous quote.[56] While there are some additions to it in the medieval and post-Reformation periods that contribute to its rejection by Protestants (discussed below), it is important to note here how early, widespread, and virtually universal the doctrine is, and how much it aligns with our biblical exploration in the previous chapter.

THE EASTERN ORTHODOX VIEW(S)

The descent doctrine is more closely tied to a postmortem opportunity for salvation and/or an implicit universalism, especially in the East, after the fifth century. In some cases it is difficult to ascertain how strongly Eastern writers held to an implicit universal salvation in the descent due

---

Dead and Trinitarian Relations in Second Century Christian Texts and Hans Urs von Balthasar," *SJT*, forthcoming.

[53]One reason that such a wide variety of contemporary views exist on the descent is that there are an equally wide variety of views on the meaning of Hades, Sheol, Gehenna, hell, and Death, as well as into which of these places Jesus descended. On the biblical language about death and the afterlife, see Dimitris J. Kyrtatas, "The Origins of Christian Hell," *Numen* 56 (2009): 282-97; and Gary Yamasaki, "Jesus and the End of Life in the Synoptic Gospels," *Vision* (5.1): 40-47.

[54]Bass, *Battle for the Keys*, 11.

[55]I only say "nearly" (and, elsewhere, "virtually") to acknowledge that some Christian somewhere may have denied the doctrine. But in the extant writings we have from this period, to my knowledge, no one denies the descent.

[56]On the development of the descent in the medieval period and particularly in England, see Colleen Donnelly, "Apocryphal Literature, the Characterization of Satan, and the *Descensus ad Inferos* Tradition in England in the Middle Ages," *Religion & Theology* 24 (2017): 321-49.

to the poetic nature of their writings. This is the case, for instance, with the Syrian hymn writer Romanos the Melodist, who penned a number of his *kontakia* with reference to the descent. In *Kontakion 44*, for example, he writes, "For not only myself [Adam] but also my descendants and all men you [Death] will lose; you will be deprived of all."[57] Maximus the Confessor, a seventh-century Byzantine theologian, seems to suggest that the descent provides an opportunity for postmortem salvation for the unrighteous dead.[58] But according to Vladimir Lossky, charges that Maximus secretly follows Origen on his understanding of apocatastasis (the renewal of all things, with the implication of universal salvation) are overblown. Critiquing Balthasar's understanding of Maximus, Lossky notes that while some of Maximus's statements about Christ's work and particularly his descent have universal overtones, these passages are set in a context in which Maximus clearly delimits the effects of Christ's work for all human beings "proportionately for each one."[59]

On the other hand, John of Damascus, writing in the late eighth and early ninth centuries, says that Christ in his descent "became to those who believed the Author of everlasting salvation and to those who did not believe, a denunciation of their unbelief, so he might become the same to those in Hades: 'That every knee should bow, in heaven and on earth and under the earth.'"[60] It appears, then, that Eastern theologians in the late patristic or early medieval period (depending on whether one divides those eras in the fifth or eighth centuries) carried on the earlier traditional understanding of the doctrine. Additionally, some of those same theologians also were more explicit about

---

[57]Romanos the Melodist, *Kontakion* 44, 7 (SC 128, 558), as quoted by Alfeyev, *Christ the Conqueror of Hell*, 149.

[58]See Maximus the Confessor, *Questions-Answers to Thalassius* 7 (PG 90:284bc), as quoted in Alfeyev, *Christ the Conqueror of Hell*, 79.

[59]The passage Lossky references regarding the descent is *Questions-Answers to Thalassius* 64 (CCSG 22:195, II. 147-51), while the referent for the proportionate nature of Christ's work is *Questions-Answers to Thalassius* 47 (CCSG 7:325, II. 214-16). See Vladimir Lossky, *The Mystical Theology of the Eastern Church* (1957; Crestwood, NY: St. Vladimir's Seminary Press, 2002), 249-50.

[60]John of Damascus, *An Exact Exposition of Orthodox Faith* 3, 29 (PG 94:1101a), as quoted in Alfeyev, *Christ the Conqueror of Hell*, 80.

postmortem salvation opportunities or an implied universal salvation in the descent.

This tendency continues in the East through the medieval and Reformation periods to today. Like their early medieval (or late patristic) forebears, contemporary Orthodox theologians share many of the same views of the early Christian view, and many of them are also much more willing to proclaim a general or universal effectiveness of Christ's descent for all humanity.[61] This effectiveness is still usually tied to the faith response of the individual, but there is much more hope of universal salvation in the Orthodox tradition than there is in the early views of the descent or in Protestantism and Roman Catholicism. Metropolitan Hilarion Alfeyev, for example, says that,

> We do not know if everyone followed Christ when he rose from hell, nor do we know if everyone will follow him to the eschatological heavenly kingdom when he will become 'all in all.' We do know that, since Christ's descent, the way to resurrection has been opened for 'all flesh,' salvation has been granted to every human being, and the gates of paradise have been opened for all who wish to enter through them.[62]

Similarly, Sergius Bulgakov links an implicit universalist hope with the supposed evangelistic preaching of Christ in his descent to hell, saying,

> God has left us ignorant of the destinies of those who have not known Christ and have not entered into the church. A certain hope is given us by the teaching of the Church on the descent of Christ into hell and His preaching from hell, addressed to all pre-Christian humanity. The word stands firm that God 'wishes all men to be saved and to come to the knowledge of the truth' (I Tim. 2:4). Nevertheless, the Church has never officially defined the destiny of non-Christians, adult or infant.[63]

---

[61]See, for instance, Kukota, "Christ, the Medicine of Life," 17-56.

[62]Alfeyev, *Christ the Conqueror of Hell*, 218.

[63]Sergius Bulgakov, *The Orthodox Church*, rev. ed., trans. Lydia Kesich (1935; Crestwood, NY: St. Vladimir's Seminary Press, 1988), 183. Although not Eastern Orthodox and while careful not to imply universalism per se, Brent A. Strawn appears to combine both the victorious and what he calls "revival" elements of the descent in his treatment of the topic for preaching. He

And although Alfeyev, Bulgakov, and other Orthodox theologians attempt to root their implied universalism in the early Christian view,[64] we should be clear here that this was not the standard view of the early Christian theologians (see the discussion above). In fact, the only theologian in whom it is close to explicit, Origen,[65] was condemned for exactly that universalist tendency in his explication of apocatastasis.[66] And although many draw on Clement of Alexandria in this vein as well, even his comments are attenuated conjecture.[67] So while the Eastern Orthodox view has close affinities with the early Christian view, especially since they continue to tie it explicitly to the victorious aspects of Christ's work and to the beginning of his exaltation,[68] we should not equate the two, and we should be clear that the former

---

says that in his descent Jesus preaches "the greatest revival the world—or the *under*world—has ever seen, and in doing so 'the disobedient ones' who, according to 1 Peter, are in prison but . . . now have a chance to hear and decide to repent and believe the good news." See Brent A. Strawn, "My Favorite Part of the Creed: 1 Peter 3:13-22," *Journal for Preachers* 38.3 (2015): 22.

[64]E.g., the very next sentence in Alfeyev's conclusion: "This is the faith of the early church, inherited from the first generation of Christians and cherished by Orthodox tradition." Alfeyev, *Christ the Conqueror of Hell*, 218. See also, for instance, Timothy Ware's discussion of apocatastasis, albeit without reference to the descent, in Ware, *The Orthodox Church*, rev. ed. (London: Penguin, 1964), 266-67.

[65]On Origen's view of the descent, see Origen, *Cels.* 2:43; cf. also *Comm. Matt.* 35; *Comm. Jo.* 5.37; 6.18; *Hom. Exod.* 6.6; *Hom. Lev.* 9.5(4); *Hom. 1 Reg.* 28.6. See also the comments by Bass, *Battle for the Keys*, 13; and Wicks, "Christ's Saving Descent," 302-7.

[66]On apocatastasis in Origen's thought and its subsequent impact on Christian theology, see Ilaria L. E. Ramelli, *The Christian Doctrine of* Apokatastasis: *A Critical Assessment from the New Testament to Eriugena*, VCSup 120 (Leiden: Brill, 2013).

[67]Clement of Alexandria, *Strom.* 6.6; *Exc.* 18, in R. P. Casey, ed., *The Excerpta ex Theodoto of Clement of Alexandria*, ed. K. Lake and S. Lake, Studies and Documents (Cambridge: Harvard University Press 1934), 54-55. See the comments in Bass, *Battle for the Keys*, 12. Further, Clement still affirmed the necessity of faith for salvation, even if it came via a postmortem offer in Christ's descent. See Wicks, "Christ's Saving Descent," 302. While a postmortem offer is not, in my opinion, warranted by Scripture or common in evangelical thought (see chapter seven), we should at least be clear that Clement's so-called universalism is still not universalism per se, as it seems to be in Origen, but rather still an articulation of salvation tied to an explicit confession of faith.

[68]See on this John Behr, *The Mystery of Christ: Life in Death* (Crestwood, NY: St. Vladimir's Seminary Press, 2006), 98. Behr points to the iconographic tradition, in which the *Anastasis* icon "does not actually depict Christ's bodily rising out of the tomb. It seems, instead, to portray Christ's descent into the underworld . . . portraying the effect of Christ's Passion, destroying of death by death, giving life to those in death. This is, moreover, something that has not yet been fully completed: Adam is in the process of being pulled out of the realm of death" (Behr, *Mystery*, 98).

departs from the latter in its willingness to imply that the descent makes universalism probable.[69]

THE ROMAN CATHOLIC VIEW(S)

Another view related to the early Christian view but also in some ways distinct from it, albeit for different reasons than the Eastern Orthodox view, is the traditional Roman Catholic understanding of the descent. This is commonly referred to as the Harrowing of Hell.[70] Here, Christ descends to the uppermost part of Hades (and not to the supposed lower three regions), the limbo of the fathers (*limbus patrum*). Its inhabitants are faithful Jews (and, in some versions, virtuous pagans) who died before Christ's first advent and therefore did not have the opportunity to respond to the gospel in the fullness of time but nevertheless expressed faith in YHWH and his coming Messiah.[71] Christ's descent, understood as the referent of 1 Peter 3:18, is for that very purpose—to proclaim the good news to those who have already died. Christ liberates those who believed—Jews and non-Jews—prior to their death (as well as, in some articulations, virtuous pagans). In distinction from what became standard in Eastern Orthodoxy, Jesus does not in this view lead every human being out, but instead saves those who were prepared for it in the era before Christ. There is less emphasis on universal possibilities (although that is certainly not excluded)[72] and more on culminating the salvation of those who waited for the Messiah but died before Jesus' first advent.[73] Alyssa

---

[69]For more on this, see the discussion of universalism and the descent in chapter seven.

[70]See, for example, Martin Connell's summary of Aquinas's view, for a representative Roman Catholic understanding. Connell, *"Descensus Christi ad Inferos,"* 271-75. See also Pitstick's summary of the "traditional" Roman Catholic view in Alyssa Lyra Pitstick, *Light in Darkness: Hans Urs von Balthasar and the Catholic Doctrine of Christ's Descent into Hell* (Grand Rapids: Eerdmans, 2007), 1-86. Note, though, Paul J. Griffiths's rejoinder concerning Pitstick's alleged overreach in "Is There a Doctrine of the Descent into Hell?" *Pro Ecclesia* 17.3 (2008): 257-68.

[71]See Pitstick, *Light in Darkness*, 15, 45-48. See also Herzog, *"Descensus Ad Inferos,"* 68-82.

[72]See Thomas Joseph White, "On the Universal Possibility of Salvation," *Pro Ecclesia* 17.3 (2008): 269-80; and See Steffen Lösel, "A Plain Account of Christian Salvation? Balthasar on Sacrifice, Solidarity, and Substitution," *Pro Ecclesia* 13.2 (2004): 153.

[73]"The typical "Catholic" position, at least since the time of the Catechism of Trent, has been to define Christ's descent into hell as simply the triumphal rescue of the dead awaiting the Messiah's

Lyra Pitstick summarizes the Roman Catholic view, "as set forth by John Paul II and the two universal catechisms," thus:

> The sinless human soul of Christ, united to his divine person, descended only to the realm of the dead reserved for the souls of holy individuals, called the limbo of the Fathers.
>
> He liberated those holy souls from there by conferring on them the glory of heaven. Having accomplished humanity's redemption in the blood of his cross, Christ distributes the first fruits of his sacrifice.
>
> In doing so, his power and authority were made known to all the dead, both good and evil, and to the fallen angels.
>
> Because Christ descended in His sinless soul as the all-holy redeemer, His descent was glorious in a way similar to His resurrection, and He did not suffer in His descent.[74]

As should be apparent from this summary, the Roman Catholic view (or at least, the one articulated by Pitstick[75]) is in some ways similar to the summary we gave at the end of the biblical section, to both the early church's and Luther's views, and to the summary we will give at the end of this section.

Matthew Levering's (and Aquinas's) view is typical of this Roman Catholic view and its similarity to the biblical view articulated in chapter one and the Lutheran view articulated below, with the exception of the relation of the descent to purgatory in Roman Catholic thought. Levering and Aquinas make clear that Jesus descends in his human soul, is therefore by virtue of the hypostatic union victorious over Death and Hades, only descends to paradise (the place of the righteous dead), and

---

advent, resulting in an enumeration of different hells, where the 'hell of the damned' is that designated for those without faith in Christ (as either coming or having come)." Joshua R. Brotherton, "Hans Urs von Balthasar on the Redemptive Descent," *Pro Ecclesia* 22.2 (2013): 168.

[74]Alyssa Lyra Pitstick, *Christ's Descent into Hell: John Paul II, Joseph Ratzinger, and Hans Urs von Balthasar on the Theology of Holy Saturday* (Grand Rapids: Eerdmans, 2016), 71.

[75]On the question of whether or not there is *one* Roman Catholic view of the descent, see Griffiths, "Is There a Doctrine of the Descent into Hell?"

only liberates those faithful Jews ("holy Israel") who awaited him. Further, they affirm that those faithful Jews (and, presumably, Gentile proselytes) awaited Christ "in a place of joy for those who love God," but that

> the waiting of holy Israel in the intermediate state, like that of Simon and Anna in the Temple, must have entailed some suffering "through their glory being delayed." Aquinas adds, however, that their suffering would have been mitigated by "great joy" from the faithful hope with which they awaited the Messiah's victory [here they cite John 8:56].[76]

There are at least three main differences, though, between versions of the Roman Catholic view and what I am calling an evangelical view. First, there is some variation within Roman Catholic doctrine regarding the status of those "holy souls" in the limbo of the Fathers prior to Christ's descent. Are they in the presence of God,[77] or are they cut off from him until Christ appears? The latter option does not lack proponents, and, in my view, should be rejected as an evangelical position (more on this in later chapters). The second difference between Roman Catholic versions of the descent and an evangelical position concerns those whom Christ "liberates" in his descent. Is the descent effective only for those who awaited the Messiah in faith prior to his first coming, or is it effective for those who express faith in the Messiah (Jew or Gentile) *and* "virtuous pagans," e.g., Greek philosophers? Again, the latter option occurs among some Roman Catholic articulations and is dependent upon an understanding of the descent that allows for a postmortem opportunity to respond to the gospel message (proclaimed by Christ in his descent).[78]

---

[76]See also Matthew Levering's articulation of the descent, largely based on the view of Aquinas, in his *Jesus and the Demise of Death: Resurrection, Afterlife, and the Fate of the Christian* (Waco, TX: Baylor University Press, 2012), 15-25. Levering, *Jesus and the Demise of Death*, 24, citing Aquinas *Summa Theologica* III. q. 52, a. 5, ad. 1.

[77]So Levering and Aquinas in the previous footnote.

[78]On these complicated questions about the relationship of the descent, a postmortem offer, the inhabitants of the *limbus patrum* (and therefore the scope of the effect of Christ's descent), and the relation of the descent to purgatory in Roman Catholic thought, and the various options for how to answer them, see Edward T. Oakes, "*Descensus* and Development: A Response to Recent Rejoinders," *IJST* 13.1 (2011): 3-24, esp. 21-22.

The third difference is related: in many Roman Catholic articulations of the descent, it is related to their doctrine of purgatory. Matthew Levering, summarizing and quoting Aquinas's view on the descent, says,

> When Christ entered the intermediate state . . . his presence did not compel the dead to love him. Those whose love is still divided (even after the scourging of death) undergo in the intermediate state a further purification of their loves. Aquinas comments that "they who were such as those who are not in Purgatory, were not set free from Purgatory by Christ's descent into hell." This does not mean that Christ's presence had no impact among those who as yet could not fully welcome him. It simply means that they were unable to fully welcome him, and his love worked, as it always does, to heal them gradually of this deficiency.[79]

In other words, purgatory is a place to heal humans' deficiency of perfect love for God. In traditional Roman Catholic thought,[80] it is a place (where "place" is understood in a spiritual, not spatiotemporal, sense) that exists prior to Christ's advent, but its purpose—namely, entry into Christ's heaven upon perfection of love for God—is made possible specifically through Christ's defeat of death, since that is when Christ opens the gates to heaven. This exit from purgatory into heaven may have happened for some at the descent, and the descent opens heaven's gates for the rest in purgatory both then and now so that they, too, might enter in once their love for God is transformed and perfected completely.[81] Based

---

[79]Levering, *Jesus and the Demise of Death*, 25. He is quoting from Aquinas, *Summa Theologica* III, q. 52, a. 8. See also, for instance, Oakes, "*Descensus* and Development," 20; and Joseph Ratzinger and William Congdon, *The Sabbath of History* (Washington, DC: William G. Congdon Foundation, 2000), 21-22. For a detailed discussion of Aquinas's view of the descent, see Harm J. M. J. Goris, "Thomas Aquinas on Christ's Descent into Hell," 93–114 in Marcel Sarot and Archibald L. H. M. van Wieringen, eds., *The Apostles' Creed: 'He Descended into Hell,'* Studies in Theology and Religion 24 (Leiden: Brill, 2018). Unfortunately this text was published after submission of the final draft of the manuscript and so I am only able to reference it here, rather than interact with it in more detail.

[80]Balthasar is a notable exception here, as he posits that purgatory is created via Christ's descent. See the discussion of von Balthasar elsewhere in this volume.

[81]I am grateful to Matthew Levering for dialogue on this section. I have tried to be more precise in my language thanks to his feedback. Any remaining deficiencies, imprecisions, and mistakes in my description of the Roman Catholic position are, of course, my own.

on our biblical argument in chapter two, as well as the argument regarding purgatory in chapter five and universalism in chapter seven, we reject this view as out of bounds for a properly "evangelical" account.

REFORMATION VIEWS:
LUTHER, CALVIN, AND BUCER

The sixteenth-century Reformation addressed many beliefs and practices of the medieval church, and the descent was one of the centers of doctrinal reform and revision. For Luther, Christ's descent is almost entirely couched in victorious terms. Jesus, in descending to the dead, has broken the gates of Sheol and triumphed over the devil. According to Richard Klann, "Luther taught that after Christ's burial, after He became alive again in the grave and before His emergence from the grave, the God-man descended to hell in a supernatural manner, conquered the devil, destroyed hell's power, and took from the devil all his might (Article IX, Tappert ed., p. 610)."[82] And in Luther's own words, in the descent, "for us, through Christ, hell has been torn to pieces and the devil's kingdom and power utterly destroyed; that to accomplish this He died, was buried, and descended thither, so that it should no longer harm or overwhelm us, as He Himself says, Matthew 16:18."[83]

The Formula of Concord, which, as Bass notes,[84] alludes to Luther's Torgau Sermon on the descent, says, "We believe simply that the entire person, God and human being, descended to Hell after his burial, conquered the devil, destroyed the power of Hell, and took from the devil all his power." While there may be some sense of liberation in Luther and the Formula of Concord, it is not emphasized and certainly does

---

[82]Richard Klann, "Christ's Descent into Hell," *Concordia Journal* (1976): 43. Also Martin Luther, "Third Sermon at Torgau, April 17, 1533," in *Luther's Works*, vol. 57: *Sermons IV*, ed. Benjamin T. Mayes (St. Louis: Concordia, 2016), 127-38. For wider discussion of Luther and later Lutheran views of the descent in relation to the development of the Formula of Concord, see Robert Kolb, "Christ's Descent into Hell as Christological Locus in the Era of the 'Formula of Concord,'" *Lutherjarbuch* 69 (2002): 101-18.

[83]Klann, "Christ's Descent into Hell," 47.

[84]Bass, *Battle for the Keys*, 17.

not have the universalism implicit in Eastern Orthodoxy. Notice also that Luther and the Formula of Concord place Christ in Hades *after* his resurrection; this is rare in terms of timing. Loofs connects this idiosyncratic view of the timing of Christ's descent with the Lutheran doctrine of the ubiquity of Christ's exalted humanity.[85] It is difficult to tell exactly what Luther is getting at with respect to the timing of Christ's descent, given his insistence on the metaphorical nature of the language that must be used to describe it. Here Luther helps with the cosmology, as he makes clear it is a spiritual (i.e., Christ's human spirit, or soul) descent into the realm of the dead, not necessarily a geographical descent, even if we use spatial terms to describe this distinction. In any case, with Luther the meaning of the descent remains relatively the same even if the timing appears to shift slightly (although it remains prior to exiting the tomb).[86] Nevertheless, the emphasis on Saturday's victory proclamation means that his view "is the only interpretation that provides the theological safeguard of catholicity with the ancient church in her pervasive belief in Christ's spatial descent into hell . . . and does not reduce *descendit* to needless repetition."[87]

Calvin's view, on the other hand,[88] which is virtually unattested prior to his own articulation of it,[89] understands the descent clause to be a

---

[85]Loofs, "Descent into Hades (Christ's)," 657.

[86]For more on the relation between Luther's view of the descent and his christological ubiquitarianism, see David R. Law, "Descent into Hell, Ascension, and Luther's Doctrine of Ubiquitarianism," *Theology* 107.838 (2004): 250-56.

[87]Hamm, "*Descendit*: Delete or Declare?" 115.

[88]For more on the distinction between Calvin's and Luther's views, as well as the differences that subsequently arose in the respective traditions that followed them, see Richard A. Muller, *Dictionary of Latin and Greek Theological Terms: Drawn Principally from Protestant Scholastic Theology* (Grand Rapids: Baker, 1985), 89-90. I am grateful to Bobby Grow for this reference.

[89]The idiosyncrasy of Calvin's position is commonly acknowledged in histories of the descent doctrine. Loof's rather dramatic statement that "the view of the Reformed Churches [as inheritors of Calvin's, Jud's, and Bucer's views] . . . is characterized by a complete abandonment of the Roman dogma," is nevertheless accurate in the sense that Calvin's position on the descent is virtually unheard of prior to his articulation of it in the *Institutes*. See Loofs, "Descent to Hades (Christ's)," 657-58, for an overview of the Reformed position on the descent and how it differs from the early Christian, Orthodox, and Roman Catholic views. See also Russ Leo, "Jean Calvin, Christ's Despair, and the Reformation *Descensus ad Inferos*," *Reformation* 23.1 (2018): 53-78, on the idiosyncrasy of Calvin's position and the theological motivations for his shift.

reference to Christ's substitution for sinners on the cross rather than to a victorious descent in his human soul to the place of the dead. This does not mean, though, that Calvin did not see any victorious elements in Christ's burial. Rather, Calvin's interpretation of the *descensus* creedal affirmation in particular has the substitutionary interpretation. In the previous section, on the phrase "he died and was buried," Calvin very clearly affirms that Christ's death and burial is victorious over death and the grave.[90] Calvin's view is comparatively idiosyncratic; he is "the first to understand the phrase metaphorically for Christ experiencing (descending to) hell on the cross *before* his burial instead of after his burial."[91] In his view, the descent happens on the cross as Jesus experiences the full separation from the Father due to bearing the weight of sin, expressed in the cry of dereliction. Jesus, in his humanity, experiences the torments of hell, most notably the separation from God, on the cross in the place of those who receive him by faith.[92] Calvin, and later Lightfoot, saw the descent doctrine not only as teaching substitutionary atonement but also as anti-Apollinarian.[93] Christ did not only suffer in his body but in his body and his soul, thus maintaining the unity of his human person. It thus has implications in Calvinist thought for the intermediate and eternal states.

It is also important to remember here that Calvin's view is entirely novel with respect to the views of those that preceded the Reformation. Never before had anyone placed Christ's descent on Friday or made it an instance of torment. All before Calvin had affirmed that Christ descended to the place of the dead but not to the place of the unrighteous dead to be tormented. One might ask why Calvin came up with his view. At least two points should be considered. First, it is possible that Calvin adapted

---

[90]John Calvin, *Institutes of the Christian Religion*, vol. I, The Library of Christian Classics, trans., Ford Lewis Battles, ed., John T. McNeil (1960; Louisville, KY: Westminster John Knox, 2006), 511-12.

[91]Bass, *Battle for the Keys*, 17.

[92]Calvin, *Institutes*, 512-20.

[93]Calvin, *Institutes*, 520; Chad B. van Dixhoorn, "New Taxonomies of the Westminster Assembly (1643–49): The Creedal Controversy as Case Study," *RRR* 6.1 (2004): 93. See also Lucas W. Sharley, "Calvin and Turretin's Views of the Trinity in the Dereliction," *RTR* 75.1 (2016): 21-34.

some of what Augustine says in his letter to Evodius.[94] A second point is admittedly conjectural but still worth mentioning; it may be that Calvin articulated his view based on a variety of factors: a rejection of the so-called three-tiered universe, which was a central facet of early Christian views of the doctrine but also a target of scientists and biblical commentators since the Copernican Revolution; a rejection of the Roman Catholic and Eastern Orthodox aspects of the descent, including implicit universalism and purgatory; *and* a rejection of Bucer's suggestion of redundancy (see below). We might also point to the evolving definitions of *hell* and its cognates; perhaps Calvin merely equated *inferna* with torment. In other words, Calvin thought the creedal clause meant something (he says as much in the *Institutes*) but he did not think it meant all that it had come to mean in Eastern and Roman thought, and he also may have simply equated *inferna* with torment. Unfortunately, it appears that Calvin overcorrected, so to speak, the Eastern and Roman views.[95] To quote Bass again, "This understanding of Christ's descent seemed to be sourced solely in Calvin's ingenuity."[96] And according to Hamm, this unique view arose largely due to a mistaken reading of Rufinus (who was also incorrectly identified as Pseudo-Cyprian) by Erasmus.[97] Thus while Calvin deserves the sole credit for his view of the descent, there are certain precursors to it (namely, Erasmus's misreading of Rufinus and certain ambiguous statements by Augustine).

---

[94]See Augustine, *Letters of St. Augustin* CLXIV, "To Evodius" 515-21 (*NPNF*[1] 1:515). See comments on this text in chapter two. On Augustine's view of the descent, see Paul J. J. van Geest, "Augustine's Certainty in Speaking about Hell and His Reserve in Explaining Christ's Descent into Hell," pp. 33-53 in Marcel Sarot and Archibald L. H. M. van Wieringen, eds., *The Apostles' Creed: 'He Descended into Hell,'* Studies in Theology and Religion 24 (Leiden: Brill, 2018). Unfortunately this text was published after submission of the final draft of the manuscript and so I am only able to reference it here, rather than interact with it in more detail.

[95]See, again, Loofs, "Descent to Hades (Christ's)," 657-58 and Leo, "Jean Calvin," 53-78, for references concerning Calvin's potential motivations in articulating an idiosyncratic meaning for the creedal clause.

[96]Bass, *Battle for the Keys*, 18. It may also be attributed to Calvin's aversion to early Christian (and the later modification of it in Roman Catholic) cosmology. See Loofs, "Descent into Hades (Christ's)," 657.

[97]Hamm, "*Descendit*: Delete or Declare?" 101-103. "[W]hat begins as a mistaken view of *descendit* continues to be disseminated and eventually becomes urban legend among the Reformers" (103).

We should also mention in this regard Martin Bucer, who appears to be among the first to posit that the descent clause in the Creed is equivalent to "he was buried" *as bodily burial* and should thus be excised. But this is a category mistake, and one that is, perhaps, rooted in "a pre-Bultmannian attempt to demythologize the NT text because Bucer and those who followed him could no longer accept an underworld beneath the earth."[98] As we argued in our discussion of Grudem and his understanding of Rufinus, the early church did not see these two clauses as equivalent, at least with respect to both indicating mere bodily burial, nor did theologians in the medieval period. Calvin's and Bucer's positions are idiosyncratic up to that point in the descent's history. Thus during the Reformation we find divergent views, with Luther affirming the doctrine's historic meaning while rejecting its more problematic developments during the medieval period, whereas Calvin and Bucer radically revise the content of the creedal clause, albeit in different ways.[99]

BALTHASAR'S VIEW

Calvin's penal substitutionary view, Luther's victorious view, and the Eastern and Roman versions of the liberating victorious view of the descent carry through the post-Reformation and modern periods on three essentially separate tracks. While we could trace out the development of these separate tracks during the post-Reformation and Enlightenment periods, it is essential in our brief survey to consider the most important development regarding the descent doctrine since the Reformation, as articulated by the Roman Catholic theologian Hans Urs von Balthasar. In the twentieth century, he attempts to combine three main tracks of the descent doctrine, namely, the Eastern, Roman Catholic, and Calvinist views. His explanation of the descent has provided an opportunity for much contemporary reflection and debate.

---

[98]Bass, *Battle for the Keys*, 18.

[99]For discussion of the various Reformed understandings of the descent clause and their reception at the Westminster Assembly, see Mark Jones, "John Calvin's Reception at the Westminster Assembly (1643–1649)," *CHRC* 91.1-2 (2011): 223-27.

Depending on one's perspective, he has either radically departed from Roman Catholic orthodoxy[100] or provided a legitimate explication of the doctrine that furthers the Roman Catholic Church's understanding of it.[101] In any case, Balthasar combines many of the themes in early Christian, medieval, and Reformation theology and provides a unique picture of Christ's descent. Balthasar desires to unite some of the disparate models of the atonement in his understanding of soteriology, especially victory, liberation, and substitution.[102] The climax of Christ's atoning work, especially in terms of substitution, comes for Balthasar on Holy Saturday. Unlike Calvin (and, later, Barth[103]), Balthasar places Christ's descent on Saturday in the tomb instead of on Friday on the cross. Like Calvin, though, the purpose of the descent is to stand for humanity, experiencing the pains of hell with them and for them.[104]

While this may seem rather innocuous, since all that has happened is a date change to this point, there is a reason Balthasar's position is considered radical by some. He posits that Jesus, in his descent to hell, experiences all that is included in the torment of hell, and especially the separation from the Father due to the presence of sin.[105] Problematic for many is the fact that, unlike Calvin, Balthasar wants to place this separation not only between the human spirit of Jesus and God but between Christ's divine nature and the Father as well.[106] His motivation seems to

---

[100]I.e., Pitstick, *Light in Darkness*. For another critical view of Balthasar's position, see Gavin D'Costa, "The Descent into Hell as a Solution for the Problem of the Fate of Unevangelized Non-Christians: Balthasar's Hell, the Limbo of the Fathers, and Purgatory," *IJST* 11.2 (2009): 146-71.

[101]Edward T. Oakes, "The Internal Logic of Holy Saturday in the Theology of Hans Urs von Balthasar," *IJST* 9 (2007): 184-99. See also his response to critics of Balthasar (including Pitstick and D'Costa), in *"Descensus* and Development," 3-24.

[102]Hans Urs von Balthasar, *Theo-Drama: Theological Dramatic Theory, Part IV: The Action,* trans., Graham Harrison (San Francisco: Ignatius, 1994), 317-19.

[103]Karl Barth, *Church Dogmatics* IV/1 §59.2. See also David Lauber, *Barth on the Descent into Hell: God, Atonement and the Christian Life,* Barth Studies (Burlington, VT: Ashgate, 2004), who notes that Barth "basically endorses Calvin's position" (80).

[104]There is some shifting in language in Balthasar between "solidarity" with humanity and "substitution" for humanity. See Lösel, "A Plain Account of Salvation?" esp. 150-54.

[105]Balthasar, *Theo-Drama* IV, 335. See also Lauber, *Barth on the Descent into Hell,* 74.

[106]For a highly critical articulation of Balthasar's position on this issue, see Pitstick, *Light in Darkness,* 205-7.

be to head off Nestorianism.[107] According to Balthasar, this is the culmination of Jesus' abandonment by the Father, and "if Jesus can be forsaken
by the Father, the conditions for this 'forsaking' must lie within the
Trinity, in the absolute distance/distinction between the Hypostasis who
surrenders the Godhead and the Hypostasis who receives it."[108] Balthasar
does attempt to defeat any criticism here by first arguing that there is
already separation between Father and Son vis-à-vis eternal generation,
a separation that does not negate fellowship within the Godhead.[109]
Second, he argues that the separation experienced is only subjective, not
objective; that is, the persons of the Father and the Son experience or
"feel" (my word, not Balthasar's) separation but that separation is not at
the metaphysical level. There is not an ontological break in the being of
God, and thus the descent is not technically an ontological split between
persons of the Trinity.[110] Third, he argues that the entire point of this
separation is so that it might be defeated via the love that exists between
Father and Son as expressed in the Spirit.[111] Hell and its effects are thus
swallowed up and transformed by being taken into the life of the Trinity.
Here again we hear echoes of the universalism[112] of the Eastern Orthodox
view combined with his own Roman Catholic views[113] and the

---

[107]Oakes, "The Internal Logic," 192-93.

[108]Balthasar, *Theo-Drama* IV, 333. See also Hans Urs von Balthasar, *Mysterium Paschale: The Mystery of Easter* (San Francisco: Ignatius Press, 1990), 49-88. Balthasar is clear that this divide is experiential, not ontological (71-88), but the point here is that there is still a divide between the hypostases of Father and Son.

[109]Balthasar, *Theo-Drama* IV, 330-32.

[110]Balthasar, *Theo-Drama* IV, 338. Balthasar also argues that, in descending to the dead in both his humanity and divinity, Christ is totally passive. Balthasar, *Theo-Drama* IV, 335. This is yet another point of contention among contemporary theologians about the validity of Balthasar's approach and whether or not he departs from the tradition. For a sympathetic assessment, see Oakes, "Internal Logic," 192.

[111]Balthasar, *Theo-Drama* IV, 338, 349-51.

[112]See Oakes, "Internal Logic," who argues that Balthasar's universalism is necessarily inclusivist because of the centrality of Christ's work within its schema. See also the discussion of the universalist implications of Balthasar's views of the descent, and specifically its timelessness, in Joshua R. Brotherton, "The Possibility of Universal Conversion in Death: Temporality, Annihilation, and Grace," *ModTheo* 32.3 (2016): 307-24.

[113]Again, it is up for debate how faithful Balthasar is to the Roman Catholic tradition on the descent. See, for instance, Pitstick, *Christ's Descent into Hell*; and, for a more sympathetic view

substitution language explicit in Calvin. Balthasar is also clear that the descent destroys hell,[114] and so the victory element, so prominent in the Fathers and Luther, is retained as well.[115]

CONTEMPORARY EVANGELICALS AND THE DESCENT

Finally, there are some evangelical theologians who would abandon the descent doctrine altogether, most notably Wayne Grudem.[116] Grudem's primary arguments, discussed in detail at the beginning of this chapter, are exegetical in the first place—he disagrees that 1 Peter 3:18-21 teaches a descent to the dead—and theological in the second place, in that he ties it almost exclusively to the Harrowing of Hell and to Jesus experiencing torment, and thus at least to a view of justification and the salvation of OT saints alien to Protestant theology. It is unclear, though, how Grudem deals with Jesus' burial apart from denying particular views about it.

This is not to say that all contemporary evangelicals deny the descent doctrine. On the contrary, David Scaer responds directly to Grudem, arguing for retention of the creedal formula.[117] Millard Erickson, while not endorsing the doctrine, does note that there is room for confessing evangelicals to affirm it,[118] and Tom Nettles gives a contemporary Calvinist understanding of the *descensus*.[119] Keith Johnson provides a unique perspective by arguing that, rather than importing the events of Good Friday or Easter Sunday into Holy Saturday, we should understand it on its own terms. This

---

of Balthasar that still contrasts his view with Ratzinger's, Joshua R. Brotherton, "Damnation and the Trinity in Ratzinger and Balthasar," *Logos* 18.3 (2015): 123-50.

[114]This does not preclude, in Balthasar's view, the creation of purgatory in the descent. Balthasar here seems to go farther than traditional Roman Catholicism, which does not see purgatory created in the descent, but only opened to the possibility of exiting it and moving into heaven. See Brotherton, "Hans Urs von Balthasar on the Redemptive Descent," 183-84.

[115]In this regard, Moltmann also attempts to combine these major themes and to follow in a combined fashion Luther, Calvin, and Balthasar on the descent. See Nigel G. Wright, "Universalism in the Theology of Jürgen Moltmann," *EvQ* 84.1 (2012): 33-39. See also Jürgen Moltmann, "'Descent into Hell,'" *Duke Divinity School Review* 33.2 (1968): 115-19.

[116]Grudem, "He Did Not Descend." See also Grudem, "Christ Preaching Through Noah," and John S. Feinberg, "1 Peter 3:18-20, Ancient Mythology, and the Intermediate State," *WTJ* 48 (1986): 303-36.

[117]David P. Scaer, "He Did Descend to Hell: In Defense of the Apostles' Creed," *JETS* 35.1 (1992): 91-99.

[118]Millard J. Erickson, "Did Jesus Really Descend into Hell?" *Christianity Today* 44.2 (2000): 74.

[119]Tom J. Nettles, "He Descended into Hell," *Modern Reformation* 11 (2002): 38-41.

means seeing it as Jesus' willingness to descend even to the depths of hell to rescue his people, which then allows his people to "confront any evil . . . with full confidence that Christ himself . . . has gone before us into the depths and goes with us still."[120] And aside from excising the clause altogether, perhaps the most popular view today is to appropriate Balthasar's focus on Christ experiencing abandonment and use that for pastoral counseling in situations where people feel abandoned and without God.[121]

Table 3.1. Historical views of the descent

View	Timing	Location	Purpose	Christological Aspect
Early Church	Saturday	Place of the Dead, Righteous Compartment	Victory Over Death, Victorious Proclamation, Release of Righteous Dead	Human Soul
Eastern Orthodox	Saturday	Place of the Dead (Righteous Compartment?)	Victory Over Death, Victorious Proclamation, Release of all in Hades	Human Soul
Roman Catholic	Saturday	Place of the Dead, limbus patrum	Victory Over Death, Victorious Proclamation, Release of those in limbus patrum	Human Soul
John Calvin, Karl Barth	Friday	Crucifixion	Substitutionary Atonement	Human Soul
Martin Bucer, Leo Jud	Friday	Bodily Burial	Solidarity with Humanity	Human Body
Martin Luther	Sunday(?)	Place of the Dead	Victorious Proclamation	Resurrected Body
Hans Urs von Balthasar	Saturday	Hell, the Place of Torment	Solidarity with Humanity, Substitutionary Atonement, Victorious Proclamation, Destruction of Hell and Release of its Inhabitants	Divine Nature
Contemporary Evangelicals	Friday or Saturday	Usually Bodily Grave or Crucifixion	Solidarity with Humanity (especially in feeling abandoned by God) or Substitutionary Atonement	Human Body or Soul

---

[120]Keith L. Johnson, "'He Descended into Hell,'" *Christian Reflection* 50 (2014): 27-34.

[121]The most well-known recent treatment of the descent, Alan Lewis's *Between Cross and Resurrection: A Theology of Holy Saturday* (Grand Rapids: Eerdmans, 2001) takes this approach.

EVALUATING HISTORICAL POSITIONS
IN LIGHT OF BIBLICAL EVIDENCE

What do we do, then, with these options in light of the biblical evidence analyzed in the previous chapter? Given what we saw in the New Testament regarding Christ's descent, we can summarize it in the following manner:

- Christ in his humanity experienced death as all humans do, in body and in soul, his body being buried and his soul consciously remaining in the place of the dead;

- Christ, as the God-Man, defeated death in his descent (as well as in his crucifixion and resurrection);

- Christ proclaimed victory—achieved through his death, descent, and coming resurrection—over death, Hades, Satan, and the fallen angels;[122]

- Christ "releases" the OT saints, by which we mean simply that, rather than dwelling in Abraham's bosom (or paradise) awaiting the Messiah, they now dwell in the presence of the risen Christ;[123]

- and, therefore, Christ's descent is primarily the beginning of his exaltation, and only secondarily a part of his humiliation (he remained human and experienced the state of being dead but did not experience substitutionary torment or wrath in his descent).[124]

---

[122]This proclamation of victory in the descent is easily related to two of Christ's offices, prophet and king. Whether or not the descent includes the office of priest as well is not a question I intend to answer fully in this book. Suffice it to say here that I think the argument could be made, especially in relation to the priests going ahead of the ark through the Jordan in Joshua 3–4. Christ as our high priest goes before us through the waters of death and then upward into the holy place (on the latter, see Heb 9:24). Thanks to Fred Sanders for this question and the observation about the priests in the Jordan. For a recent treatment of the *munus triplex* and the interrelation and continuity between the three offices, see Jeremy Treat, *The Crucified King: Atonement and Kingdom in Biblical and Systematic Theology* (Grand Rapids: Zondervan, 2014), 165-73.

[123]See Bass, *Battle for the Keys*, 2, 8, 55, 70, 85. See also the discussion on the cosmological shifts brought about by the descent in the previous chapter, as well as chapter five.

[124]Again, I leave to a later chapter an extended analysis of the question of whether the descent is for only OT saints or more universal in its salvific scope. For now, it is enough to note that I

This summary leads us to the following conclusions about the historical options with respect to the *descensus*.

- There is no biblical warrant to reject the *descensus* or excise the descent clause from the creeds.

- Calvin's view, and subsequently that of Barth and Balthasar insofar as they appropriate it, are not consistent either with the biblical evidence or the historical articulation of the descent doctrine. As Bass notes, it was not until Martin Bucer that anyone questioned whether the descent was separate from Christ's burial, and it was not suggested that Christ's descent was equal to his crucifixion.[125] This notion of torment in the descent seems to have arisen due to both a misunderstanding of the Latin and German terms for "the dead"[126] and a desire to extirpate any redundancy between the burial and descent clauses of the Apostles' Creed.[127] Regarding the former, the simple fact is that those who follow Calvin in their interpretation of the descent clause, i.e., those who see it as depicting Christ's torment on the cross, not only miss the narrative structure of the Apostles' Creed but also miss the meaning of *inferna/inferos* and *hölle*. In Latin and German, respectively, these are all originally generic terms related to the place of the dead, a place to which both righteous and unrighteous people go in their souls upon death.[128]

---

do not affirm an understanding of the descent that entails universalism. Additionally, see the previous chapter for discussion of the relation between humiliation and exaltation. Christ still experiences humiliation in the descent (as well as in the entirety of his work) as he remains incarnate. But the *primary* state of the descent, resurrection, and ascension is that of exaltation.

[125]Bass, *Battle for the Keys*, 17-18.

[126]On the distinction between these terms and their development, as well as similar issues regarding Sheol and Hades, see Hamm, *Descendit*: Delete or Declare?" 94n7; and Laufer, *Hell's Destruction*, 30.

[127]Even when Augustine *may* suggest that Christ's soul was in hell, i.e. the place of torment, he makes it clear from the beginning of his speculations on 1 Pet 3:18-22 that he was not tormented there, but rather went in order to defeat death and hell and (perhaps; Augustine is consistently cautious on this point) release some of its inhabitants. See Augustine, *Letters* CLXIV, "To Evodius," 515-21 (*NPNF*¹ 1:515).

[128]There also may be some incipient reaction in the Reformation against the three-tiered cosmology underlying the Greco-Roman and Second Temple Jewish contexts of the New Testament,

Calvin's view is an innovative departure from the tradition and one that uniquely places Christ's descent on the cross as part of his humiliation.

- Regarding Bucer's rationale above (that the descent clause is redundant), if our biblical examination has led to correct conclusions about the nature of Christ's descent, it is clear that it does not mean the same thing as "died and was buried," if the latter is taken to mean mere bodily burial. Additionally in this respect, if the origin of the phrase was to combat Apollinarianism, this adds emphasis to the descent clause and its impact on theological anthropology. Given that Calvin's view, and that of those who follow him, is dependent on these assumptions, it seems that a Calvinist understanding of the *descensus* is unwarranted, or at least idiosyncratic historically, biblically, and creedally. This of course does not mean that Calvin's view of the atonement—that Christ suffered God's wrath on the cross—is incorrect, only that it is not the meaning of the *descensus* clause or in accord with what has historically been seen as its biblical-theological basis in the New Testament. To clarify further, I fully affirm penal substitutionary atonement. Christ bears the full wrath of God on our behalf on the cross. I just do not believe the descent is part of that aspect of Christ's work. We should note here that, in particular, Balthasar's view seems out of step with the biblical and historical evidence, as well as with classic Christian theism.

- Grudem and those who follow him within contemporary evangelicalism, who wish to excise "he descended into hell" from the creeds, are also making a claim about what the descent means that is unfounded when considering the meaning of the clause in its early iterations. Contrary to Grudem and others, and likewise

---

which may have led some to reject the descent (it relies, in some respects, upon their being a third tier, an underworld). See Laufer, *Hell's Destruction*, 75-76, 88-89.

contrary to Calvin, the phrase did not originally mean that Christ suffered in hell either on the cross or on Holy Saturday, but that he experienced death as all humans do, body and soul, and in doing so as the God-Man, defeated death, Hades, and Satan and his angels. It also originally meant that Christ proclaimed his victory to these defeated captives on Holy Saturday, a notion that Grudem rejects based on his interpretation of 1 Peter 3:18-22. But, as we have seen, this rejection is exegetically tenuous at best. Further, the main claim of the descent doctrine is not dependent upon the exegesis of this one verse. It seems best, then, given the biblical evidence, to dispense with the notion that the descent clause has no biblical warrant and the church should no longer confess it.

- Given the biblical evidence, in fact, it seems that Luther's view holds most closely to what is expressed in the New Testament and later confessed by the early church. Christ descended qua human, his human body to the grave and in his human soul to the place of the dead, all the while remaining the incarnate Son.[129] In doing so, he continued to achieve victory over his enemies and proclaimed that victory to them and to his righteous saints. As we have seen from texts like Matthew 12:40; Romans 10:7; and Revelation 1:18, this is entirely consistent with what the New Testament teaches about Christ's descent to the dead.

- The Eastern Orthodox and Roman Catholic views teach something similar to Luther, on the one hand.[130] On the other, they each differ in one way or another from the view articulated by Luther and in this chapter. For Eastern Orthodoxy, there is a tendency

---

[129]By this latter phrase here and elsewhere I simply mean that the hypostatic union between Christ's human nature and divine nature does not cease during his death and descent.

[130]We could also add here individual early Christian writers, like Origen. But, as we have seen, the *collective* witness of the early church does not follow Origen or Clement of Alexandria in their universalist tendencies. These are only picked up collectively later on in (some strands of) Eastern Orthodoxy.

toward universalism, never fully supported but always tantaliz-ingly suggested, a tendency brought about by emphasizing Christ's release of Adam and thereby the entire human race from Hades. For Roman Catholicism, there are versions that affirm a more in-clusive view of the *limbus patrum*, as well as versions that see the *limbus patrum* as a place where the righteous dead did not expe-rience torment per se but where they also were considered as suf-fering the effects of Adam's sin and waiting without experiencing the beatific vision. Most consistently and therefore most problem-atically, the Roman Catholic view of the descent is directly related to the doctrine of purgatory. While I will delay covering these issues in detail until subsequent chapters (namely, those on cre-ation, soteriology, and eschatology), to anticipate my conclusions there I do not think either of these capture message of the biblical witness on the descent. While Christ's descent and subsequent ascent change the nature of the OT saints' experience of God's presence with them, this is not the same thing as confessing what the Eastern Orthodox or Roman Catholic Church does.

CONCLUSION

With these biblical and historical considerations in mind, then, the con-fession that Christ "descended to the dead" can be summarized like this:

Christ, in remaining dead for three days, experienced death as all humans do: his body remained in the grave, and his soul remained in the place of the righteous dead. He did not suffer there, but, remaining the in-carnate Son, proclaimed the victory procured by his penal substitu-tionary death to all those in the place of the dead—fallen angels, the unrighteous dead, and the OT saints. Christ's descent is thus primarily the beginning of his exaltation, not a continuation of his humiliation.[131]

---

[131]At least, it is not a continuation of his humiliation with respect to experiencing suffering and achieving penal substitution. See again Treat's discussion of the two states of Christ in *The Crucified King*, 156-65. Some current work on the descent attempts to hold these two together,

The remainder of this book will explore what this confession means for the life of the church, both in its confession and in its practice. I hope to demonstrate how this doctrine impinges upon other dogmatic loci, and thus also hope to show how Christian theology is a tightly knit fabric. Each of the threads connects to and supports the others. This is no less true of the descent. Additionally, theology is immensely practical, and so throughout the following chapters but especially in chapter ten, I attempt to show how the descent doctrine bears upon our lives as Christians, especially in light of our impending deaths and the deaths of our loved ones.

---

although for the historical reasons discussed above, I find this untenable. See, for instance, Carl P. E. Springer, "Of Triumph and Triumphalism: Etymological and Poetical Considerations," *Logia* 26.1 (2017): 5-13. I agree with Springer's historical survey, but he appears to attempt to combine these (in my opinion) contradictory notions of the descent (see esp. p. 8).

THE DESCENT AND CHRISTIAN DOGMATICS

"GOD THE FATHER ALMIGHTY . . . JESUS CHRIST, HIS ONLY SON, OUR LORD . . . AND THE HOLY SPIRIT"

Classical Trinitarianism and the Descent

The primary doctrine for Christians is the Trinity. God is one God who exists in three persons: Father, Son, and Holy Spirit. This confession is often pitted against the descent as the polar extremes of doctrinal importance; while the Trinity is of primary importance, the descent is of little or no importance at all, especially comparatively speaking. And yet, while I would maintain the primacy of our confession of the Triune God, the descent is not unimportant, not least because it bears on how we actually think about the Triune God and his inseparable work of redemption.[1]

In this chapter we will explore this relationship between the doctrine of the Trinity and the doctrine of the descent

---

[1]And it bears on many other Christian doctrines, as we will see in subsequent chapters. As I mentioned in the preface and in the conclusion to the previous chapter, this book is thus an exercise in demonstrating what Richard Lints calls the "fabric of theology," its interwoven character in which pulling on one thread affects all other threads. See Richard Lints, *The Fabric of Theology: A Prolegomena to Evangelical Theology* (Grand Rapids: Eerdmans, 1993).

PART TWO: The Descent and Christian Dogmatics

and in two ways. First, I will show how the classic view of the descent both shaped and is shaped by the Trinitarian doctrine of inseparable operations and its corollary, the doctrine of appropriation. Second, I will return to the twentieth-century Trinitarian and descent theology of Hans Urs von Balthasar, so that we can see how derivations from a classic view of the descent deviate from the traditional view of that doctrine but also from traditional articulations of Trinitarian orthodoxy.

INSEPARABLE OPERATIONS AND THE DESCENT

Was Jesus alone—abandoned by the Father, bereft of the Spirit, even if only in an existential sense—during his descent? Consideration of this question needs to occur in the wider context of Trinitarian theology. The doctrines of inseparable operations and appropriation are crucial to a biblically and historically faithful account of the descent. Together, these doctrines emphasize the unity of God's action while also maintaining appropriate distinctions between the persons in that unified action. As Gilles Emery puts it,

> The three divine persons act inseparably, in virtue of their common divine nature, and the whole Trinity is the source of all their works. But each person acts within the distinct mode of his relationship to the other persons within this common action.[2]

The first sentence is an affirmation of inseparable operations, that God's actions as the one God are always one. The Triune God acts with one will to accomplish his purpose.[3] This is not acting in concert or agreement, but acting truly as the one God. Nevertheless, the one God is Triune, and so God's oneness must not be emphasized to the point

---

[2]Gilles Emery, OP, *The Trinitarian Theology of St. Thomas Aquinas*, trans. Francesca Aran Murphy (Oxford: Oxford University Press, 2007), 349. On the doctrines of appropriations and missions, see also Scott R. Swain, "Divine Trinity," 78-106 in *Christian Dogmatics: Reformed Theology for the Church Catholic*, ed. Michael Allen and Scott R. Swain (Grand Rapids: Baker Academic, 2016), 103-4.

[3]For a contemporary defense of dyothelitism (that Christ's human nature possesses one will while his divine nature shares the one divine will), see R. Lucas Stamps, *"Thy Will Be Done": A Contemporary Defense of Two Wills Christology* (Minneapolis: Fortress, forthcoming).

that his triunity is forgotten. This is where the doctrine of appropriation, affirmed in Emery's second sentence, is important.[4] The three persons act as the one God but in a manner consistent with their eternal relations of origin, or their mode of subsistence in the divine essence: the Father as Unbegotten, the Son as Begotten, and the Spirit as Proceeding from the Father and the Son.[5]

The import of these doctrines is in God's acts of creation and redemption, where we make affirmations such as, "God the Father predestines" or "God the Son alone becomes incarnate." While it may sound as though each person is acting distinctly, or separate, from one another— e.g., it is the Son who takes on a human nature, not the Father—we need to be clear that these are not separate acts taken on individually by one of the three persons of the Godhead. Rather, the one God acts with one will to accomplish one work, whether it is creation or redemption. Yes, these actions are appropriated to each person in a manner fitting to their eternal relations of origin, but they are not individual actions carried out only by individual persons of the Triune God. As Scott Swain puts it,

> The reason distinct divine acts are appropriated to distinct persons is not because God's actions toward his creatures are divided between the persons: *opera Trinitatis ad extra indivisa sunt* ["The operations of the Trinity outside itself are indivisible."] The reason is due to the ways in which the personal properties and characteristics of the three manifest themselves within their common, indivisible action.[6]

So we say, "God the Father creates the world through his Word (Son) and Spirit," or, "The Father sends the Son, the Son becomes incarnate, and the Spirit anoints the Son."

---

[4]On the doctrine of appropriations in Thomas, see *Summa Theologica* I.39.7-8.
[5]For an introduction to the eternal relations of origin, see Emery, *The Trinitarian Theology of St. Thomas Aquinas*, esp. 51-102. See also Fred Sanders, *The Triune God*, New Studies in Dogmatics (Grand Rapids: Zondervan Academic, 2016), 126-29; and Scott Swain, "Divine Trinity," 94-99.
[6]Swain, "Divine Trinity," 103-4. On inseparable operations, see also the forthcoming book by Adonis Vidu, *Opera ad Extra: The Inseparable Works of the Triune God* (Grand Rapids: Eerdmans, forthcoming).

For the descent, this means that we need to affirm both that the one God is acting as one in this particular aspect of the divine drama of redemption, and also that it is particularly (appropriately) the incarnate Son who descends. It is not uncommon for Christians—lay persons and theologians alike—to describe the descent in ways that suggest Jesus' ontological isolation from the Father. "Divine abandonment" is often employed in describing Jesus' actions on Holy Saturday.[7] But the doctrine of inseparable operations, and its foundation in the doctrine of God, does not allow us to separate Father and Son in this fashion.[8] Instead, we should affirm that the descent, like all other divine activity, is part of the one redemptive act of the one God, appropriately attributed to the Son but carried out by all three persons in unity of act and will. Early Christian texts affirmed this. Second-century writers and works such as Ignatius,[9] Polycarp,[10] Shepherd of Hermas,[11] *Ascension*

---

[7]This is one of the foundational aspects of the most recent attempt to retrieve the descent, Alan Lewis's *Between Cross and Resurrection: A Theology of Holy Saturday* (Grand Rapids: Eerdmans, 2001). Lewis relies on the view of Balthasar, which we will explore in detail below. For an examination of Lewis's view that coalesces with many aspects of this chapter, see Myk Habets, "Putting the 'Extra' Back into Calvinism," *SJT* 62.4 (2009): 441-56.

[8]For an exploration of how the affirmations of penal substitution, the hypostatic union, divine impassibility, and Trinitarian inseparable operations relate to one another in light of the Cry of Dereliction, see Steven J. Duby, "Atonement, Impassibility and the *Communicatio Idiomatum*," *IJST* 17.3 (2015): 284-95; and Duby, "The Cross and the Fullness of God: Clarifying the Meaning of Divine Wrath in Penal Substitution," *SBET* 29.2 (2011): 165-76. For a discussion of these issues in particular relation to the descent (especially in the writings of Alan Lewis and Jürgen Moltmann) and the application of the *extra Calvinisticum* to them, see Habets, "Putting the 'Extra' Back into Calvinism." See also the response to Habets's article by Darren O. Sumner, "The Twofold Life of the Word: Karl Barth's Critical Reception of the *Extra Calvinisticum*," *IJST* 15.1 (2013): 42-57. Thanks to Bobby Grow for pointing me to the latter two essays.

[9]E.g., Ign. *Trall.* 9:1-2; Ign. *Magn.* 9.2; and Ign. *Eph.* 18.2. On this latter passage and its interpretation, see William R. Schoedel, *Ignatius of Antioch: A Commentary on the Letters of Ignatius of Antioch*, Hermeneia (Minneapolis, Fortress, 1985), 84-86. Schoedel identifies a parallel with *Odes* 22:5 (cf. 24:1-4) as well. Schoedel, *Ignatius of Antioch*, 85. For introductions to critical issues and studies for each of the AF mentioned here and elsewhere in the text, including Ignatius, Polycarp, and Shepherd of Hermas, see Michael W. Holmes, *The Apostolic Fathers: Greek Texts and English Translations*, 3rd ed. (Grand Rapids: Baker Academic, 2007).

[10]Pol. *Phil* 1.2. On this passage and its interpretation, see Paul Hartog, ed., *Polycarp's Epistle to the Ephesians and the Martyrdom of Polycarp: Introduction, Text, and Commentary*, Oxford Apostolic Fathers (Oxford: Oxford University Press, 2013), 100-102.

[11]Herm. *Sim.* 9.16. On this passage and its interpretation, see Carolyn Osiek, *The Shepherd of Hermas: A Commentary on the Shepherd of Hermas*, Hermeneia (Minneapolis, Fortress, 1990), 238.

of Isaiah,[12] *Odes of Solomon*,[13] *Teachings of Silvanus*,[14] *Dialogue with Trypho*,[15] and *Against Heresies*[16] all emphasize on the one hand that it is *God* (in the person of the incarnate Son) who descends to the place of the dead. For instance, *Ascen. Isa.* 10:7-11; 11:19 emphasizes that Christ's descent is effective precisely because it is as *God* in the flesh that he descends. We will return to the "in the flesh" portion of that equation in a moment, but for now it is particularly important that we notice how *Ascen. Isa.* (along with many other second-century and early Christian texts[17]) emphasizes that the descent is effective precisely because it is the

---

[12]*Ascen. Isa.* 10:7-11; 11:19. See also similar, if truncated, statements about the descent in 4:21; and 9:12-17. For an introduction to *Ascen. Isa.*, including critical issues, thematic and theological issues, and a translation, see P. Bettiolo et al., eds., *Ascensio Isaiae: Textus*, CCSA 7 (Turnhout: Brepols, 1995); and E. Norelli, *L'Ascensione di Isaia: Studi su un apocrifo al crocevia dei cristianesimi*, Origini NS 1 (Bologna: Centro editorial dehoniano, 1994).

[13]*Odes Sol.* 15:9-10; 17:10-17; 22; 24:5-7; 29:4-6; 31:1; and 42:6-20 all clearly speak of the Messiah's descent to and overthrow of Hades. On these passages and their interpretation, see Michael Lattke, *The Odes of Solomon: A Commentary*, Hermeneia (Minneapolis, Fortress, 2009). For an introduction to the *Odes* including critical issues, thematic and theological issues, and a translation, see James H. Charlesworth, 'The Odes of Solomon,' 725-74 in *The Old Testament Pseudepigrapha*, vol. 2: *Expansions of the 'Old Testament' and Legends, Wisdom and Philosophical Literature, Prayers, Psalms, and Odes, Fragments of Lost Judeo-Hellenistic Works*, ed. James H. Charlesworth (1983; Peabody, MA: Hendrickson, 2015).

[14]*Teach. Silv.* 103.23–104.14; 110.14–111.4. See Malcolm L. Peel, "The 'Descensus ad Inferos' in 'The Teachings of Silvanus' (CG VII, 4)," *Numen* 26.1 (1979): 23-49, esp. 30-31.

[15]Justin Martyr, *Dial.* 74. For an introduction to *Dial.* including critical issues, thematic and theological issues, and a translation, see Miroslav Marcovich, *Iustini Martyris Dialogus cum Tryphone*, Patristische Texte und Studien 47 (Berlin: Walter de Gruyter, 1997).

[16]Irenaeus, *Haer.* III.20.4; V.31.1. See also *Epid.* 78. For an introduction to *Haer.* including critical issues, thematic and theological issues, and a translation, see the following four volumes: A. Rousseau and L. Doutreleau, *Irénée de Lyon: Contre le Hérésies, Livre I* (SC 263-64); A. Rousseau and L. Doutreleau, *Irénée de Lyon: Contre le Hérésies, Livre II* (SC 293-94); A. Rousseau and L. Doutreleau, *Irénée de Lyon: Contre le Hérésies, Livre III*, 2 vols. (SC 100); and A. Rousseau et al., *Irénée de Lyon: Contre le Hérésies, Livre IV* (SC 210-11). For an introduction to *Epid.* including critical issues, thematic and theological issues, and a translation, see K. Ter-Mekerttschian and S. G. Wilson, with Prince Maxe of Saxony, eds., Εἰς ἐπίδειξιν τοῦ ἀποστολικοῦ κηρύγματος; *The Proof of the Apostolic Preaching, with Seven Fragments*, trans J. Barthoulot (PO 12.5). On Irenaeus and the descent, see Jared Wicks, SJ, "Christ's Saving Descent to the Dead: Early Witnesses from Ignatius to Origen," *Pro Ecclesia* 17.3 (2008): 294-309.

[17]There are ample resources on the descent in the early church and even in the second century. Some of the most important include Jean Daniélou, *The Theology of Jewish Christianity*, A History of Early Christian Doctrine before the Council of Nicaea 1 (Philadelphia: Fortress Press, 1964), 233-48; Aloys Grillmeier, "Der Gottesohn im Totenreich: soteriologische und christologische Motivierung der Descensuslehre in der alteren christlichen Überlieferung," *ZKT* 71 (1949): 1-53, 184-203; Josef Kroll, *Gott ünd Hölle: Der Mythos vom Descensuskampfe* (1932; Darmstadt: Wissenschaftliche Buchgesellschaft, 1963); and J. A. MacCulloch, *The Harrowing of Hell*:

one God who descends in the person of the Son.[18] These texts of course recognize that it is God the Son incarnate particularly, but they also affirm that the Son is divine in the same way as the Father and Spirit are.[19] Because it is God the Son incarnate who descends to the place of the dead, Death and Hades are defeated as God, in the person of the incarnate Son, enters their midst.

But it is appropriate, on the other hand, that the *incarnate* Son descends. Father, Son, and Spirit are all active here in the one act of redemption—the Father sending, the Son sent, the Spirit the agent of sending[20]—so that we can say that all three persons are acting in the descent. But it is the incarnate Son who descends particularly, since the descent requires a human nature—a human nature to which God the Son is now hypostatically united in the incarnation. Thus the continuity of the incarnation is crucial to the descent as well; only as the God-Man can the Son descend, and do so both victoriously and vicariously. The descent is only victorious because the Son descends as God, and it is only vicarious because he descends as a human being, as *the human being*.

Here one final reminder, which will be crucially important when we turn to analyzing Balthasar's view below, is that Christ's descent qua human is via his human soul. We have already analyzed 1 Peter 3:18-22 and other relevant texts in chapter two, so here we simply need to remember that the Petrine, Matthean, and Acts texts indicate that Christ's descent happens via his human soul. His human body, dead in the grave,

---

A Comparative Study of An Early Christian Doctrine (Edinburgh: T&T Clark, 1930), 83-173. These works do not, though, address the question of this chapter, nor do they (necessarily) deal with Balthasar's position (the subject of the latter half of the chapter), since he wrote his major works dealing with the descent subsequent to the works listed here.

[18]On the descent as both human and divine, not merely, on the one hand, docetic or Gnostic, or, on the other hand, an event exclusive to Christ's human nature, see Peel, "The 'Descensus ad Inferos' in 'The Teachings of Silvanus,'" 34, 36-39.

[19]This is not to claim that their thinking in the second or third centuries was as precise as it would become as a result of the fourth-century Nicene debates, but only to say that they use the same names and attributes to refer to Father, Son, and Spirit.

[20]On sending in the Godhead, see Sanders, *Triune God*, 121-54.

remains there, but his human soul descends to the place of the dead.[21]
The incarnate Son descends qua divinity via the human soul's descent
to the dead.

BALTHASAR, THE DESCENT,
AND CLASSIC TRINITARIANISM

The twentieth-century Roman Catholic theologian Hans Urs von
Balthasar has done much to bring the descent back to the forefront of
Christian theology, at least in some circles. Particularly among Roman
Catholic theologians, Balthasar's position on the descent is one that
brings polar opposite reactions. And for good reason: at the very least,
Balthasar's position stretches the boundaries of classic Christian doc-
trine regarding the descent.[22] In short, Balthasar posits that, in the
descent, the divine hypostases of Father and Son existentially (not

---

[21]We should also remember that this is the official Roman Catholic position, a position to which
Balthasar claims to be faithful. For a summary of the Roman Catholic position, see Alyssa Lyra
Pitstick, *Christ's Descent into Hell: John Paul II, Joseph Ratzinger, and Hans Urs von Balthasar on
the Theology of Holy Saturday* (Grand Rapids: Eerdmans, 2016), 71.

[22]For an analysis of where Balthasar's position fits in Roman Catholic tradition, see Pitstick,
Christ's Descent into Hell, esp. 85-112. See also Pitstick, *Light in Darkness: Hans Urs von Balthasar
and the Catholic Doctrine of Christ's Descent into Hell* (Grand Rapids: Eerdmans, 2007),
esp. 279-348. Although, at least in my view, Pitstick has accomplished the most thorough
comparative analysis of Balthasar's view and the rest of the Roman Catholic tradition, other
Roman Catholic theologians do not universally follow her conclusions. Her most ardent de-
tractor appears to be Edward T. Oakes, who has contributed the following to the discussion:
"The Internal Logic of Holy Saturday in the Theology of Hans Urs von Balthasar," *IJST* 9.2
(April 2007): 184-99; and *"Descensus* and Development: A Response to Recent Rejoinders,"
IJST 13.1 (January 2011): 3-24. See also the dialogue between Oakes and Pitstick, "Balthasar,
Hell, and Heresy: An Exchange," *First Things* 168 (December 2006): 25-32. Additionally, Paul
J. Griffiths has critiqued Pitstick's reading of Balthasar in "Is There a Doctrine of the Descent
into Hell?" Others who have waded into the discussion include Joshua R. Brotherton, "Hans
Urs von Balthasar on the Redemptive Descent," *Pro Ecclesia* 22.2 (2013): 167-88; Gavin D'Costa,
"The Descent into Hell as a Solution for the Problem of the Fate of Unevangelized Non-
Christians: Balthasar's Hell, the Limbo of the Fathers and Purgatory," *IJST* 11.2 (2009): 147-71;
Stefen Lösel, "A Plain Account of Christian Salvation? Balthasar on Sacrifice, Solidarity, and
Substitution," *Pro Ecclesia* 13.2 (2004): 141-71; and Thomas Joseph White, "On the Universal
Possibility of Salvation," *Pro Ecclesia* 17.3 (2008): 269-80. D'Costa is the most critical of
Balthasar's position, and on a number of fronts (which we will encounter throughout this
chapter and in others), while the rest attempt to steer a *via media* in various ways between
Pitstick and Oakes. Brotherton and White attempt to do so with respect to the question of
universalism, while Lösel's focus is on the question of whether or not the descent is substitutionary, as it is for Balthasar.

ontologically) experience separation from one another, as the Son bears the Father's wrath and experiences the torments of hell. This separation is bridged in intra-Trinitarian fashion, as the love of the Spirit overwhelms that gulf and reunites Father and Son, thereby defeating death, sin, and hell. It may also be an implication of this view that the incarnation is temporarily suspended, or at least unimportant, in Balthasar's view, since the key elements of the descent occur between the divine hypostases of the Triune God. In his own words,

> Jesus does experience the darkness of the sinful state, not in the same way as the (God-hating) sinner experiences it (unless the sinner is spared such experience), but nonetheless in a deeper and darker experience. This is because it takes place in the profound depths of the relations between the divine Hypostases—which are inaccessible to any creature.[23]

Balthasar further grounds this existential separation between Father and Son in what he calls the previous two kenotic moments in the life of God—the eternal generation of the Son and the incarnation of the Son.[24] For Balthasar, these two moments mark both the self-giving emptying of the Father and also, therefore, a separation, or "distance," between Father and Son. In the eternal generation of the Son, the Father empties himself into the Son, but is also therefore separate (distinct) from the Son. In the incarnation, the Father sends the Son, emptying himself. The Son, too, empties himself in the incarnation, taking on the form of a servant (Phil 2:5-7). The descent thus marks a third kenotic moment in the life of God, when the self-giving of the Father—by delivering up his own Son to bear his wrath—separates Father and Son but also ends in their redemptive, Spirit-wrought reunion.

Theological influences for Balthasar's view. There are a few different theological streams flowing into Balthasar's position on the descent. First, he seeks to be faithful to the Fathers by keeping the descent on

---

[23]Hans Urs von Balthasar, *Theo-Drama: Theological Dramatic Theory* IV: *The Action* (San Francisco: Ignatius, 1994), 336.
[24]See Pitstick's summary in *Light into Darkness*, 240-43. See also Balthasar, *Theo-Drama* IV, 323-26.

Saturday and insisting that it empties hell.[25] In this sense, he also attempts to draw from the doctrine's development in the Eastern Orthodox tradition, where there is a very strong sense of the descent's universal redemptive significance.[26] At the same time, as a Roman Catholic, at least two other streams bear on his articulation of the descent. On the one hand, he continually asserts that his position is in line with the Roman Catholic tradition. But, on the other hand, he also draws on the mystical tradition of Roman Catholicism,[27] and particularly the "dark night of the soul" of his Swiss Catholic mystic contemporary, Adrienne von Speyr.[28] In this mystical experience, the medical doctor and theologian von Speyr feels complete abandonment by God, separated entirely from him, a feeling that she connects with the abandonment Christ felt on the cross. Balthasar also posits that this abandonment is what Christ feels in the descent, not only qua human but particularly qua divine.

Both Alan Lewis and Jürgen Moltmann go beyond even Balthasar in this aspect. Lewis says, riffing on Moltmann, that

> there is a dying of the Son which, by the principle of *perichoresis*, mutual indwelling, intrudes death into the whole Godhead. This, for Moltmann, is not "the death of God," for that would blur the Trinitarian distinctions: the Father and the Spirit do not die. But this is death *in* God, since through the cross death and its division *does pierce the life and heart of the triune family.*[29]

Moltmann is perhaps even more explicit, saying,

> The cross [and with it, presumably, the descent] stands at the heart of the trinitarian being of God; it divides and conjoins the persons in their

---

[25]See on this chapter seven, where we discuss the descent and universalism.

[26]See Metropolitan Hilarion Alfeyev, *Christ the Conqueror of Hell: The Descent into Hades from an Orthodox Perspective* (Crestwood, NY: St. Vladimir's Seminary Press, 2009), esp. 213-18.

[27]On Balthasar's supposed connection with the tradition, as well as particular reliance upon von Speyr, see, for example, Brotherton, "Hans Urs von Balthasar on the Redemptive Descent," 169, 179; Lösel, "A Plain Account of Christian Salvation?" 153; and Pitstick, *Light in Darkness*, 273-74, 292.

[28]For an introduction to von Speyr's life and thought, see Hans Urs von Balthasar, *First Glance at Adrienne von Speyr,* 2nd ed. (San Francisco: Ignatius, 2017).

[29]Lewis, *Between Cross and Resurrection,* 224-25. Emphasis in the final clause is mine.

relationships to each other and portrays them in a specific way. For . . . the theological dimension of the death of Jesus on the cross is what happens between Jesus and his Father in the spirit of abandonment and surrender. In these relationships the person of Jesus comes to the fore *in its totality as the Son*, and *the relationship of the Godhead and the manhood in his person fall into the background.*'[30]

While Lewis and Moltmann are not Balthasar, and while Balthasar is sometimes more careful to avoid their extremes, these quotes do show how other theologians, and particularly Lewis, have taken this supposed separation between the Father and Son in Christ's passion (and particularly in his descent).

The final stream that flows into Balthasar's position is that of Calvin via Karl Barth.[31] For Calvin and subsequently for Barth, Christ's descent occurs not on Holy Saturday but on Good Friday at the cross. For Calvin and for Barth, Christ *"descendit ad inferos"* means that he experienced the wrath of God in his humanity during the crucifixion. Christ bore the weight of sin's penalty in his body on the tree (Gal 3:13) and thus felt abandoned by God, expressed via the cry of dereliction. Balthasar finds commonality between his mysticism—especially expressed in von Speyr—and Barth's articulation of the descent but shifts its timing to Saturday and location to hell. Rather than the separation occurring in Christ qua human on Friday on the cross, it occurs in Christ qua divine on Friday in hell. Thus for Balthasar, the descent is an amalgam of Eastern Orthodoxy, Roman Catholicism, mysticism, and Barth's particular brand of Calvinism, resulting in what we could summarize as a universally redemptive kenotic moment in the life of God, in which the

---

[30]Jürgen Moltmann, *The Crucified God: The Cross of Christ as the Foundation and Criticism of Christian Theology* (1974; Minneapolis: Fortress Press, 1993), 207, emphasis mine. See also Moltmann, *Crucified God*, 217, 243, 277. The examples in Lewis and Moltmann could be multiplied. See both Habets, "Putting the *Extra*," and Pitstick, *Light into Darkness*, for sustained discussion.

[31]For Barth's view of the descent, see Karl Barth, *Church Dogmatics* II/2, 496, and *Church Dogmatics* IV/1, §59.2. On the relationship between Balthasar's view of the descent and Barth's, see David Lauber, *Barth on the Descent into Hell: God, Atonement, and the Christian Life*, Barth Studies (Surrey: Ashgate, 2004).

Son suffers the torments of hell and is existentially separated from the Father, only to be reunited via the bond of love that is the Spirit.

Evaluating Balthasar's views on the descent. What, if anything, can be retrieved for evangelicals from Balthasar's position, and what must be rejected on biblical and historical grounds? We will continue to answer these questions in subsequent chapters in various ways; for instance, we will deal with the issue of universalism in chapter seven, while cosmology and exactly where Jesus descended will be covered in chapter five. Here, our focus is specifically on what can be said about Balthasar's position with respect to its Trinitarian shape and implications.

First, with respect to the doctrines of inseparable operations and appropriation, it appears to us that Balthasar's position on the descent explicitly departs from both of these. In classic Trinitarianism and classic Christology, theologians have been very careful to discuss the crucifixion in such a way that it does not posit a breach either in the Trinity or the hypostatic union. As Fleming Rutledge puts it,

> The Son and the Father are doing this [the crucifixion] in concert, by the power of the Spirit. This interposition of the Son between human beings and the curse of God upon Sin is a project of the three persons. The sentence of accursedness has fallen upon Jesus on our behalf and in our place, *by his own decree* as the second person.[32]

Son and Father are not separated in the act of redemption, but rather acting "in concert," as Rutledge puts it, pouring out the wrath they share as the first and second persons of the one God, on Christ Jesus qua human. Of course, the man Christ Jesus is God the Son incarnate, and so in another sense "The wrath of God has lodged in God's own self."[33] And so, again, we must be careful in our talk of redemption not to posit

---

[32]Fleming Rutledge, *The Crucifixion: Understanding the Death of Christ* (Grand Rapids: Eerdmans, 2015), 100. She footnotes here the classic statement from Augustine (*Trin.* 1.5) regarding inseparable operations: *Opera trinitatis ad extra indivisa sunt.*

[33]Rutledge, *Crucifixion*, 132.

a break either between the Trinitarian persons or between the human and divine natures of the incarnate person of the Son.

And yet this is exactly what Balthasar does, and for a variety of reasons. The first move Balthasar makes is that he places Christ's torment on Saturday, not Friday. This is innovative from the perspective of the traditional doctrine of the atonement, to say the least. Traditionally speaking, Christ's humiliation in his work of redemption ends on Good Friday, while the exaltation phase of his redemptive work *begins* with the descent and culminates with the ascension. There is good biblical reason to support this traditional distinction between the phases of Christ's work, most notably Jesus' own cry of "It is finished" (Jn 19:30) and Paul's description of Jesus' humiliation that climaxes in death on a cross (Phil 2:8). Both of these texts seem to indicate that the humiliation of Christ climaxes and, at least in the sense of suffering, finds its completion at the cross. Regarding the beginning of his exaltation, Christ first proclaims his victory to the dead ones in his descent, then rises bodily from among them and proclaims his victory to the apostles and five hundred witnesses in the resurrection, and finally ascends to heaven where he sits at the right hand of the Father and rules and reigns over all things.[34] Balthasar, though, extends Christ's humiliation *in the sense of suffering for sin* to continue through Holy Saturday, and precisely because he sees Christ as descended to the place of the damned (instead of just the generic place of the dead) *in order to be tormented*, something that simply is not found in the history of Christian thought prior to his work.[35]

---

[34]See the iconographic history that supports this understanding of the traditional view of the descent discussed in John Behr, *The Mystery of Christ: Life in Death* (Crestwood, NY: St. Vladimir's Seminary Press, 2006), 98.

[35]For a critique of Balthsar's position on the descent and torment, see Lösel, "A Plain Account of Christian Salvation?" Again, we should note that Augustine speculates about Christ's exact location in "hell," and even suggests that he *may* have descended to the place of torment. But in doing so he does not go there to be tormented, but to "loose the bonds" of hell—that is, he destroys hell by virtue of his completed work on the cross. See Augustine, *Letters of St. Augustin* CLXIV, "To Evodius" 515-21 (*NPNF*[1] 1:515–21).

The second shift that Balthasar makes is to see the effects of death related to the penalty of sin happening not to Christ qua human but qua divine. While Balthasar does not explicitly state that the incarnation is put on hold, negated, or otherwise temporarily suspended in the descent, the fact that its actions and effects occur between the divine hypostases strongly suggests that it is qua divine that Christ experiences death, not qua human.[36] But if we look at the history of the doctrine, this is again completely innovative. Christ's descent is effective because he is divine, but the tradition makes clear that he descends to the place of the dead qua human.

These two shifts lead to the third and most important one for our purposes in this chapter, namely, that Balthasar sees the descent effecting existential separation between the divine hypostases of Father and Son. Since Christ's humanity is God-forsaken, and since Balthasar appears to be intent on avoiding Nestorianism in his position,[37] the Son qua divine must experience this God-forsakenness, this separation from the Father, in some sense as well. Of course, it is for this reason that the descent is effective in Balthasar's thought; nevertheless, it is still an innovation on the tradition and also a departure from the doctrine of inseparable operations. As D'Costa perceptively remarks, "What is at stake is the unity of the Trinity. If Christ is ontologically alienated from his own divinity when Christ is ontologically God-forsaken, there is also a rupture in the divine Trinitarian life which destroys the nature of God."[38]

Recall that the doctrine of inseparable operations posits that each act of the one God is one act. Thus for God to pour out his wrath means that the Triune God pours out his wrath—Father, Son, and Spirit together. Further, God's role as Judge is affirmed of both Father

---

[36]On this reading of Balthasar's position, see both D'Costa, "The Descent into Hell," 154; and John Saward, *Mysteries of March: Hans Urs von Balthasar on the Incarnation and Easter* (Washington, DC: Catholic University of America Press, 1990), 55-56.

[37]See Oakes, "The Internal Logic," 198.

[38]D'Costa, "The Descent into Hell," 154.

and Son (and, by implication, the Spirit; see, e.g., Jn 5:22-23). That Jesus, the God-Man, is both the Just and the Justifier—and therefore the one who executes justice through pouring out his divine wrath (cf. Rom 3:23-26)—was one of the key affirmations in the fourth century that led to the pro-Nicene doctrine of the Trinity.[39] For Balthasar, however, it is not the one God who pours out his wrath, but only the Father. This is a bifurcation between the persons of the Trinity not only at the level of action but also at the level of attributes, since now only the Father is wrathful.[40]

We of course need to bear in mind both biblical language about the atonement and the doctrine of appropriations here; the Father does "deliver up" the Son (cf., e.g., Acts 2:23; Rom 4:25), and it is appropriate to speak of the Father as the one who pours out wrath. But if we strip those affirmations away from the corollary affirmation of inseparable operations, we will end up very close to tritheism. The biblical passages that speak of the Father delivering up the Son and the Father pouring out his wrath should not be divorced from the Shema: "the LORD our God, the LORD is one." His actions and attributes are one, and when we speak about him, we must be careful not to do so in a way that sounds as if there is not one God but three. But this is exactly what Balthasar does in his explication of the descent. While his anti-Nestorian aims are admirable, ultimately something like Luther's position—or even the classic version of his own Roman Catholic tradition—would have better served him in this regard. Both Luther and the traditional Roman Catholic position posit that Christ descended in body and soul, and as human and divine—thus avoiding both Docetism and Nestorianism—but they do not posit any existential separation (as Balthasar does) between

---

[39]For a discussion of the relationship between the Son's and Father's authority in the context of early Christianity's Jewish roots, see Richard Bauckham, *Jesus and the God of Israel: God Crucified and Other Studies on the New Testament's Christology of Divine Identity* (Grand Rapids: Eerdmans, 2008), esp. 107-26.

[40]For a recent exploration of wrath as one of the perfections of the Godhead, see Jeremy J. Wynne, *Wrath Among the Perfections of God's Life*, T&T Clark Studies in Systematic Theology (London: T&T Clark, 2012).

Christ's humanity and divinity or between the divine hypostases of Father and Son.

CONCLUSION

The descent is part of the one act of redemption accomplished by the one God through the God-Man, God the Son incarnate, Jesus Christ. When speaking about it, therefore, we need to be careful to do so in such a way that we maintain God's tri-personal oneness through the doctrines of inseparable operations and appropriation. While Hans Urs von Balthasar's position on the descent has given the doctrine a certain revival in recent years, unfortunately it fails to stay within these two Trinitarian guardrails. Regarding inseparable operations, by positing a separation between the hypostases of Father and Son, Balthasar fails to maintain the unity of God's action. For him, it is only the Father who has and pours out wrath. Regarding the doctrine of appropriation, the Son does assume a particular role in Balthasar's view, but it is outside the boundaries of inseparable operations since the Father and Son are in some sense acting independently of one another. Further, Balthasar does not maintain the unity of the incarnate Son, since the hypostatic union seems to be temporarily suspended, or at least negligible in importance, for the existential separation between the divine hypostases of Father and Son to occur. While there may be some sense of poetry to Balthasar's position, it does not ultimately bear up under biblical, historical, or theological scrutiny.

"MAKER OF HEAVEN AND EARTH"

The Descent and the Doctrine of Creation

"We still have not had a death," [José Arcadio Buendía] said. "A person does not belong to a place until there is someone dead under the ground."

GABRIEL GARCÍA MÁRQUEZ,
ONE HUNDRED YEARS OF SOLITUDE

The Triune God who defeated death through the descent of the God-Man Jesus Christ is the same Triune God who made heaven and earth. Since the descent is described in spatiotemporal language—that is, language that references specific places and times—it is necessary for us to explore not only what God is doing in the descent but also the nature of creation to which he descends. Further, if, as chapter two concluded, human beings in the intermediate state experience a temporary disunion between their bodies, which lay in the ground and decay, and their souls, which exist in a conscious, albeit temporary and abnormal, intermediate state, this has many implications for the doctrine of creation. Additionally, because the New Testament speaks of paradise, heaven, Gehenna, Hades, and the abyss with at least some correlation to Christ's descent, not only human death in general but

Christ's descent to the dead in particular have implications for cosmology, emplacement, and embodiment. With respect to cosmology, we must ask exactly *where* (in a spatially metaphorical sense) Christ's human soul, along with all human souls, goes. We must also ask whether or not the victory achieved in Christ's descent has any bearing on cosmology and the location of disembodied souls. And while most of our attention in this book so far has been on disembodied souls, we must also remember that the descent says something about Christ's body, along with all human bodies, as well—that it is buried. What does burial have to do with embodiment? Specifically, what does Scripture tell us about burial and emplacement, and particularly about the place where Jesus' body is laid? I will argue in this chapter that Christ's descent to the dead requires a particular cosmology, one that allows for disembodied souls to exist together and, for the righteous dead, in the joyful presence of YHWH.[1] I will also argue that the description of Christ's tomb in the Gospel of John presents us with a doctrine of place, one that is both unique to Jesus as the God-Man but also that has implications for human burial.

COSMOLOGY

The scriptural witness to the realm of the dead is admittedly varied,[2] especially between the Old Testament and New Testament, but this does not mean that it is self-contradictory. To the contrary, while I might be

---

[1]We should note again here, as I did in chapter two, that all spatial language is metaphorical. Immaterial souls are not spatially extended, to put it in dogmatic and philosophical terms. I owe that phrase to Luke Stamps.

[2]For two different understandings of the OT teaching on the afterlife, and therefore of how the Old Testament and New Testament relate to one another in this regard, see John W. Cooper, *Body, Soul, & Life Everlasting: Biblical Anthropology and the Monism-Dualism Debate* (Grand Rapids: Eerdmans, 1989); and Philip S. Johnston, *Shades of Sheol: Death and Afterlife in the Old Testament* (Downers Grove, IL: IVP Academic, 2002). While Cooper takes what we might call the "traditional" view (the Bible, and particularly the Old Testament, teaches that humans exist as a body-soul unity and that there is an intermediate state between death and resurrection), Johnston argues that the Old Testament does not (at least explicitly) teach a conscious intermediate state or speak of human beings in such a way that would warrant a separation between body and soul. See, e.g., the conclusion in Johnston, *Shades of Sheol*, 215.

willing to say that clear teaching on the afterlife becomes more prevalent throughout Israel's history, progression in terms of specificity is not the same thing as a shift in either what Israel confessed or what is true in reality (more on this below).[3]

"From the Dead (Ones)." As I mentioned in chapter two, a significant term for understanding exactly what the New Testament teaches about Christ's descent is τῶν νεκρῶν and its synonyms (e.g., ἐκ νεκρῶν; "from the dead"). While the basic point made earlier about these phrases does not need more explanation,[4] it does have consequences for cosmology.[5] Especially pertinent are the phrase's implications for the existence of an invisible (and non-spatial) realm; its inhabitation not only by angels and demons but also disembodied souls; and, with respect to the realm of the righteous, a shift in location (if I can use such a term non-spatially).

In the Old Testament we find at least two interrelated themes concerning the afterlife: (1) the language of ascending and descending, and (2) Sheol. Regarding the former, the Old Testament speaks both of YHWH ascending and descending from earth to heaven and vice versa, and of YHWH bringing humans down to Sheol and back up again (albeit metaphorically in many cases, i.e., with reference to sickness, violence, and other threats as a threat of death).[6] In other words, the Old Testament can use ascending/descending language to refer to the passing of God and angels from the spiritual realm to the physical realm

---

[3]On the progression in and continuity of Israel's thought from exclusive polemics against the common ANE perspective to the view of the afterlife found in Second Temple Judaism and the New Testament, see Joseph Ratzinger, *Eschatology: Death and Eternal Life*, 2nd ed. (Washington, DC: Catholic University of America Press, 1988), 81-83. Note also though Feldman's comment that "theologies and speculations about death tend to be very conservative, and late texts can reflect much older beliefs. Even the later prophetic utterances in this area are not necessarily reflections of later development." Emmanuel Feldman, *Biblical and Post-Biblical Defilement and Mourning: Law as Theology* (New York: Yeshiva University Press/KTAV Publishing, 1977), 17.

[4]Namely that they should be translated "to/from among the dead ones" and therefore demonstrate that Christ's human soul departed to the realm of the dead.

[5]Additionally, and again as argued in chapter three, the fluctuation in the language of the Apostles' Creed—*descendit ad inferos* becoming the preferred wording, rather than *ad inferna*—aligns with the interpretation of τῶν νεκρῶν above.

[6]See Ratzinger's discussion of threats of death as metaphors for the experience of death and the intermediate state in *Eschatology*, 81-83.

and back again (e.g., Gen 28:10-22). It is also used to refer to death and resurrection, e.g., 1 Sam 2:6: "The LORD kills and brings to life; he brings down to Sheol and raises up." As far as Sheol is concerned, there is some disjunction, to put it mildly, between the traditional view of the afterlife—body in the grave, disembodied soul—and the consensus of critical biblical scholarship. Both of these uses, while distinct, impinge upon the descent and its implications for the afterlife.

Regarding the descent and ascent of YHWH, the New Testament uses this language to speak of both Christ's incarnation and descent to the dead. These include clear uses of descent language, such as Ephesians 4:9, as well passages that speak of Christ coming down from heaven even if the word *descent* or its correlates are not used (e.g., Phil 2:7). But this is not the only instance in which descent language is used; as we saw in chapter two, Romans 10:6-7 refers to ascending to heaven "to bring Christ down" and descending to the Abyss "to bring Christ up from the dead." Our exegetical exploration also concluded that Ephesians 4:8-10 refers both to Christ's ascent to heaven and to his descent to the dead. We will return to this pattern of language below in our discussion of angels, demons, and the spiritual realm.

Exactly where Christ descends is dependent on which terminology best captures the sense of the texts above. In chapter two, I noted somewhat briefly that Christ descends to the "place of the dead" in body and soul, and that "the place of the dead" for the soul meant the generic realm of the dead to which all human souls go. It is worth exploring here in more detail what the biblical text means by "the place of the dead" and the different terms it uses to refer to it. These terms do not all mean the same thing or refer to the same place, but they are all used to refer in some sense to the place of the dead. These references to the afterlife include Sheol, paradise, heaven, Gehenna, Hades, abyss, and Tartarus;[7]

---

[7]For a discussion of each of these "compartments" in the Second Temple period, see Justin W. Bass, *The Battle for the Keys: Revelation 1:18 and Christ's Descent into the Underworld*, Paternoster Biblical Monographs (Eugene, OR: Wipf and Stock, 2014), 45-61.

we could also add metaphorical references to subterranean realms, whether under the earth or the sea.[8]

Gehenna and Tartarus are almost always references to postmortem torment, while paradise and heaven are almost always references to postmortem blessing. Sheol is commonly thought to refer to the place of the dead in general, although Johnston has persuasively argued that it more often refers to a place where the unrighteous spend their post-mortem existence.[9] The same can be said for the abyss, although for both "abyss" and "Sheol" it is possible that in at least some cases it is referring to a more general realm of the dead. Whether the metaphorical uses of "under the earth/sea" are to be taken as general references to all the dead or as a reference only to the unrighteous dead is unclear.[10]

For our purposes, it is important to note first that, whatever term is most appropriate to use of Christ's descent, many ANE and Greco-Roman cultures thought of the universe as having three tiers: the heavens, the earth, and the underworld.[11] The latter tier was, in Second Temple Judaism and in some Greco-Roman texts, divided into compartments for the righteous and unrighteous (and potentially subdivided even more from there).[12] While it is true that Israel's expressions about the afterlife appear to become more specific over the course of its history, this does not mean that there are contradictions within the scriptural witness or that Israel's earliest attested beliefs about the afterlife constitute the entirety of the truth about or the scriptural witness to an

---

[8]See here Johnston, *Shades of Sheol*, 83-84,114-126. On the synonymous relationship between "the sea," "abyss," and "Hades," see James D. G. Dunn, *Romans 9–16*, WBC 38B (Dallas: Word, 1988), 606.
[9]Johnston, *Shades of Sheol*, e.g., 81.
[10]See the discussion in Johnston, *Shades of Sheol*, 81-85; For a more positive assessment of their synonymous relationship, see Richard Bauckham, *The Fate of the Dead: Studies on the Jewish and Christian Apocalypses*, NovTSup 93 (Atlanta: SBL Press, 1998), 33-38; and Dunn, *Romans 9–16*, 606.
[11]For an introduction to these concepts, see John H. Walton, *Ancient Near Eastern Thought and the Old Testament: Introducing the Conceptual World of the Hebrew Bible* (Grand Rapids: Baker Academic, 2006), 165-78. It is important to point out, as Walton does, that, for ANE peoples, "cosmic geography was predominantly metaphysical and only secondarily physical/material." Walton, *Ancient Near Eastern Thought*, 167.
[12]See again Bauckham, *Fate of the Dead*, 19-49.

intermediate state. The arguments we make in chapter six concerning this progression of thought with respect to an intermediate state of the human soul also bear on a progression in how Israel understood Sheol.

Progressive revelation and the concept of Sheol. The OT witness to Sheol is a difficult topic, made more difficult by the relative lack of explicit mention or discussion of an intermediate state in Israel's Scriptures. Despite the numerous texts that mention Sheol or its synonyms, we are left with only a few passages that can give us a clear indication of what Israel thought about it. And even then, the conclusions we can draw are tenuous at best. The important point to make here is that the cosmological beliefs of Israel appear to follow the same textual and theological lines drawn in the next chapter. That is, Israel's thought about the afterlife, both theologically in terms of the character of YHWH and textually in terms of increasing mention of bodily resurrection, entails increasing specificity in their thought about the cosmology of afterlife.

This helps us to place in historical and theological context many of the OT passages in which Sheol is used to refer to the general place of the dead without bifurcation between righteous and unrighteous. While it is characterized in such texts as a place of silence, these passages probably reflect a situation in Israel in which their main objective was to argue against the popular ANE notions of the afterlife as they related to magical intervention of the dead and the like.[13] As discussed in the next chapter, it also held commonalities with their ANE neighbors, in that the place of the dead was generally conceived of in terms of contrast to the living and with similarity to a grave—dark, shadowy, dirty, and the like.[14] This

---

[13]On ANE cosmography with respect to the netherworld, ANE cults of the dead, and Israel's relation to both, see Walton, *Ancient Near Eastern Thought*, 316-24. On Israel's primary concern as rejecting ANE neighbors' cults of the dead, see Walton, *Ancient Near Eastern Thought*, 320.

[14]We should point specifically here to Ps 6:5 which reads, "For in death there is no remembrance of you; in Sheol who will give you praise?" It is important to note here, as we also do in the next chapter, that this passage and others like it do not *teach* dogmatically the nature of the afterlife and Sheol, but may merely reflect the writers' desire to reject the occult-like ways in which Israel's ANE neighbors thought about the dead. We may additionally suggest that the texts that

common starting point included not only its belief about the fate of individual souls but also about where these souls existed after their separation from the body at death.[15] Israel's thoughts about Sheol become more explicit (in continuity with previous biblical data) over time, though through specific textual reflection on YHWH's character as the God over all places and people, including the inhabitants in and place of the dead. We also hear Israel expressing hope in return from exile in terms of death and resurrection, as well as the hope for final judgment expressed proleptically in the judgment of the dead during the intermediate state. This means that, if we look at the Old Testament diachronically, we see a movement from speaking of Sheol as an undifferentiated place of silence to a compartmentalized, conscious state where all souls go upon death,[16] but to either the righteous or unrighteous compartment. This diachronic movement may reflect a shift in primary concern, from polemics against ANE neighbors to reflections on YHWH's impending return, Israel's resurrection, and the final judgment.

In this regard, it is important to recognize that Israel's reflections about the intermediate state grow in number and specificity not only as

---

appear more dogmatic could just as easily be explained phenomenologically. That is, to the living, it *appears* that the dead do not participate in praising YHWH, since they are not with the living in the congregation and, most importantly, do not have access to the tabernacle/temple. Finally, texts like Is 38:18—"For Sheol does not thank you; death does not praise you; those who go down to the pit do not hope for your faithfulness"—may reflect the use of Sheol to refer to the place of the unrighteous dead rather than all the dead. This is more than likely the case given the judgment context of Isaiah 38. In any case, this polemical stance of Israel does not contradict later explicit language about the afterlife, but rather progresses in step with Israel's theological reflection and further revelation from YHWH about his own character, his interaction with his people, and his plan for eschatological renewal.

[15]Another important source for understanding Israel's views about death comes from burial practices. For a helpful analysis, including discussion of the term *Sheol* and its relation to the grave, see Matthew J. Suriano, "Sheol, the Tomb, and the Problem of Postmortem Existence," *JHS* 16.11 (2016): 1-31. See also Roland de Vaux, *Ancient Israel: Its Life and Institutions*, trans., John McHugh (1961; London: Darton, Longman and Todd, 1998), 56-61; and Philip J. King and Lawrence E. Stager, *Life in Biblical Israel*, Library of Ancient Israel (Louisville, KY: Westminster John Knox, 2001), 363-82 for a summary of Israel's burial practices and their relation to a belief in the afterlife.

[16]Again, the view of "silence in Sheol" and later articulations of a conscious state do not contradict one another, especially if we recognize the inherently phenomenological nature of living persons' reflections about death.

they theologically reflect on YHWH's character and his promises of the eschatological renewal of Israel and the world, but also as they use different literary techniques. Most importantly, we should acknowledge that the increasingly specific references to Israel's beliefs about the intermediate state coincide with the development of prophetic writing, and especially apocalyptic material. Regarding prophetic writing generally, it is especially in the prophets that we see the hope of future restoration, and out of this comes more explicit mention of belief in the resurrection of the dead. This resurrection of the dead, promised first with the respect to the restoration of Israel (Ezek 36–37) and distinguished as it is (in Dan 12:2-3 especially), naturally leads to reflection on what happens to persons in between death and that promised resurrection. Because YHWH's future resurrection of his people also entails the judgment of his enemies, apocalyptic works during the Second Temple period like *1 Enoch* (e.g., *1 En.* 50:1-11) explicitly relate proleptic judgments. Sheol/Hades is compartmentalized: the righteous dead dwelling in paradise, or Abraham's bosom, and the unrighteous dead dwelling in Gehenna, or Tartarus.

This brings us to a second and related important cosmological point with respect to Sheol and the biblical concept of the underworld, namely that nowhere does the biblical text proclaim that Christ in his human soul descended into Gehenna or Tartarus;[17] instead, the references are to "Hades" (Acts 2:27; cf. Rev 1:18), "the abyss" (Rom 10:7), and "the lower regions, the earth" (Eph 4:9). The only reference to a synonym of Gehenna and/or Tartarus is in 1 Peter 3:19, where Christ "proclaimed" his work to "the spirits in prison." Given texts like Luke 16:19-31 and its parallels in Second Temple Judaism,[18] as well as

---

[17]While 1 Pet 3:19 refers to Christ declaring his victory to "the spirits in prison" (cf. 2 Pet 2:4-5 for a possible parallel to those fallen angels imprisoned in Tartarus), this does not demand an interpretation in which Christ suffered along with Tartarus's inhabitants. Rather, if the realm of the dead includes all the dead but in a bifurcated sense (i.e. Lk 16), communication across underworld compartments is possible.

[18]See Matthew Ryan Hauge, *The Biblical Tour of Hell*, LNTS 485 (London: Bloomsbury, 2013).

the purpose of Christ's proclamation as articulated in chapter two (namely to proclaim his victory), it is not demanded by this text that Christ actually descended into Gehenna or Tartarus. And, as we saw in chapter three, early Christian theologians did not understand Christ's descent as extending to the place of torment, only to the place of the righteous dead. While this is not an open-and-shut case, it does suggest that Christ's descent is *not* one in which he experiences torment. Rather, he descends into the righteous compartment of Hades in order to proclaim victory to all the dead and to the evil spirits in the lowest compartment, Tartarus.

Another means by which the early church reflected cosmologically on Christ's descent is their comparison of the three descents of Jesus. It was common in the early church to see Christ's incarnation, baptism in the Jordan, and descent to the dead as parallel to one another both cosmologically and soteriologically. In soteriological terms, they are each part of Christ's defeat of his enemies: broadly in the incarnation, and more specifically the chaos monsters in his baptism and Death and Hades (and everything else) in his descent. This is why the icons of Jesus' baptism many times include pictures of monstrous fish underneath his feet, and why the early church also saw these three descents as cosmologically parallel.[19] The sea in the Old Testament was the place where the chaos monsters dwelt, from the beginning in Genesis 1:2 as well as throughout Israel's history (cf. Job 40:23 for reference to Behemoth [a dragon?], who is described as having the Jordan rush "against his mouth," as well as the poem about Leviathan in Job 41). In descending, Jesus went down into the waters—the place of chaos—first into the waters of Mary's womb, then into the waters of

---

[19]This is reflected not only in the writings of early Christians, as discussed in chapter three, but also in the liturgical texts and practices related to baptism in the early church. See Everett Ferguson, *Baptism in the Early Church: History, Theology, and Liturgy in the First Five Centuries* (Grand Rapids: Eerdmans, 2009), 11, 120-22, 213. cf. also Ferguson, *Baptism*, 223-24, 226, 415, and 730 for more connections between baptism and the descent in the early church. Finally, see Per Lundberg, *La typologie baptismale dans l'ancienne église* (Uppsala: Lorentz, 1942).

Figure 5.1. Icon of Jesus' baptism

the Jordan, and finally into the abyss, the place of the dead, the ul-timate chaotic realm.[20] And, in doing so, he crushes chaos in each of the three tiers of the universe: from heaven to earth in the incarnation, on earth in his baptism, from earth to the underworld in his descent, and then victoriously upward to earth and then heaven in his resur-rection and ascension.

This pattern of descent and ascent, seen especially in the angels descending and ascending Jacob's ladder—the way to and from God's dwelling place—in Genesis 28:10-22, is now fulfilled in Christ. Jesus both descends and ascends in his incarnation, baptism, de-scent, resurrection, and ascension, thus paving the way for his human sisters and brothers to come after him in faith to be restored to God. But he also is now the ladder as well, the means by which not only angels (Jn 1:51) but also human beings, by faith alone, will be able to dwell once again with God in the heavenly places. Christ's descent, the nadir of his descent in the incarnation and baptism, is thus the culmination of a pattern of descent in the Old Testament. But instead of descent into exile, as with Israel, Jesus' descent is vic-torious over the chaos monsters, over sin, and over Death and Hades, so that now those who follow Christ in faith can ascend to dwell again with God.

What, then, does the doctrine of the descent have to do with the doctrine of creation? I suggest that, in the first place, it affirms the three-tiered universe implied and assumed by all of the biblical writers, the Greco-Roman world, the ancient Near East, and Second Temple Ju-daism. I do not wish to imply, though, that this means that to affirm the descent one must also affirm that heaven and the underworld are physical locales accessible to living human beings. What Scripture de-scribes with locative and spatial terms is a spiritual reality, not mappable

---

[20]In this regard we think of Jonah, who not only descended into the waters but into the belly of a "great fish." Could Jonah's three-day journey into the underworld also be a journey into the belly of a chaos monster? See the discussion in chapter two on the parallels between the fish's belly and the abyss.

on geographic or cosmographic terms.[21] We will discuss this further in the section on angelology below.

Paradise Cubed. Another cosmographic implication of the descent is how the New Testament speaks about paradise, the righteous compartment of Hades. The word *paradise* (παράδεισος) only occurs three times in the New Testament: Luke 23:43; 2 Corinthians 12:2-4; and Revelation 2:7. While Luke 16:19-31 does not use the term *paradise*, it does refer to Lazarus sitting by "Abraham's side" (Lk 16:22-23), and the rich man and Lazarus can see and speak to one another across the chasm. This description, parabolic though it is, matches the common view of the afterlife in Second Temple Judaism: the unrighteous are consigned to torment in Hades (again, this term can be used of both a general place of the dead and of the place of torment), while the righteous experience peace in paradise (or Abraham's bosom). This is the most socioculturally sensible explanation of Jesus' statement to the thief on the cross in Luke 23:43 that, "today you will be with me in paradise." In the Gospel of Luke, and in Luke's sociocultural context, Abraham's bosom and paradise were synonymous, and they were part of the common underworld where all the dead lived, albeit in separate compartments.

The presence of Jesus in paradise, though, changes its entire constitution. Rather than being a place where the righteous dead await the coming of Israel's promised Messiah, the Christ is now in their midst. First, in the descent, he is present with them in his human soul, and then, after the ascension, he is present with them bodily. This change in paradise's constitution, from one of messianic expectation to one of christological reality, is mirrored in the New Testament by a change in spatial description. The second reference to paradise in the New

---

[21]It is worth noting in this regard that, unlike Greco-Roman depictions of descents to the dead, the New Testament does not speak of Christ's descent in lengthy narratives. There is no mention of an entry to the place of the dead, no "tour of heaven and hell" (apart from the abbreviated one in Lk 16), etc. These only come later in the apocryphal literature, such as *Gos. Bart.* In other words, the NT authors' use of spatial terms is comparatively scant, meaning that their focus is on what the descent accomplished rather than on its physical location (or lack thereof).

Testament comes in 2 Corinthians 12:2-4, when Paul describes his out-of-body experience. Here, he refers to the place of the righteous dead, where Christ now dwells bodily, as both paradise and "the third heaven" (2 Cor 12:2). The spatial description of paradise shifts from the underworld to the third heaven, not because it has been physically moved (it is a spiritual, not physical, realm) but because its spiritual reality has changed. While it is not yet the paradise of the new heavens and new earth,[22] the restored Eden, the ultimate paradise, it is nevertheless the place where Christ dwells bodily.

This final, eschatological renewal of God's creation, the new heavens and new earth, is the referent of the third use of *paradise* in the New Testament. In Revelation 2:7, Jesus promises that "the one who conquers" will be able to eat from the tree of life in the paradise of God. While this paradise has not yet arrived, it is clear that John is referring to the new heavens and new earth described in Revelation 21–22 (see the references to the tree of life in Rev 22:2, 14, 19). Paradise comes down to earth in the renewal of God's creation and his dwelling place with his people.

Thus the descent once again confirms this three-tiered thinking of the biblical writers and their sociocultural context, but it also inaugurates a shift in cosmography. Paradise, because of the descent and the coming resurrection and ascension, experiences a shift in its reality. It is no longer full of the righteous dead waiting for the Messiah but is now a place where the resurrected and ascended Messiah dwells with his people.[23] They still wait but with the resurrected Second Adam—the first fruits of their own coming resurrection—in their midst. As we will see in the next chapter more fully, this is why the early church spoke of

---

[22]This should be apparent by the fact that Paul refers to being "caught up" to "third heaven," whereas the new heavens and new earth consist of heaven "coming down" to earth, i.e. heaven and earth collapsing into one another.

[23]For a Roman Catholic articulation of this aspect of the descent's effects, see Alyssa Lyra Pitstick, *Light in Darkness: Hans Urs von Balthasar and the Catholic Doctrine of Christ's Descent into Hell* (Grand Rapids: Eerdmans, 2007), 45-48.

the descent as a release of the captives of Hades. It is not because they believed the righteous dead to be in torment prior to Christ, or because they thought that all the dead were tormented but only those who responded to Christ's evangelistic preaching were released. Rather, they used this terminology to describe the change in paradise's constitution, from messianic hope to christological reality.[24] Or, as Charles Hill puts it reflecting on Hebrews 11:39-40 and 12:22-24,

> These spirits of the just [those in Paradise, the righteous compartment of the place of the dead] are now perfected, and have received the promise of the better country, the heavenly one, the city that has foundations, whose builder and maker is God.
>
> What has intervened? Of course, what has intervened and what has "perfected" them is that Christ has offered for all time a single sacrifice for sins. For by that single offering he has perfected for all time those who are being sanctified (10.12-14).
>
> And what brings them *to heaven* is their union with the one who is now *in heaven*. He has "tasted death for everyone" (2.9) and then passed through the heavens (4.14), to the heavenly Mt. Zion, into the heavenly temple, and through the greater and more perfect tent, not made with hands (9.11), entering once for all into the holy of holies by means of his own blood. The saints of old have now received what was promised! They are in the heavenly city, and now surround the throne.[25]

What Hill describes here is the cosmographic shift explored above. While it is difficult to portray these kinds of shifts visually, since we are talking about movement between things "visible and invisible" (Col 1:16), I have attempted nevertheless to portray Christ's movement from the heavenly realm to the earthly realm to the realm of the dead and then

---

[24]Douglas Farrow describes the act of redemption in Christ as "U-shaped," moving from baptism to death in his humiliation and from resurrection to ascension in his exaltation. See his *Ascension and Ecclesia: On the Significance of the Doctrine of the Ascension for Ecclesiology and Christian Cosmology* (Grand Rapids: Eerdmans, 1999), 15-40.

[25]Charles E. Hill, "'He Descended into Hell,'" *RFP* 1.2 (2016): 10.

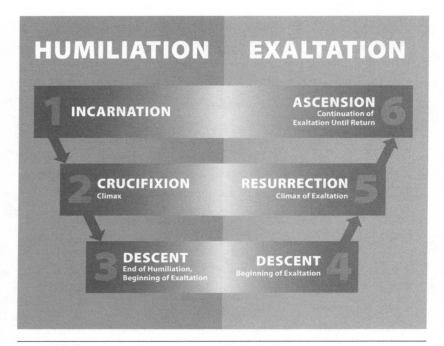

Figure 5.2. Descent and the humiliation and exaltation of Christ

back up through each of those realms in the image above. Notice also that the image traces these cosmographic movements in Christ's work in conjunction with his shift from humiliation to exaltation.

Angels, Demons, and the Intermediate State. One final implication of the descent for the doctrine of creation, at least insofar as it relates to cosmology and the intermediate state, is that it helps clarify the relationship between the metaphysics of angels and theological anthropology. We will give a defense of substance dualism that affirms an intermediate state in the next chapter; here, I only wish to draw the line from that conclusion to cosmology and angelic metaphysics. The affirmation of an intermediate state for human beings can be compared metaphysically to the nature of angels. Angels are creatures with a spiritual nature, creatures who can appear to living human beings (that is, they can be extended into timespace), but who normally exist in non-extended ways. This helps us to think about cosmology, because it means that there is a non-physical realm, an invisible, spiritual realm in which at least angels (and, given the next chapter, I would also say human souls) dwell. We cannot empirically experience it, but its inhabitants (or, at least God and angels[26]) can show themselves to us. Again, this points to the descent's affirmation of the biblical worldview concerning the universe and its makeup. There is the physical world, the second tier, earth; and then there is the spiritual world, consisting of heaven and the underworld, the first and third tiers.

DEAD BODIES, BURIAL, AND THE DESCENT

Another main way that the descent relates to the doctrine of creation is through burial practices. While the clause "he was buried" is syntactically separate from the descent clause in the Apostles' Creed, these two clauses were seen in some early Christian reflections as synonymous.[27] Burial and descent are two anthropological sides of the same coin, the former reflecting bodily realities and the latter spiritual ones. In both the Old Testament and the New Testament, burial communicates something about spiritual—or heavenly—realities. Here, I will mention two: resurrection hope and embodiment.

Facing the East. First, burial practices, especially those of historic Christianity, reflect the hope of resurrection. This hope is reflected in the spiritual realm by the martyred souls' cry in Revelation 6:10. The intermediate state for Christ followers is *intermediate*: it is not the final eschatological state of eternal bliss, but rather the proleptic presence of the bodily, risen Christ while they remain disembodied, awaiting their

---

[26]I say "at least" because there are a few instances in Scripture where not just God or angels show themselves, but, seemingly, the souls of deceased persons, namely Samuel (1 Sam 28) and Moses and Elijah (Mt 17 and par.). These appearances do not appear to be of their own volition, though.

[27]Not in the sense that "descended" simply refers to bodily burial, but in the sense that both clauses implicitly contain the other in them. See the discussion of Rufinus in chapter three.

resurrection from the dead.[28] The practice of burying bodies facing east is the earthly reflection of the disembodied soul's hope: that one day Christ will come again, from the East, and raise us bodily. Christ's descent to the dead, the inauguration of his victory over death, is the starting point of his exaltation, the basis for this resurrection hope.

Burial practices and embodiment. Christ's descent to the dead also has implications for how we speak of human beings, especially in burial practices. At death, human beings do not cease to exist. I will discuss this again in the next chapter, but here I want to connect this with burial practices. This is reflected in Israelite (specifically Judahite) burials, where the three days' waiting period prior to anointing with spices was related to allowing the human spirit to depart from the body.[29] These three days are thus a liminal space, in between life and the afterlife, much like Holy Saturday is a liminal space between Christ's death and resurrection. The continued existence of human beings even in death is also reflected in the phrase "gathered to their Fathers" in the Old Testament, which is said of Jacob *before* burial (Gen 49:33, "gathered to his people"; 50:13), implying that the burial of the body cannot be univocally equated with the gathering. This, in turn, implies that "gathering" has something to do with the human person's soul, not just with the body.[30]

These biblical and theological realities have implications for human burial. I have discussed graves facing east, waiting for Christ, but I should also mention here the practice of cremation. While I do not want to be dogmatic on this point,[31] the fact of continued human existence

---

[28]So Matthew Levering (summarizing Thomas Aquinas) in *Jesus and the Demise of Death: Resurrection, Afterlife, and the Fate of the Christian* (Waco, TX: Baylor University Press, 2012), 22, 25.

[29]See Suriano, "Sheol, the Tomb, and the Problem of Postmortem Existence," 5-7.

[30]On this and related phrases in the Old Testament and their relation to the afterlife, as well as the explicit case of Jacob, see Johnston, *Shades of Sheol*, 33-35. We could also mention in this regard 1 Thess 4:13-18, where the dead are called "those who have fallen asleep." They bear some relationship to the living, still exist, but are not alive. Thanks to Patrick Schreiner for this observation.

[31]For a more pointed argument against cremation, see David Jones, "To Bury or To Burn? Toward an Ethic of Cremation," *JETS* 53.2 (2010): 335-47.

in death and the reality of the resurrection should, I believe, lead one to avoid cremation. I realize that this is a delicate issue, and I do not wish to pass judgment on those who have chosen cremation upon their own death or at the death of their loved ones, or upon those who required cremation (or any other non-terrestrial mode of burial) due to the nature of their death. I also do not wish to suggest that those who have been cremated cannot be raised from the dead; far from it![32] But I do wish to say that I believe bodily burial is the option more consistent with the Christian confession of Christ's descent to the dead, his bodily resurrection, and our bodily resurrection at his second coming.

THE TOMB AND THE TEMPLE

One final way in which Jesus' descent relates to the doctrine of creation is with respect to our understanding of Israel's Promised Land. In our justifiable focus on Christ's crucifixion, along with our rush to get to the resurrection, Christians often neglect the fact that Jesus was buried. Of course, that has been the major burden of this book: to demonstrate that neglect and provide a corrective. But our focus thus far has been on Jesus' human soul and his descent to the dead. We have not spent much time meditating on his bodily burial, aside from the previous brief sections. John's Gospel and its description of Jesus' tomb gives us ample reason to do so, and especially in the context of creation. Creation in the Bible is not merely universally cosmic but concentrated particularly on the Promised Land. For John, Jesus' burial is indicative of Christ's purchase of the Promised Land and therefore of his purchase for the entire creation. For as Israel goes, so goes the world; as Israel is saved, so is the world saved. In redeeming the Land, Jesus is redeeming the entire cosmos, and so in purchasing the Land, he is purchasing the entire cosmos.

---

[32]This would be akin to saying that those who have been long dead and have thus almost completely disintegrated cannot be raised, a statement which is clearly contrary to the biblical witness. On the metaphysics of bodily resurrection, especially for those long dead, see Nichols, *Death and Afterlife*, 135-50.

How exactly does Jesus purchase the Promised Land in his burial? To answer this question, we need to first look back at how the Land was purchased in the Old Testament.[33] In Deuteronomy 30:5, the author declares that YHWH will "bring [Israel] into the land that your fathers possessed, that you may possess it." Israel's fathers are here described as proleptically possessing the Promised Land prior to the conquest. In the Genesis narratives, this appears to occur via burial sites[34] and/or altar sites.[35] Thus, while the comment in Deuteronomy 30:5 is brief, it is plausible that it is referring to Abraham, Isaac, and Jacob possessing the land through burial and worship.[36] Further, given that Macpelah is the first piece of land purchased and Arunah's threshing floor the last (2 Sam 24:18-25; cf. 1 Chron 21:18-30), we could also say that the entire Promised Land narrative moves from a burial site to a temple site. Ezekiel may mirror this pattern, as, in his prophecy, Israel's restoration begins at a burial site (Ezekiel 36–37) and ends at the temple (Ezekiel 40–48).

Building on this twofold possession pattern of burial and altar/ temple in the Hebrew Bible, Jesus' burial in both Matthew 27–28 and John 19–20 is portrayed as a land claim. Previous work has demonstrated that the Fourth Gospel describes Jesus' tomb using temple language,[37] and that Matthew's crucifixion narrative is related to the temple, but it has not asked how these might relate to claims over the Promised Land.

---

[33]The following two paragraphs are taken or modified from my "Land, Burial, and Temple: Deuteronomy 30:5, John 19–20, and Jesus' Burial as a Land Claim" (paper presented at the Annual Meeting of the Society of Biblical Literature, "Intertextuality in the New Testament" Program Unit, Boston, November 19, 2017).

[34]On Machpelah as the first piece of land purchased, see Victor P. Hamilton, *The Book of Genesis: Chapters 18–50*, NICOT (Grand Rapids: Eerdmans, 1995), 135. On the larger point that burial sites are tied to land ownership, and particularly in Genesis, see, e.g., Benjamin D. Cox and Susan Ackerman, "Rachel's Tomb," *JBL* 128.1 (2009): 138-39.

[35]On altar sites in Genesis and their relation to possession of the land, see e.g., R. R. Reno, *Genesis*, Brazos Theological Commentary on the Bible (Grand Rapids: Brazos, 2010), 146.

[36]On the relation between burial, land ownership, and belief in an afterlife in the patriarchal narratives, see King and Stager, *Life in Biblical Israel*, 365.

[37]See, for instance, Rowan Williams, "Between the Cherubim: The Empty Tomb and the Empty Throne," 183-96 in *On Christian Theology* (Oxford: Blackwell, 2000). See also Nicholas P. Lunn, "Jesus, the Ark, and the Day of Atonement: Intertextual Echoes in John 19:38–20:18," *JETS* 52.4 (December 2009): 731-46 for a more detailed and exegetical inquiry into this issue.

Because of the intricate relationship between the restoration of the Promised Land and the restoration of the temple in the OT Prophets, we can plausibly say that this temple language in the Gospels is implicitly a land claim.[38] Second, textual features in John 19–20, such as the temple-like spices brought by Joseph of Arimethea and Nicodemus[39] and the presentation of the burial site as a garden,[40] only further intensify the temple, and thus land claim, language. For instance, the spices in Song of Solomon 4:14 are commonly acknowledged by commentators to be the ones used in making the holy oil that anointed the tabernacle (Ex 30:23).[41] We could also point out that, while Jesus goes "outside the camp" (Heb 13:12-13) and takes the curse of the law for us (Gal 3:13) for us in the crucifixion, and thus under Roman law and Jewish custom deserves a traitor's burial in a mass grave, he is instead buried like a king by Joseph of Arimathea and Nicodemus (Jn 19:38-42).[42] Finally, not only in the Hebrew Bible but also in a variety of cultures,

---

[38]On the relation of land and temple, and even of the metonymy of temple for land, especially in Second Temple Judaism, see, e.g., W. D. Davies, *The Territorial Dimensions of Judaism* (Berkeley: University of California Press, 1982), 33, 64. See also Norman C. Habel, *The Land is Mine: Six Biblical Land Ideologies*, Overtures to Biblical Theology (Minneapolis: Augsburg Fortress, 1995), 100-101. Habel notes that the reason for this link between temple and land ownership is because the temple serves as the residence for the national deity.

[39]The description of the spices has intertextual resonance with texts like Num 24, 1 Kings 7, and Song 4:14-16. On temple language in Songs, including Song 4:14, see Edmée Kingsmill, *The Song of Songs and the Eros of God: A Study in Biblical Intertextuality*, Oxford Theology and Religion Monographs (Oxford: Oxford University Press, 2010), 155-78.

[40]On the comparison between the garden in John, the Garden of Eden, and the Solomonic Temple, see, for instance, Nicolas Wyatt, "'Supposing Him to Be the Gardener' (John 20,15): A Study of the Paradise Motif in John," *ZNW* 81 (1990): 21-38.

[41]See, for instance, G. Lloyd Carr, *The Song of Solomon*, TOTC 19 (Downers Grove, IL: IVP Academic, 2009), 92, 119, 137-38; Duane Garrett, *Song of Songs*, WBC 23B (Grand Rapids: Zondervan, 2004), 197; Paul J. Griffiths, *Song of Songs*, Brazos Theological Commentary on the Bible (Grand Rapids: Brazos, 2011), 114; and Marvin H. Pope, *Song of Songs: A New Translation with Introduction and Commentary*, AB (New York: Doubleday, 1977), 350, 427, 439, 493-95.

[42]See, for instance, Gerald R. Borchert, *John 12–21*, NAC 25B (Nashville: Broadman and Holman, 2002), 281n187; Craig S. Keener, *The Gospel of John: A Commentary*, vol. II (Peabody, MA: Hendrickson, 2003), 1163-64; and Leon Morris, *The Gospel According to John*, rev. ed., NICNT (Grand Rapids: Eerdmans, 1995), 729n113. We could also note Jesus' potential defilement of the land if he had hung on the cross much longer (Deut 21:23), and so the movement is from exile and (potential) defilement to kingship and restoration *via burial*. On defilement, see Raymond E. Brown, *The Gospel According to John XIII–XXI: A New Translation with Commentary*, AB 29 (New Haven, CT: Yale University Press, 1970), 933-34.

burial is understood as a land claim.[43] While exploring and defending these claims would require a separate essay or book; here our only purpose is to suggest that, based on these intertextual, theological, and sociocultural factors, Jesus' bodily burial is portrayed as a claim on the Promised Land in John's Gospel.[44] This matters for the descent since his bodily burial is a part of his descent. While the historical focus of the doctrine is on the descent of his human soul to the place of the dead, his human burial is also a part of the doctrine and, in that respect, the descent is related to understanding Jesus' fulfillment of God's promises to Israel about the land.

CONCLUSION

Jesus' descent helps us understand a number of different aspects of the doctrine of creation. First, it allows us to see the intricate relationship between the spiritual, or non-bodily, realm of existence and the earthly, or corporeal, realm. We see this in the continued relationship between Jesus' human soul and his body as well as in his "movement" throughout the descent act, namely through descending into the place of the dead and then transforming it through his bodily resurrection and ascent into the third heaven. Second, the descent helps us to understand the importance of the body, both with respect to Jesus' implicit land claim via his bodily burial and also through the fact that the descent is only the beginning of Jesus' exaltation. The intermediate state is *not* the ultimate destination of the righteous. Jesus rises from the place of the dead and ascends bodily. This emphasis on the body in turn may suggest a third way in which the descent can help us to reflect theologically, specifically on the ethics of burial. While I do not want to suggest that the descent automatically excludes cremation, I do think it should give Christians pause in how we treat our bodies in burial given the

---

[43]Robert Pogue Harrison, *The Dominion of the Dead* (Chicago: The University of Chicago Press, 2003), 17-36.
[44]This is an abbreviated version of the argument made in my "Land, Burial, and Temple."

connection during the descent and in the resurrection between Christ's human body and human soul. Ultimately, though, the descent of Christ is part of his redemptive work, and while that work includes creation, it is specifically acted out on behalf of his image bearers, human beings. This brings us to the way the descent impinges upon the doctrine of anthropology.

"CONCEIVED BY THE HOLY SPIRIT, BORN OF THE VIRGIN MARY"

Christological Anthropology in Descent Perspective

Theological anthropology is a notoriously difficult field.[1] On the one hand, many modern scholars have moved on from dualist conceptions of the human person, whether philosophically, scientifically, or biblically. Many philosophers consider dualism to be logically and conceptually untenable, opting instead for monism, typically of the physicalist sort. Scientific research also consistently points toward the human person as a psychophysical being, one that does not require some non-physical substance, i.e., a "soul."[2] And with respect to biblical

---

[1] For an introduction, see Marc Cortez, *Theological Anthropology: A Guide for the Perplexed* (London: T&T Clark, 2010).

[2] For an introduction to these issues from biblical scholars and theologians who take a nonreductive physicalist, or monist, approach to theological anthropology, see Joel B. Green, "'Bodies–That Is, Human Lives:' A Re-Examination of Human Nature in the Bible," 149-73 in Warren S. Brown, Nancey Murphy, and H. Newton Malone, eds., *Whatever Happened to the Soul? Scientific and Theological Portraits of Human Nature*, Theology and the Sciences (Minneapolis: Augsburg Fortress, 1998); as well as the discussions of biblical anthropology, resurrection, and the intermediate state (or lack thereof) in Green, *Body, Soul, and Human Life: The Nature of Humanity in the Bible*, Studies in Theological Interpretation (Grand Rapids: Baker Academic, 2008), 46-71, 140-70. See also Nancey S. Murphy, *Bodies and Souls, or Spirited Bodies?* Current Issues in Theology (Cambridge: Cambridge University Press, 2006), esp. 24-26, 137-41. Of course, we should note that science cannot provide

studies, the charge is often leveled that dualism is absent from the Old Testament and, therefore, that later Platonic, Aristotelian, and Thomistic dualist conceptions of anthropology are developments that arose out of Greco-Roman philosophy, not out of a Jewish worldview.[3] In this account, the OT picture of the human person is holism; body and soul are not separate substances, but rather human beings are one, always seen as unified. When the body dies, the person ceases to exist in any meaningful sense.[4]

Table 6.1. Major views on theological anthropology.

View	Human Persons Consist of:	Intermediate State?
Substance Dualism	Body and Soul	Yes
Non-Reductive Physicalism; Constitutionalist	Body	No
Hylemorphic Dualism of the Animalist Sort	Body and Soul, where "soul" = form of the body	No

On the other hand, much of the Christian tradition, from at least the Apostolic Fathers to the Reformation and post-Reformation theologians,

---

all the answers to the anthropological question either; for instance, Eric LaRock admits that neuroscience still cannot explain consciousness adequately. See LaRock, "Neuroscience and the Hard Problem of Consciousness," 151-80 in Thomas M. Crisp, Steven L. Porter, and Gregg A. Ten Elshof, eds., *Neuroscience and the Soul: The Human Person in Philosophy, Science, and Theology* (Grand Rapids: Eerdmans, 2016). For a discussion of these issues from the perspective of anthropological dualism, see the succinct summary of these objections, as well as resources for further study, in Terrence Nichols, *Death and Afterlife: A Theological Introduction* (Grand Rapids: Brazos, 2010), 77-90. As Nichols argues, these challenges revolve primarily around evolution (when did and how could a soul "evolve"?) and neuroscience (why would there be a soul when most of our human functions, including emotions and decision making, have been mapped in the brain?). See also John W. Cooper, *Body, Soul, & Life Everlasting: Biblical Anthropology and the Monism-Dualism Debate* (1989; Grand Rapids: Eerdmans, 2000).

[3]For a description of this objection and a response to it, see Joseph Ratzinger, *Eschatology: Death and Eternal Life*, 2nd ed. (Washington, DC: Catholic University of America Press, 1988), 75-79. For a defense of anthropological dualism from within the context of modern biblical scholarship, see Robert Gundry, *Soma in Biblical Theology: With Emphasis on Pauline Anthropology*, SNTS 29 (Cambridge: Cambridge University Press, 1976).

[4]For a theological account that sees the cessation of human existence at death but that also affirms a future bodily resurrection, see Paul J. Griffiths, *Decreation: The Last Things of All Creatures* (Waco, TX: Baylor University Press, 2014).

has affirmed some kind of dualism.[5] Thomas is seen by many as the pinnacle of Christian reflection on the nature of the human person, arguing for a hylemorphic dualism. In this variety of dualism, the body and soul, while distinct, are distinct as the matter and form, respectively, of the human person. All creatures have matter and form; for humans they exist as body (flesh) and soul. They are, as with all creatures, ordinarily a unit, a hylemorphic whole. Thus Thomas seems to affirm the holistic view of human nature in the Old Testament while also giving space for what many see in the biblical data, a distinction between body and soul.

Recent proposals regarding hylemorphic dualism, however, have followed Thomas's conception of the person while rejecting his affirmation of an intermediate state after death. They are "hylemorphic dualists, of the animalist sort"—that is, when the body ceases to function, the person does not exist in any meaningful sense.[6] This is because, while body and soul are distinct, they cannot and do not exist without one another. And while these sorts of hylemorphic dualists tend to disagree with some of the conclusions of John W. Cooper (namely, the ability of the soul to exist consciously apart from the body), Cooper's point still stands: the presence of an intermediate state determines what kind of theological anthropology one affirms.[7] If Scripture gives evidence of an intermediate state, some sort of dualism is required, and if that intermediate state includes a conscious soul, then a hylemorphic dualism of the non-animalist sort is required. We should be able, then, to pursue

---

[5]I include the trichotomist view in the "dualism" side of this broad distinction between monism and dualism, as the primary difference is the affirmation of a soul that survives beyond death in dichotomist (or trichomomist) views and the denial of such in monist views. For a succinct history of theological anthropology in the Christian tradition, see, e.g., the summaries in Cooper, *Body, Soul & Life Everlasting*, 7-33; and Nichols, *Death and Afterlife*, 55-76. For theological anthropology in the early Christian period, see J. Patout Burns, SJ, trans. and ed., *Theological Anthropology*, Sources of Early Christian Thought (Philadelphia: Fortress, 1981).

[6]See especially the recent dissertation of James T. Turner, Jr., *On the Resurrection of the Dead: A New Metaphysics of Afterlife for Christian Thought*, Routledge New Critical Thinking in Religion, Theology, and Biblical Studies (Philadelphia: Routledge, 2018).

[7]Cooper, *Body, Soul, & Life Everlasting*, xv-xvi.

exegetical analysis of the biblical data and make a decision about whether or not an intermediate state exists and in what capacity.

The problem with this approach is that, as biblical scholars note, the biblical data on the intermediate state (or lack thereof) is notoriously difficult to interpret. Both OT and NT scholars, in their respective disciplines, are split on whether or not either testament teaches an intermediate state, and, if so, what kind. For instance, John W. Cooper's classic study argues that the Bible, both Old Testament and New Testament, teaches holistic dualism and affirms an intermediate state.[8] On the other hand, many contemporary biblical scholars and theologians would argue that this classic model is unwarranted, either because it is unbiblical, it is theologically nonsensical, or because it is philosophically and scientifically untenable.[9]

Given this lack of clarity among biblical scholars, what method can we use to arrive at even tentative conclusions about the intermediate state and, thereby, theological anthropology more generally? We will argue in this chapter that a christological approach to anthropology may serve to shed some light on these issues.[10] As Marc Cortez has argued, Barth's christological anthropology can serve as a model of theological method and as an arbiter in the current mind-body debate.[11] In his *Embodied Souls, Ensouled Bodies*, Cortez argues that given Barth's theological method, both non-reductive physicalism and holistic dualism are options for Christians with respect what they confess about anthropology. Interestingly, though, in his examination of both of these options, he appears to be noncommittal with respect to an intermediate state.

---

[8]Cooper, *Body, Soul, & Life Everlasting*, esp. 33-178.

[9]For an overview of the objections to anthropological dualism, of both the substance and emergent varieties, see Joel B. Green and Stuart L. Palmer, eds., *In Search of the Soul: Four Views on the Mind-Body Problem* (Downers Grove, IL: IVP Academic, 2005), esp. 61-74, 101-14.

[10]For a related argument that attempts to use Christ's descent to evaluate options in theological anthropology, see my "Mapping Anthropological Metaphysics with a *Descensus* Key: How Christ's Descent to the Dead Informs the Body-Mind Conversation," in *The Christian Doctrine of Humanity: Explorations in Constructive Dogmatics*, ed. Oliver D. Crisp and Fred Sanders (Grand Rapids: Zondervan Academic, 2018), 200-216.

[11]Marc Cortez, *Embodied Souls, Ensouled Bodies: An Exercise in Christological Anthropology and its Significance for the Mind/Body Debate* (London: T&T Clark, 2008).

Much like Cooper, Cortez asserts that the presence and character of an intermediate state would a) functionally rule out non-reductive physicalism and b) give us greater clarity with respect to what kind of dualism Christians can and should affirm. But, Cortez maintains, because of the supposed ambiguity of Scripture concerning an intermediate state or lack thereof, one cannot make any judgments in this respect.[12]

In other words, the determining factor in solving the mind-body debate from a theological perspective is, in many respects, what one believes about the intermediate state. My argument here is that given the biblical data about the descent, a christological approach to anthropology *via Christ's descent* can ease some of the anthropological gridlock. Because the descent involves Christ's experience of an intermediate state, and because Christ qua human is paradigmatic for all humanity, what he experiences in his time in the tomb can be said to be endemic of all human beings' intermediate state.

The argument will proceed in three parts. First, I will summarize Cortez's appropriation of Barth's christological anthropology as it relates to the mind-body debate. Second, I will apply Barth's method to Christ's descent, asking what aspects of his descent are qua divine and what aspects are qua human. The latter, if there are any, are therefore endemic to humanity per se. In other words, the third part of the argument is that if we affirm that Christ descended to the dead in both body and soul in ways consistent with each, we are in a position to affirm that humanity consists of body and soul, the latter a substance that can and does consciously exist beyond bodily death.

BARTH'S CHRISTOLOGICAL ANTHROPOLOGY AND THE MIND-BODY DEBATE

In his *Embodied Souls, Ensouled Bodies,* Marc Cortez engages the mind-body debate—a topic that garners the attention of a wide variety of

---

[12]Cortez, *Embodied Souls,* 89-92.

academic fields, including not just theology but also biology, philosophy, and psychology—via Karl Barth's christological anthropology. As Cortez argues, Barth's method is applicable to the mind-body debate because of the theological presupposition on which it rests: because Christ is the paradigmatic human being, what we can say about his human nature particularly is necessarily true of human nature in general. To say this biblically, Christ "is the image of the invisible God" (Col 1:15), "the radiance of God's glory and the exact representation of his being" (Heb 1:3 NIV). As the perfect, ultimate image of God, he is the pattern for all other image bearers. We see this in the New Testament's statements about sanctification; those who are in Christ are transformed in to the Lord's image (2 Cor 3:17-18; Rom 8:29), and when they see him, they will be like him (1 Jn 3:2). According to Cortez, the image into which believers are being transformed—Christ's—is also the image in which humans are made. When we say, therefore, that human beings are made in God's image (Gen 1:26-28; 2:15), we mean specifically that we are made in Christ's image. The key, according to both Barth and Cortez, is to determine what we can say about Christ that is a statement about him qua human and not about him qua divine or some aspect of his person that is unique to him as the incarnate Son.[13]

Cortez goes on to argue that the most important and recognizably, uniquely human aspect of Christ's portraits in the Gospels is that he exercises his own, human volition. In other words, it is evident in the Gospels that Christ makes decisions and choices, and generally operates in the world, via his will.[14] Given this aspect of Christ's humanity—and, according to Cortez, the aspect that makes Christ and all other humans truly human—what can be said about the two main options in the mind-body debate: physicalism and dualism? Regarding the former,

---

[13]On the preceding paragraph, see especially Cortez, *Embodied Souls*, 16-39.

[14]See Cortez, *Embodied Souls*, 86-89, 104-5. That Christ has a human will is currently a highly debated topic in philosophy and theology. For an introduction this issue and a defense of the traditional doctrine of dyothelitism, see R. Lucas Stamps, *"Thy Will Be Done": A Contemporary Defense of Two Wills Christology* (Minneapolis: Fortress, forthcoming).

Cortez argues that only a non-reductive form of physicalism adequately accounts for the volitional nature of human action in general and Christ's in particular. Regarding the latter, Cortez notes that any kind of dualism can account for Christ's volitional activity, but with respect to other concerns—namely the Old Testament's holistic anthropology—it seems that, if dualism is true, it must be a holistic dualism. In making both of these assessments, Cortez does not go beyond them to arguing for one anthropological outlook over the other. Instead, he simply says that both non-reductive physicalism and holistic dualism are theoretically both viable options according to Barth's method with respect to christological anthropology.

Interestingly, Cortez notes in both cases that if one affirms the traditional view of the descent (as articulated in chapters two and three of this book), unlike Barth's view, then this would entail an intermediate state. In turn, that would necessitate the rejection of all forms of physicalism and some forms of dualism (e.g., hylemorphic dualism of the animalist sort, as argued for most recently by J. T. Turner).[15] For our purposes, if, as I have argued, the biblical data teaches that Christ, in his human soul, descended to the place of the dead and there proclaimed his victory over the evil spirits and Satan, this means that Christ experienced an intermediate state between his death and resurrection. The question for anthropology, especially via Cortez's christological method, is whether or not anything regarding his descent is true of humanity in general or if this experience of an intermediate state is unique to Christ as the incarnate Son. Before I can make that kind of claim, though, I must clear some methodological ground. Here, reviewing Cortez's Barthian-inspired method provides us with fertile ground in which to answer these questions.

Christological anthropology and the intermediate state. While a full exploration of Barth's christological anthropology is not possible here,

---

[15]Cortez, *Embodied Souls*, 91n48.

Cortez summarizes it nicely via six criteria, three foci, and three theological grounds. Regarding the criteria, Cortez argues that,

[F]or Barth, true humanity must be understood as (1) being constituted by the ontological priority of Jesus in his relationship with God; (2) being conditioned by the salvation enacted in Jesus; (3) having its "true determination" in the glory of God; (4) existing under the Lordship of God; (5) freely corresponding in its proper action to the divine deliverance; and (6) freely rendering service to God as a being who is *for* God.[16]

These six criteria are used to adjudicate between various options regarding anthropology's three main foci: relationality, ontology, and temporality.[17] For Cortez and for Barth, ontology has "decisive importance for understanding the human person," and there are three ontological grounds to be considered in this regard: Christology, pneumatology, and God's covenant with his people.[18] Again, while pneumatology and covenants are vitally important, they are correlative to and derivative of the primary ground of human ontology, the person of Jesus Christ. To put the matter succinctly, for Cortez and for Barth, what can be said about Jesus' humanity as true of all humanity is indicative for human nature (ontology). That is, for our purposes here, if I can say that the human nature of Jesus is constituted of a body and a soul, and also that said constitution is not unique to his humanity as the God-Man but true of all humanity, then this body-soul dualism is indicative of human nature (ontology). And indeed, Barth affirms that "the ontological continuity of human persons is best understood as a properly ordered and *unified duality of body and soul* that is created, preserved, and regenerated by the Holy Spirit and so constituted as God's covenantal partner."[19]

Simply affirming a "unified duality of body and soul" does not solve the matter, though. As Cortez goes on to note, the features indicative of

---

[16]Cortez, *Embodied Souls*, 38.
[17]Cortez, *Embodied Souls*, 75.
[18]Cortez, *Embodied Souls*, 75.
[19]Cortez, *Embodied Souls*, 77, emphasis mine.

this unified duality, as well as the intermediate state, can be answered not only in the traditional manner via body-soul dualism—that is, the body remains in the grave while the soul departs and exists consciously in the realm of the dead—but also via at least two other anthropological options. Both non-reductive physicalism[20] and at least some forms of holistic dualism[21] can, according to Cortez's analysis via a Barthian method, account for the human nature of Jesus and its implications for all humanity. Both affirm selfhood, consciousness, continuous personal identity, agency, mental causation, freedom, agency, and contingent personhood, which are the main features Barth identifies as constituents of Jesus' paradigmatic human nature.[22]

Both also, however, have significant challenges with the intermediate state. For non-reductive physicalism (NRP), the issue is continuous personal identity. If the human person is constituted materially, what happens to their identity at death, when said material ceases to function? Further, while Christian proponents of NRP would affirm the resurrection of said persons, how is the identity of that resurrected person continuous with the identity of the person before death? Both death (the cessation of bodily function) and resurrection (the transformation into a spiritual person) are radical changes in the material, physical constitution of the human person. It is not clear how any human, Jesus included, could be said to have continuous personal identity between death and resurrection.[23] As Cortez notes, there are a number of potential rebuttals to this objection to NRP, but none of them provides a clearly satisfactory answer.

The problem of the intermediate state does not go away with holistic dualism (HD), but only shifts to a different anthropological issue. For HD proponents, according to Cortez, the problem with respect to the intermediate state is not continuous personal identity but rather wholeness

---

[20]See Cortez, *Embodied Souls*, 110-54.
[21]See Cortez, *Embodied Souls*, 155-87.
[22]Cortez, *Embodied Souls*, 100-106.
[23]On this particular objection to NRP, see Cortez, *Embodied Souls*, 146-53.

and embodiment.[24] If the human person is a whole, comprised of body and soul, how can we still affirm the whole while maintaining that one (soul) can exist without the other (body)? Further, how can the soul be said to still function in capacities that seem to require a body (e.g., perception, will) while existing without a body in the intermediate state? Cortez notes that there are two options here: either argue for the soul's continued conscious but severely truncated existence, or argue for the soul's unconscious existence that only regains consciousness upon the resurrection of the body.

How do these two proposed solutions to this problem fare when related to Christ's paradigmatic humanity? Further, how can we adjudicate between not only options within HD but also between HD and NRP? Cortez, given Barth's own views on the topic, acknowledges the difficulty yet offers a potential solution in his discussion of Barth's conclusions about Christ's three days in the tomb. Here, Cortez notes that since Barth does insist that "an adequate anthropological ontology must begin with christological reflection, decisions regarding the state of human ontology during any intermediate state would have to begin with the biblical portrayal of Christ during his entombment."[25] With Barth and Cortez, we can say, "Yes, exactly!" However, Cortez goes on to say that Barth finds biblical evidence for Christ's intermediate state completely absent from the biblical witness, and therefore we are left with an undetermined christological anthropology with respect to the intermediate state. Interestingly, however, Cortez says in a footnote that "if one differs from Barth on this point and understands these texts [e.g., Eph 4.9; 1 Pet 3.19] to affirm that Jesus was active during this time, Barth's christological methodology would require us to affirm some sort of intermediate state." Again, we can say to this, "Yes, exactly!"

The descent and common objections to the intermediate state. Without completely restating earlier exegetical points, it is still worth mentioning

---

[24]See Cortez, *Embodied Souls*, 167-68, 183-85.
[25]Cortez, *Embodied Souls*, 91.

the main arguments for the descent as they relate to common objections to the intermediate state. First, there is still significant opposition to the current scholarly consensus (the rejection of an intermediate state; see, e.g., Johnson and Green). With respect to the OT witness to the intermediate state, Johnston's interpretation is not the only one. As mentioned earlier in the chapter, John Cooper's argument continues to have an impact. And for those who believe Cooper's work is too broad and not grounded enough in history and exegesis, the recent work of Richard Steiner answers that objection ably.[26]

But as with many biblical doctrines, this one cannot be settled by exegesis of individual texts alone. There are theological parameters—what we might call meta-exegetical categories[27]—that must be taken into account when dealing with, for example, what Israel meant by *Sheol*, what happened to Samuel in the necromancy narrative (1 Sam 28), and how the OT view relates to Second Temple Judaism and the NT views of the afterlife.[28] Among these theological parameters are the nature of YHWH and his rule over all things.

First, YHWH is the God of the living. This is not an indication that he ceases to be Abraham's God upon Abraham's death; quite the

---

[26]Richard C. Steiner, *Disembodied Souls: The* Nefesh *in Israel and Kindred Spirits in the Ancient Near East, with an Appendix on the Katumura Inscription*, Ancient Near Eastern Monographs (Atlanta: SBL Press, 2015). This is not the place to relate Steiner's arguments in detail, but it is worth noting that he defends the intermediate state in the Old Testament on exegetical and sociocultural grounds.

[27]I say "meta-exegetical" because I do not wish to give the impression that these theological factors are unrelated to exegesis. Far from it. Rather, there are certain theological teachings of Scripture, of which we become aware via exegesis, that govern our exegesis of other passages of Scripture. In other words, Scripture *theologically* interprets Scripture.

[28]In addition to the theological parameters discussed below, the exegetical and historical data must also be considered. The popular notion today that Israel did not believe in some kind of existence after death does not stand up to scrutiny when one considers not only Sheol and *nephesh* but also burial customs, funeral rites, and the like. See, for instance, Roland de Vaux, *Ancient Israel: Its Life and Institutions*, trans. John McHugh (1961; London: Darton, Longman, and Todd, 1998), 56-61, for a summary of Israel's burial practices. De Vaux concludes that, "The food-offerings express, at the very least, belief in a life beyond the grave." de Vaux, *Ancient Israel*, 61. See also Philip J. King and Lawrence E. Stager, *Life in Biblical Israel*, Library of Ancient Israel (Louisville, KY: Westminster John Knox, 2001), 363-82, who include the fifth commandment (Ex 20:12), family burial, and the cult of the dead as evidence that Israel held to a belief in some sort of afterlife. King and Stager, *Life in Biblical Israel*, 365.

opposite. It means, rather, that God's being provides the ground for eternal life for human beings. He does so through both his promise to restore Israel and through his covenantal remembrance of his creatures. Regarding the latter, God cannot and does not forget those whom he has made, and so they cannot cease to exist. Regarding the former, God's promises to restore Israel, especially in the Latter Prophets, find a natural corollary in Israel's confession, especially during the Second Temple period, that God would restore—resurrect—individual human beings.[29] YHWH is God of the living, and those who die in faith will be raised again and restored to his presence.[30]

A second theological parameter stemming from YHWH's character is that he is the ruler of all things. Unlike the ANE deities, YHWH is God over all realms, including Sheol (death).[31] For this reason, Israel

---

[29]See, for instance, Donald E. Gowan, *Theology of the Prophetic Books: The Death and Resurrection of Israel* (Louisville, KY: Westminster John Knox, 1998), 144-87. While I do not agree with Gowan on his historical-critical conclusions, he does provide a helpful discussion on the relationship between national and individual resurrection.

[30]See, for instance, the discussion in Paul R. Williamson, *Death and the Afterlife: Biblical Perspectives on Ultimate Questions*, NSBT 44 (Downers Grove, IL: IVP Academic, 2018), 38-44, 74-84.

[31]E.g., Ps 139, of which verses 7-8 are particularly important for our purposes: "Where shall I go from your Spirit? Or where shall I flee from your presence? If I ascend to heaven, you are there! If I make my bed in Sheol, you are there!" On YHWH's relationship with death, the realm of the dead, and those in the realm of the dead, see Emmanuel Feldman, *Biblical and Post-Biblical Defilement and Mourning: Law as Theology* (New York: Yeshiva University Press/ KTAV Publishing, 1977), 17-20. Feldman's work as a whole is relevant to this study, given that he covers not only material in the Hebrew Bible but also in the ancient Near East as well as in rabbinic Judaism. For our purposes in this paragraph, though, it is important to note Feldman's argument in the particular pages cited, namely that Israel's theological monotheism demanded, conceptually speaking, that they acknowledge YHWH's rule over the realm of the dead. To quote Feldman,

> The dilemma of God's supreme power versus His apparent lack of dominion over death may not be a real one. The passages which seem to support a cessation of God's activity [e.g. Ps 6:6; Ps 88:11-13; Is 38:9ff., cited earlier by Feldman] have been misread somewhat. . . . God is present in death, but only in life can man have a meaningful relationship with the God of life. The desacralization of death removes man from contact with the Divine, but it is certainly recognized that He ultimately rules the underworld since He is the supreme force in the universe. Psalms 139:8 affirms the presence of God everywhere, even in Sheol. Similar ideas are expressed in Psalms 33:7, 95:4, 55:15; Job 26:6, 11:7-8, 12:22; Proverbs 15:11; Hosea 13:14; Isaiah 7:11; Deuteronomy 32:22. The dead cannot praise God, not because God is unable to be present in death, but because those without life can have no relationship with Him. R. Johanan expresses this idea very succinctly. Citing Psalms 88:6, "Among the dead I am free . . ." he interprets: "Once a man is dead, he is free from fulfilling the commandments." And in

naturally came to confess more explicitly exactly *how* YHWH would defeat Death, i.e., through resurrection. This is why Jesus can say, concerning YHWH's present relation to Abraham, Isaac, and Jacob, that he is not the God of the dead but of the living (Mt 22:32). It is also why, although Israel held some beliefs that were similar to her ANE counterparts' view of the afterlife (e.g., generic, silent), they also understood it in a much more robust sense.[32] So, when we talk about the exegetical data of the Old Testament, it is important that we refrain from assuming that because a particular belief in the afterlife is unattested at a particular time in Israel's history, it is either nonexistent or contradictory to later beliefs. Rather, Israel's earlier writings include primarily polemical remarks directed against the common ANE view, while her later Scriptures focus on explicit expression of belief in afterlife, judgment, and resurrection because of Israel's faith in YHWH, the God of the Living, and because that same YHWH is also YHWH *melek*—God the King over all things.[33]

Here I should also mention the fact that the contemporary consensus also relies in many ways on philosophical and scientific assumptions. But, we might ask, why would we follow scientific objections to the soul

---

Shabbat 30a the sages say: "As soon as a man dies he is restrained from [the practice of] Torah and good deeds." The dead cannot serve God. (Feldman, 18)

I include this long quote because it illustrates the precise language that is needed but often lacking in discourse about the Old Testament's view about the so-called intermediate state. Statements like "the dead cannot praise you," as Feldman points out, are not because Israel rejected what we would now call an anthropological dualism, but because praise of YHWH was explicitly tied to the temple cultus and obedience to Torah (note "desacralization" and "restrained from Torah" in the above quote). In other words, these statements in the Old Testament do not reflect a rejection of an intermediate state as much as they do the ability of the dead to participate in the life of Israel's worship through temple and Torah.

[32] For a discussion of YHWH as God of the Living and King over all things, including the realm of death, and those confessions' implications for Israel's view of the existence and nature of the afterlife, see Ratzinger, *Eschatology*, 80-92.

[33] The phrase "YHWH *malak!*" ("The LORD reigns!") is a central exclamation and theme in the Old Testament and particularly in the Psalms. See James L. Mays, *The Lord Reigns: A Theological Handbook to the Psalms* (Louisville, KY: Westminster John Knox, 1994), esp. 12-23; and J. Clinton McCann, *A Theological Introduction to the Book of Psalms: The Psalms as Torah* (Nashville: Abingdon, 1993), 41-52.

if we do not follow them on, say, the resurrection? As Terrence Nichols[34] and Joseph Ratzinger[35] have noted, scientific objections to the resurrection, both of the individual and of the cosmos, are just as strong as they are to the intermediate state. One wonders why, then, biblical interpreters and theologians are so ready to follow secular philosophy and science on the issue of the soul and not on the resurrection. To state it differently, like theological answers to scientific objections to the resurrection, there are also theological and philosophical answers to scientific objections to the intermediate state.

A modification of exegetes' and theologians' rejection of substance dualism in favor of non-reductive physicalism is the same rejection of substance dualism in favor of hylemorphic dualism of the animalist sort. In this view, there is no intermediate state, since the soul cannot survive separation from the body. Instead, the believer experiences time differently, resurrected immediately upon death in the new heavens and the new earth. This view is called "immediate resurrection."[36] Here, Jesus' statement to the thief on the cross that, "today you will be with me in paradise" (Lk 24:43) is understood as assurance that the believing thief will pass immediately upon death from this life to the resurrection of the dead, since *paradise* is understood to be synonymous with "new heavens and new earth." This is different from soul sleep, which posits that the soul still exists but only in a state akin to sleep during the period between death and resurrection (a position Calvin specifically rejects). It is similar, but not quite the same, as Anthony Thiselton's alternative, where the soul experiences time differently from those still living—that

---

[34]Nichols, *Death and Afterlife*, 77-90, 135-50.

[35]Thus he remarks pointedly:

> It may be concluded that the immortality of the soul removes a possible source of conflict between faith and contemporary thought. However, this scarcely saves the Bible, since the biblical view of things is even more remote by modern-day standards. Acceptance of the unity of the human being may be well and good, but who, on the basis of the current tenets of the natural sciences, could imagine a resurrection of the body?

Ratzinger, *Eschatology*, 106.

[36]On the arguments for immediate resurrection, see Murray J. Harris, *Raised Immortal: Resurrection and Immortality in the New Testament* (Grand Rapids: Eerdmans, 1985), 99, 139, 221-26.

is, the soul seems to experience time in such a way that death and resurrection are sequential, while ordinary time keeps marching on.[37] These latter two views—soul sleep and what I will call alternative soul time—both still hinge on substance dualism, even if in a modified sense. The immediate resurrection view, however, rejects substance dualism and posits that the soul cannot exist without the body.

There are good responses to each of these on anthropological grounds alone. For instance, to the immediate resurrection view, we might say, with Ratzinger and Nichols, that this view is hard to reconcile with the fact that the new heavens and new earth are not yet reality. Not only does a dead body lie in front of us, but we bury it in the yet-to-be redeemed earth. In other words, if a person is immediately upon death transported through time to the resurrected state, this necessarily requires that they be resurrected into the new heavens and new earth. But this decaying earth is still here. The cosmos has not been restored. The dead body is still in the grave in front of us, perhaps as a pastor reads Psalm 23 to us and over the deceased. The immediate resurrection view, in other words, seems to necessitate either willful ignorance of the dead body buried within the dying creation that sits in front of us, or the suggestion of alternate universes in which the new heavens and new earth already exist. This seems a bit too much like science fiction and too little like the biblical data. Instead I prefer to say, with Paul, that "we would rather be away from the body and at home with the Lord" (2 Cor 5:8).[38]

In any case, these exegetical and philosophical arguments need not detain us. I could spend the entire book discussing issues of theological anthropology and the arguments for and against immediate resurrection, soul sleep, and the like. For our purposes, I only need to bring the descent to bear upon this particular issue. And when viewed

---

[37]See Anthony C. Thiselton, *Life After Death: A New Approach to the Last Things* (Grand Rapids: Eerdmans, 2012), 69-79.

[38]This same distinction, absent in the flesh but still in the presence of Christ, also appears in Phil 1:21-24.

through the lens of christological anthropology and held up to the descent doctrine articulated in chapters two and three,[39] neither immediate resurrection nor soul sleep nor Thiselton's "alternative soul time" proposal hold up. With respect to both soul sleep and Thiselton's proposal, this would entail that Jesus did not actually consciously experience the intermediate state and therefore did not proclaim victory over Death and Hades during the time between his death and resurrection. Further, with "alternative time," neither human beings nor the Messiah who came to save them actually experience death beyond the moment of dying. This makes the joyful declaration of Acts 2:27, that God did not abandon Jesus' soul in Hades, lose its force. What would it mean for a soul to be abandoned, or never rescued, in the place of the dead if no one actually consciously experiences it in the sense of the passing of time? Even if one does not affirm the proclamation aspect of the descent, therefore, this position still has christological (and anthropological) issues.

The anthropological problems with immediate resurrection mentioned above are only exacerbated by christological considerations. First, the immediate resurrection position—and the hylemorphic dualism of the animalist sort from which it arises—entails that a person is not a person unless both the body and soul are alive. One cannot exist without the other.[40] This means one of two things with regard to Christ: either he did not exist qua human between Good Friday and Easter Sunday, or he immediately resurrected on Good Friday, presumably right after the moment of death.[41] If it is the former, then the hypostatic union is

---

[39] That is, that Jesus descended in his body to the grave and in his human soul to the place of the dead, where he proclaimed his victory over Death and Hades by virtue of the hypostatic union.

[40] This is also a conclusion of NRP and constitution views of the human person, both of which are closely related to one another, as well as to hylomorphic dualism of the animalist sort at least with respect to this particular question. Regarding the constitution view, Kevin Corcoran says, "human persons are *essentially* constituted by the biological bodies that do in fact constitute them. Therefore, if my body should ever cease to exist, I would cease to exist." Kevin Cororan, "The Constitution View of Persons," in Green and Palmer, *In Search of the Soul*, 153-76.

[41] Any moment beyond this would entail, again, that the human person of Jesus did not exist between the moment of his death on the cross and whatever subsequent moment at which he

severed for whatever time between the moment of death and resurrection, even in positions like "immediate resurrection."[42] If it is the latter, this completely removes any rationale, soteriological or otherwise, for Jesus remaining in the tomb for three days, and also lays Christianity bare to the charge that the resurrection was merely resuscitation.[43]

And beyond these christological problems lie the descent itself. If our articulation of the descent is biblically and historically accurate, then neither immediate resurrection nor soul sleep nor alternative time is viable. Each of them, and particularly immediate resurrection, deny key components of the descent—the former two the victorious proclamation, and the latter the descent itself. With immediate resurrection, there is no descent of Christ. He merely rises again. Given our considerations of the biblical and historical rationale for the descent, and given the probability of the descent clause's explicit use in the face of Apollinarianism (see chapter three), I do not find these positions tenable.

CHRIST'S DESCENT AND CHRISTOLOGICAL ANTHROPOLOGY

Given the above conclusions about the intermediate state in general and Christ's descent in particular, I am now in the position to suggest that some form of holistic dualism (HD) best accounts for the biblical and theological data. If, as I have concluded in this and previous chapters,

---

was raised. In other words, he'd have to fake it in the arms of Joseph of Arimathea until they shut the tomb on him.

[42]One recent attempt at defending hylemorphic dualism of the animalist sort and its corollary, immediate resurrection, especially with respect to the continuity of persons, comes from J. T. Turner. Turner argues that a particular view of time, "Eschatological Presentism," guards against notions of loss of personal identity between death and resurrection while also denying an intermediate state. See James T. Turner, Jr., "How to Lose the Intermediate State Without Losing Your Soul," in *Christian Physicalism? Philosophical and Theological Criticisms*, ed. R. Keith Loftin and Joshua R. Farris (Lanham: Lexington Books, 2017), 271-93; and Turner, *On the Resurrection of the Dead*. While I think Turner's argument successfully defends his theological anthropology in terms of the continuity of personal identity between death and resurrection, he does not address the issue of Christ's descent to the dead, either with respect to the biblical data or with respect to the christological issues I have raised in this section.

[43]See both Cooper, *Body, Soul, & Life Everlasting*, 129-32; and Jason McMartin, "Holy Saturday and Theological Anthropology," in Loftin and Farris, *Christian Physicalism*, 117-36.

Christ's human soul remained in the place of the dead for three days, during which time he also via his human soul proclaimed his victory over God's enemies to other dead souls, we can conclude the following:

- Because Christ's human nature is paradigmatic, his normal human experiences (that is, those human experiences common to all humanity) are paradigmatic, including his state in death.

- Christ's paradigmatic human death is such that his dead body remains in the grave, while his conscious, human soul remains in the place of the dead.

- All humans, except for those alive at the Parousia, therefore experience death as a separation of body and soul, the body remaining in the grave while the soul remains conscious in the place of the dead.

- Because of this separation of body and soul, the most biblically and theologically appropriate anthropology is one that affirms both a unified body-soul dualism and also the continuation of the human person after death via the existence of a conscious but temporarily disembodied soul.

In other words, with respect to the anthropology debate, we are left with a form of HD that affirms both the unity of the person and a temporary disembodied state.

Further, I can also provide some comments not just on theological anthropology but on Christology as well. First, in the face of what seems to be an Apollinarian *ressourcement* from at least some quarters,[44] we should again, with Cyril of Alexandria and the rest of the Christian tradition, reject Apollinarianism. While I cannot prove that the clause *descendit ad inferos* was added to the Apostles' Creed specifically to counter Apollinarianism, I can say that the content of

---

[44]See William Lane Craig and J. P. Moreland, *Philosophical Foundations of a Christian Worldview*, 1st ed. (Downers Grove, IL: IVP Academic, 2003), 610-11. For an inquiry into whether or not a materialist (or physicalist) Christology requires an Apollinarian approach, see Oliver D. Crisp, "Materialist Christology," in *God Incarnate: Explorations in Christology* (London: T&T Clark, 2009), 137-54.

the doctrine requires a rejection of the idea that God the Son assumed only a human body and not a human mind or will. And of course this also requires rejecting monothelitism, since to assume a human nature, body and soul, includes assuming human will as integral to the human soul.

A second implication of the descent for the anthropological aspect of Christology particularly is that the hypostatic union does not cease and is not temporarily put on hold during Christ's descent. Indeed, for the above anthropological conclusions to arise, one must first confess that God the Son remains incarnate and does not temporarily lay aside his humanity during the time between death and resurrection. For this reason we should once again, but for slightly different reasons than those given in chapter four, reject Balthasar's idiosyncratic understanding of the descent. While in Balthasar's view the effectiveness of the descent lies in Christ's endurance of the nadir of human experience, namely, separation from God, and while, for this view to work, only Christ qua divine can endure it such that Christ's humanity must temporarily be laid aside, neither the biblical testimony nor the anthropological implications of such a view promote, require, or even allow it.

Regarding the meaning of the descent and what Christ is doing, I have already discussed the Trinitarian issues involved. I will return to the problems with Balthasar's view as they relate to soteriology and its coherence with Christian tradition. For now, I will simply note that another problem with Balthasar's view concerns the anthropological implications. Whatever else one may say about Balthasar's position (e.g., its mysticism versus a more literalistic interpretation), on the face of it the doctrine would require a suspension of the incarnation, or at the very least a kind of ontological ignorance of it given the need for "distance" between the "naked" hypostases of Father and Son. Aside from soteriological concerns, anthropologically this seems to have the same problems as a reductive physicalist does with the doctrine of the resurrection. Namely, if any person, including Jesus, ceases to exist upon death, how can they said to be the same person at resurrection? What thread of continuity exists? Is the Messiah of Good Friday the same person as the Messiah who comes to Mary in the Garden on Easter Sunday? From an anthropological perspective, and with respect to Balthasar's position, it is impossible to know. Of course, one could argue that Jesus' humanity still experiences human death, and if Balthasar affirms some form of HD[45] then his human nature is continuous. But the problem is only moved back a step here, for if Christ's divine nature is somehow separated—existentially, temporally, even if not metaphysically (although Balthasar's position seems to require the latter)—this means that it is no longer the person of Jesus Christ, the God-Man, hypostatically united in divine and human natures, experiencing these states but rather two separate individuals. On the human side, the human person Jesus of Nazareth experiences death as all humans do: body in the grave, soul in the disembodied state in the realm of the dead.[46] On the divine side, the person of the Son experiences (however limited) separation from the Father. Neither of these experiences correlate to the historic doctrine of the hypostatic union,

---

[45]Which he certainly does as a Roman Catholic, since the *Catechism of the Catholic Church* states, "The Church teaches that every spiritual soul is created immediately by God . . . and also that it is immortal: it does not perish when it is separated from the body at death, and it will be reunited with the body at the final resurrection." *Catechism of the Catholic Church* §366 (Mission Hills, CA: Benzinger, 1994), 93.

[46]A common objection to any kind of anthropological dualism that requires an intermediate state is that this is a kind of Gnostic prioritizing of the soul over the body, that it is dependent upon Platonic conceptions of the immortality of the soul, and the like. But this ignores the *intermediate* character of the intermediate state. It is not final, it is not the new heavens and the new earth, it is not the end of those creatures who have been declared righteous before God in Christ. In other words, affirming the intermediate state does not require adopting the problems of Platonism or Cartesian dualism. On this, see, for instance, Matthew Levering, *Jesus and the Demise of Death: Resurrection, Afterlife, and the Fate of the Christian* (Waco, TX: Baylor University Press, 2012), 15-26. McMartin says in his essay that, "if we endure an intermediate state . . . , it is not comfortable or 'natural' for us (2 Cor 5)." McMartin, "Holy Saturday and Christian Theological Anthropology," 122. For a recent affirmation of the wholeness of the human person from an anthropological dualist, see John W. Cooper, "Whose Interpretation? Which Anthropology? Biblical Hermeneutics, Scientific Naturalism, and the Body-Soul Debate," in Crisp, Porter, and Ten Elshof, *Neuroscience and the Soul*, 238-57.

since it is somehow suspended. I doubt this is palatable theologically, christologically, or anthropologically.

With these conclusions in mind, the corollary question concerns exactly *what* Christ's descent accomplishes with respect to the doctrine of soteriology. It is to that question we turn in the next chapter.

"THE FORGIVENESS OF SINS"

The Descent and the Doctrine of Salvation

O Death, Death, He has come.

GERARD MANLY HOPKINS, "O DEATH, DEATH"

Recent interpretations of the descent, and particularly Balthasar's, have caused much confusion regarding how this doctrine relates to soteriology. Balthasar, as discussed in chapters three and four, expanded on Calvin's substitution model of the descent but then reoriented the descent's meaning toward a Saturday occurrence in the place of torment with universal implications.[1] Both Calvin's initial departure from the descent's traditional meaning and Balthasar's recent attempt at a synthesis of Calvin and the earlier

---

Hopkins' poem is one of the most theologically potent poetic descriptions of the descent in modern literature. Those interested in the poetic expressions of the themes of this chapter may also be interested in E. E. Cummings, "Who Were So Dark of Heart They Might Not Speak," and particularly the last couplet: "but the proud power of himself death immense / is not so as a little innocence."

[1] Recall that Calvin shifted the descent's meaning from a proclamation of victory on Holy Saturday to an event effecting penal satisfaction that occurred on Good Friday. This is not to say that I disagree with penal substitution; far from it. I think Calvin's view of the atonement, now commonly referred to as penal substitutionary atonement, is correct. God poured out his wrath against sin on Jesus on the cross. I do not believe, however, that the descent doctrine as historically and biblically understood is part of that substitutionary, satisfactory aspect of Christ's work. That happens exclusively in Christ's Passion—his arrest, trial, and, especially, death on the cross.

tradition have produced not only confusion but error in contemporary understandings of how the descent relates to soteriology, at both an academic and a lay level.

In this chapter, I seek to untangle this soteriological knot in order to show exactly how the descent is biblically, has been historically, and now should be theologically understood to relate to the doctrine of salvation. I will first explore in more depth the victorious element of Christ's descent, particularly as depicted in Christian iconography. Because the descent so emphasizes Christ's victory, I will also explore here the relationship between penal substitution and *Christus Victor*. Second, I will explore what exactly it means, soteriologically, for Christ to "preach" to the dead and to "release" them. The main question in this regard is whether or not the descent entails universalism. If not, does it nevertheless speak to the question of limited versus unlimited atonement? These soteriological questions, while not necessarily solved by the descent, are at least addressed in part by understanding what the descent does in the one act of redemption, and for whom it does what it does.

CHRIST'S DESCENT AS EXALTATION

The most important point to make regarding the descent and soteriology is that, traditionally, the doctrine is undeniably focused on Christ's victory over the powers of Death and Hades. In the early Christian and medieval theologians, Christ descends to the dead in his human soul while remaining the incarnate Son.

Every knee under the Earth will bow. By virtue of this hypostatic union, Christ's human death is victorious over our last enemy, Death, and his jailor, Hades. This is why in Revelation 1:18 Jesus says he has the keys to Death and Hades—he has descended into their realm and defeated them, their keys being the sign of his victory.[2] This is also why

---

[2] On keys and victory in the ancient world, see Justin W. Bass, *The Battle for the Keys: Revelation 1:18 and Christ's Descent into the Underworld*, Paternoster Biblical Monographs (Eugene, OR: Wipf and Stock, 2014), 31-44. On that particular aspect of Rev 1:18, see Bass, 97-114.

in Christian iconography the descent is typically pictured as part of Jesus' resurrection. You will be hard pressed to find a classic icon of Jesus' descent that pictures him among the dead ones. Instead, Christians traditionally have seen Christ's descent as the beginning point of his exaltation, and so appropriately pictured via his resurrection (and ascension). As John Behr notes, the ἀνάστασις icon, which depicts Jesus coming up from Hades while drawing Adam and Eve up with him, is properly a resurrection icon—it pictures Jesus rising bodily from the grave—but it is the icon most associated with the descent. This is because, in early Christianity, Christ's exaltation was seen as one whole cloth. His descent, resurrection, and ascension all fit together in his one victory over Death, Hades, the grave, Satan, and all rulers and principalities.[3]

It may seem odd to speak about Christ's descent as part of his exaltation, especially since *exaltation* implies an ascent, not a descent. Indeed, Christ's entire exaltation is an upward movement. But how can this be possible if Christ's descent is, as the word implies, a downward movement? In one sense, this is a fair question. The descent is not an upward movement, in a spatial (albeit figurative) sense. But in the more important, theological sense, the descent communicates not torment but victory. The descent is the first of three stops on Jesus' victory tour: first he proclaims victory in the realm of the dead, then he proclaims it in the realm of the living, and then finally and universally he proclaims it in the heavenly realm.[4] In other words, the descent begins Christ's exaltation through the universe's three tiers: the underworld, the earth, and the heavens (as may be implied by Phil 2:10-11; see again on this movement figure 5 in chapter five).

We should also add that Christ's descent is really a descent—he experiences the nadir of human life in this age, and experiences it as all humans do. But the nadir that is human death is also the starting point

---

[3]See John Behr, *The Mystery of Christ: Life in Death* (Crestwood, NY: St. Vladimir's Seminary Press, 2006), 98.
[4]On this descent-ascent pattern and the place of the descent in the exaltation phase of Christ's work, see Metropolitan Hilarion Alfeyev, *Christ the Conqueror of Hell: The Descent into Hades from an Orthodox Perspective* (Crestwood, NY: St. Vladimir's Seminary Press, 2009), 217.

for Christ's exaltation. This nadir is also clearly not part of his humiliation, though, in the sense of continuing his suffering for sin; Christ does not suffer the torments of hell in experiencing human death.[5] This is true for a number of reasons. First, Christ's work of atonement is finished on Good Friday. At the cross, Jesus bears the wrath of the one God on behalf of sinners. I want to be very clear here—Jesus' death is penal and substitutionary. He dies the death that every human being deserves because of his or her sin against almighty God. But in his death, this penal substitution is complete, and applied to those who respond to his actions in faith. There is nothing else required for God's justice to be satisfied. Jesus paid it all, thanks be to God! "It is finished" (Jn 19:30).

Therefore, in allusion to Philippians 2:5-11, early Christians believed that Christ's humiliation ends at the cross. His exaltation, in which he receives the name that is above every name, occurs when every knee bows, those in heaven and earth and *under the earth*. Paul in Philippians 2:10 thus makes reference to Christ's exaltation among those who are dead. He also clearly demarcates Christ's humiliation as beginning at his incarnation and ending with his death on the cross (Phil 2:7-8).

Victory and substitution meet. When Christians speak about how the descent intersects with soteriology, then, we need to be clear that it is not an act of atonement for sin per se[6]—that is, it is not *payment for sin*, an act which occurs in Christ's passion and is finished at the cross—but is instead an act of victory. Of course, the one act of redemption accomplished by Christ can be referred to using the term *atonement*,

---

[5]This is clear in the traditional understanding of the doctrine. See Alyssa Lyra Pitstick, *Christ's Descent into Hell: John Paul II, Joseph Ratzinger, and Hans Urs von Balthasar on the Theology of Holy Saturday* (Grand Rapids: Eerdmans, 2016), esp. 78-79.

[6]There is confusion here in the terminology used in contemporary theology and biblical studies. For theologians, *atonement* is a broad term that encompasses the whole course of Christ's work, from incarnation to Pentecost. For biblical scholars, however, the word "atonement" has a more particular meaning—human beings made right with God through the forgiveness of sins. There are various terms used to describe exactly how this occurs in Scripture (e.g., redemption, justification, propitiation, etc.), but in this use of *atonement*, the point is that it refers to a particular aspect of Christ's work and not the whole. When I say, then, that the descent is not part of the atonement per se, I mean *atonement* in this latter sense. It is not part of what Christ does to atone for sin.

and in that sense the descent and payment for sin should not be parceled out to the point that its different aspects are seen as incompatible, mutually exclusive, or wholly separate. In this sense, speaking clearly about the descent may actually be a means to solve the seemingly perennial debate about penal substitution or *Christus victor*. This is not to say these are the only two ways to understand the atonement, but the contemporary debate over models often focuses on them.

This debate is in part a result of the fragmentation that plagues not only contemporary discussion of the atonement or even systematic theology as a whole but also human experience and thought in general. Private and public life, work and home, faith and science—we fragment our lives in a variety of ways.[7] We also fragment theology similarly; it has become less frequent to see systematic theology that is truly systematic. Instead, the different pieces of the theological puzzle are explored on their own, while other disciplines and areas of theological inquiry are held at bay.[8] This is antithetical to the way in which Christians approached the theological task for over a millennium. Rather than treating these doctrines like oil and water, therefore, Christians should be clear that penal substitution and *Christus victor* are not mutually exclusive options; indeed, the

---

[7]On the fragmentation of the academic disciplines in late medieval life, see G. R. Evans, *The Language and Logic of the Bible: The Road to the Reformation* (Cambridge: Cambridge University Press, 2009). As an aside, it is interesting to hear the Reformers continually blamed for fragmentation, individualism, and other modern ills, when the separation of academic disciplines, nominalism, and other precursors to modernity were clearly at work prior to Luther, Calvin, and the rest.

[8]While I am indebted to G. K. Beale in a variety of ways, both methodologically and interpretively, and while one can detect how influential he is on my own thought in other pieces I've written, he gives a perfect example of the kind of compartmentalization of which I speak in his *New Testament Biblical Theology: The Unfolding of the Old Testament in the New* (Grand Rapids: Baker Academic, 2011), 25, when he emphasizes that his book "focuses on biblical interpretation and biblical theology and much less on practical application of these truths in the modern world." He goes on to say that he hopes his book will help in that regard, and he includes a very brief chapter at the end on it, but he is clear that his task remains almost exclusively within the field of biblical theology, *not* in determining the practical application of his biblical-theological conclusions. While one can appreciate that each of us are trained in certain areas, I am much less inclined to treat those other areas as different compartments in which I should only lightly tread, if I do at all. This book is evidence of how I conceive of each discipline bearing upon one another. One could speak not only of the fabric of theology but the fabric of the theological disciplines.

very structure of the New Testament places emphasis on both of these aspects (as well as others) of Christ's saving work.[9]

We could say, in fact, that it is precisely because Christ's death is penal and substitutionary that his life, death, descent, resurrection, and ascension are vicarious and victorious. And, vice versa, we can also say that Christ's penal, substitutionary death is only ultimately effective because of his victorious resurrection. Victory and substitution go hand in hand. For our purposes, Christ can proleptically proclaim victory in his descent, a victory seen ultimately in his impending resurrection, because he has already accomplished what is necessary to defeat the powers of sin and death on the cross. His penal, substitutionary crucifixion provides freedom from bondage to Satan (*Christus Victor*) precisely because it solves the problem that lies at the root of humanity's imprisonment to the powers: enmity with God through our sinful nature and choices (e.g., Col 2:14-15).[10] Or, as Jeremy Treat puts it, "penal substitution addresses the 'how' of the atonement and *Christus Victor* addresses its effects on Satan, demons, and death—both within the broader aim of reconciliation for the glory of God."[11] To unduly fragment these elements from one another is, then, to succumb to the temptations of modernity.[12]

On the other hand, achieving victory through substitution is not the same thing as proclaiming the victory achieved, much like the crucifixion and the descent are not the same thing. They are clearly interrelated and dependent upon one another as part of the one act of salvation wrought by Christ while also speaking about different aspects of that one act. For our purposes here, the important point to make is that the crucifixion is the zenith of Christ's humiliation, while the descent is the beginning of his

---

[9]See my "Victory, Atonement, Restoration, and Response: The Shape of the New Testament Canon and the Holistic Gospel Message," *STR* 3.2 (2012): 177-94.

[10]Jeremy Treat, *The Crucified King: Atonement and Kingdom in Biblical and Systematic Theology* (Grand Rapids: Zondervan Academic, 2014), 204.

[11]Treat, *Crucified King*, 223. On this entire section relating penal substitution to victory, see 174-226.

[12]See on this Fleming Rutledge, *The Crucifixion: Understanding the Death of Christ* (Grand Rapids: Eerdmans, 2015), 462-535, esp. 530-33.

exaltation.[13] As the climax of Christ's humiliation, the crucifixion is primarily about the penal substitution and vicarious solidarity accomplished there. It accomplishes victory, yes, but through humiliation—the culmination of Christ's humiliation. And, while there is a certain aspect of humiliation retained in remaining dead (as there is in remaining incarnate throughout Christ's exaltation), the descent, as the starting point of Christ's exaltation, is primarily about the victory accomplished on the cross and proclaimed to the underworld, the earth, and the heavenly places.

When we place these two acts side by side and see them as part of the one act of redemption accomplished by Christ at the direction of the Father and in the power of the Spirit, it becomes clear that penal substitution and *Christus Victor* stand together as well. It is precisely because Christ has paid the penalty for sin on the cross that he can proclaim victory over Death and Hades, those oppressive masters of sinners, in the descent. And it is because Christ descends to and rises from the dead that we can speak of the cross, with Paul, as victory (Col 2:15). Concerning the relationship between penal substitution and *Christus victor*, the descent gives us explicit cause to say, "What therefore God has joined together, let no man put asunder" (Mt 19:6, RSV).

"PREACHING" AND "RELEASE" IN THE DESCENT

"God of Second Chances"? Once we come to understand the descent as victory over Death and Hades, as the biblical and historical evidence suggests, a number of questions arise as to the scope of this victory's effect. Many of the early Christian theologians speak of the descent as the "release" of, at least, OT saints.[14] One common contemporary

---

[13]Here see again Treat, *Crucified King*, 156-65, although I still see warrant from Phil 2:7-8 for seeing the crucifixion as primarily the climax of Christ's humiliation (even while it achieves victory) and his ascension as primarily the climax of his exaltation (even while it remains in a state of humiliation given the continuation of the incarnation). This is why I am still comfortable saying that the descent is the beginning, so to speak, of Christ's exaltation, even though it continues to contain aspects of humiliation (i.e. the state of death, the continuation of the incarnation).

[14]By this they mean simply that, rather than dwelling in Abraham's bosom awaiting the Messiah, they now dwell in the presence of the risen Christ. See Bass, *Battle for the Keys*, 2, 8, 55,

objection to the descent is that, in at least some versions, the doctrine gives a postmortem opportunity for salvation. This is particularly a concern with respect to the Eastern Orthodox view, where Jesus goes to Hades and draws out Adam and Eve as representative of all the dead. This at least implies that his proclamation there was evangelistic and effective in drawing everyone in Hades to himself, both the unrighteous and the righteous.[15] Two questions arise at this point: whether or not this implication is endemic of the descent no matter the tradition in which it is articulated, and whether or not the idea of a postmortem opportunity of salvation is biblical. For Protestants, the latter question takes precedence, but I will deal with the historical question first, since we need to be clear if we are rejecting just one (historically deviant) version of the descent or an aspect of the traditional doctrine itself.

While it is popular in contemporary theology to assert that the descent implies both universalism and a postmortem opportunity for salvation, a historical survey of the doctrine's development shows that neither of these options must be the case. Regarding a postmortem gospel proclamation, the ancient development of the descent did not universally include this element.[16] Confusion on this issue occurs

---

70, 85. See also the discussion on the cosmological shifts brought about by the descent in chapter five.

[15]See on this Eastern Orthodox perspective Alfeyev, who says,

> The implications [of Christ's descent into Hades] depend on the way in which the preaching of Christ in hell and its salutary impact on people is understood. Were the preaching addressed only to the Old Testament righteous, the soteriological implications of the doctrine would be minimal, but were it addressed to all in hell, its significance would be considerably increased.

This kind of equivocation is typical in Alfeyev, who goes on after this passage to quote another Eastern Orthodox theologian, I. Karmires, to say, "according to the teaching of *almost* all the Eastern fathers, the preaching of the Saviour was extended to all without exception and salvation was offered to all the souls who passed away from the beginning of time, whether Jews or Greeks, righteous or unrighteous." (Alfeyev, *Christ the Conqueror of Hell*, 213). The quote is from I. Karmires, *He eis haidou kathodos Christou* (Athens: n.p., 1939), 107. As I've said a number of times, Eastern Orthodox theologians, like Alfeyev here, want to suggest as much as they can the universal scope of the descent without stating it outright.

[16]It is interesting that when this issue arises, Clement of Alexandria and Origen seem to be the primary examples, and yet, as D'Costa notes, both Clement's and Origen's positions on universalism were later rejected: Clement's after Augustine turned the interpretive tide on 1 Pet 3–4

because many early Christian theologians use poetic, figurative, and lofty language to describe the descent. For instance, Metropolitan Hilarion Alfeyev says of Ephrem the Syrian's Nisibene Hymn 36 that "this hymn presents a clear theological statement: Death tries in vain to impede Christ's entrance into Sheol. Having descended into it, he resurrects everyone there and leads them out. Sheol is left bare and destitute; there are no longer any dead inside."[17]

Alfeyev draws these universalist implications from the last line and others like it: "let us give great praise to him who died and came to life again, so that he might give life and resurrection to all." But genre and purpose need to be taken into account in these situations. Poetry does not do the same thing dogmatically as a prosaic account of a particular doctrine. And regarding the latter, many early church theologians, when they write dogmatically about the descent, are clear that there is no postmortem opportunity for salvation during Christ's time in the tomb. In fact, Alefeyev admits in a footnote in the same paragraph as the quote above that "other hymns by Ephrem refer to the removal of the righteous from Hades (*De Azymis* 3, 7)."[18] And elsewhere in his book, he notes in a number of places where early Christian writers explicitly state that the descent was only effective for the righteous dead.[19]

It is important to get a sense of how clearly early and medieval theologians stated that Christ's descent was effective only for the righteous who believed prior to Christ's coming. An example comes from Gregory the Great, whom many would consider—along with Ambrose, Augustine, and Jerome—one of the four "Doctors" of the Western Church. He says,

---

and Origen more broadly for his position on apocatastasis (among other things). See Gavin D'Costa, "The Descent into Hell as a Solution for the Problem of the Fate of Unevangelized Non-Christians: Balthasar's Hell, the Limbo of the Fathers and Purgatory," *IJST* 11.2 (2009): 158-60. Ironically, D'Costa acknowledges the later rejection of Clement's and Origen's views while citing them as evidence to make the point that the descent was acknowledged by the early church as including a postmortem offer and having universal effects.

[17] Alfeyev, *Christ the Conqueror of Hell*, 116.

[18] Alfeyev, *Christ the Conqueror of Hell*, 116n15.

[19] E.g., Alfeyev, *Christ the Conqueror of Hell*, 84, 86, 89, 91, 94-96.

When he descended into hell, He delivered through His grace those only who both believed that He should come and observed His precepts in their lives. . . . Hold ye nothing but what the true faith teaches through the Catholic Church: namely, that the Lord in descending into hell rescued from infernal durance those only whom while living in the flesh He preserved through His grace in faith and good conduct.[20]

We could add to this very clear demarcation similar statements[21] from Chrysostom,[22] Jerome,[23] Augustine,[24] Aphrahat,[25] and Aquinas,[26] for example. Augustine, in fact, refers to a universal understanding of the descent as heresy.[27] And then of course there is the statement of the Council of Toledo (AD 633): "He descended into hell in order to release from it those saints who were detained there."[28] Others, like Gregory Nazianzen,[29] bring up the question but do not provide a clear answer. And, as I have noted, some, like Clement and Origen, explicitly affirm a universal effectiveness for the descent. But given the testimony of Chrysostom, Jerome, and Augustine (among others) that the descent is only effective for the righteous dead, it is difficult to conclude that early Christian and medieval theologians ubiquitously—or even mostly—saw the descent as universal in its scope. Instead, many of them, and indeed many who are later deemed "Doctors" of the church, conclude that one's eternal fate is sealed by faith in Christ or lack thereof in this life. The descent, at least according to many of the major early Christian

---

[20]Gregory the Great, *Letter* VII, 4 in *S. Gregorii Magni Opera, Registrum epistularum*, libri I–VII, CCSL 140, ed. D. Norberg (Belgium: Brepols, 1982), 447-52, as quoted in Alfeyev, *Christ the Conqueror of Hell*, 96.

[21]These are all quoted extensively in Alfeyev, if the reader needs access to them in one location. I have relied on Alfeyev for the citation of these texts.

[22]John Chrysostom, *Homilies on Matthew* 36, 3 (*NPNF*[1] 10:236).

[23]Jerome, *Interpretation of the Epistle to the Ephesians*, book 2.

[24]Augustine, *Letter* 164, II, 5, (PL 33.710-711).

[25]Jacob Aphrahat, *Demonstration* 22, 4.

[26]Thomas Aquinas, *Summa Theologica* III, q. 52, a. 4 and a. 5.

[27]Augustine, *Haer.* 79.

[28]H. D. Bruns, *Canones Apostolorum et Conciliorum Veterum Selecti*, t. I (Berlin: G. Reimeri, 1839), 221, as quoted in Alfeyev, *Christ the Conqueror of Hell*, 97.

[29]Greogry Nazaianzen, *Discourse* 45, 1–2, PG 36:624ac.

theologians, did not change the postmortem state of those who died prior to Christ's first advent.[30]

Biblically speaking, a universalist understanding of the descent via either a postmortem offer or a complete destruction of Hades is not an option, either. The writer of Hebrews reminds us that, "it is appointed for man to die once, and after that comes judgment" (Heb 9:27).[31] And thinking once again about Luke 16, the parable of the rich man and Lazarus seems to indicate that one cannot "cross the chasm" from Gehenna to Abraham's bosom. On this passage, I. Howard Marshall comments: "Not only is help unavailable because of the action of retributive justice; it is also impossible because of the eternal separation between the two parts of the abode of the dead."[32] We could add to these texts other passages like Daniel 12:1 and Revelation 20:11-13, where persons' names are written in either the book of life or other "books" (Rev 20:12).[33] These persons' names reflect not only their eternal destiny but also their intermediate state, since they are about "the dead" who are raised to stand before the throne at the final judgment (Rev 20:11, 13). Those

---

[30]Bass makes this point even more strongly, saying,

> The Fathers (except for Clement of Alexandria and Origen) overwhelmingly condemned the teaching that Christ proclaimed a second chance to repent in the underworld. Instead, they consistently taught that Christ preached the Gospel to the righteous dead who had looked forward to him when they were alive on earth.

Bass, *Battle for the Keys*, 85.

[31]As Ellingworth notes, the syntax of this phrase is ambiguous with respect to whether or not judgment occurs immediately or at the second coming of Christ, but the context of Heb 9:27 links the two together.

> Μετὰ . . . τοῦτο leaves entirely open the question of whether or not the judgment immediately follows death. The parallel with ὀφθήσεται in v. 28 suggests a link between judgment and the return of Christ, but v. 26 suggests that the author believed himself and his readers to be living already in the last times.

In other words, what we could say here is that the judgment that immediately follows death is a precursor to the judgment that will occur on the Day of Judgment. Paul Ellingworth, *The Epistle to the Hebrews: A Commentary on the Greek Text*, NICGT (Grand Rapids: Eerdmans, 1993), 486.

[32]I. Howard Marshall, *The Gospel of Luke: A Commentary on the Greek Text*, NICGT (Grand Rapids: Eerdmans, 1978), 638.

[33]On inclusivism, see Christopher W. Morgan and Robert A. Peterson, eds., *Faith Comes by Hearing: A Response to Inclusivism* (Downers Grove, IL: InterVarsity Press, 2008). On the final judgment in Rev 20:13-15, see G. K. Beale, *The Book of Revelation: A Commentary on the Greek Text*, NICGT (Grand Rapids: Eerdmans, 1999), 1033-38.

dead-but-now-raised ones whose names are not written in the book of life are thrown into the lake of fire (Rev 20:15). In other words, the state of the dead prior to the final resurrection and judgment appears to reflect their final eternal state.

One could argue here that, even if one agrees with our reading of Daniel 12 and Revelation 20, this does not preclude Christ from offering a second chance to those in the realm of the dead at the time of his descent. Perhaps, one might say, even if at all other times the dead do not receive a postmortem offer, they could have received one at Christ's descent. The question at this point is, then, whether or not any of the biblical texts related to the descent surveyed in chapter two warrant believing that Christ evangelized the dead during his descent. In my estimation, the only text that could possibly indicate such a view is 1 Peter 3:18-22, and that is only if "preaching" is taken to mean "evangelistically preaching and inviting the dead to repent and believe." But, as Bass has noted, the verb here is not εὐαγγελίζω, but κηρύσσω. While the former could indicate some form of gospel preaching that allowed the dead to repent, believe, and be saved, the latter can be used more generically for proclamation that is not also a gospel invitation.[34] Admittedly, it is used "sixty-one times and . . . in the vast majority of cases to speak of the proclamation of the 'kingdom of God' or the 'Gospel.'"[35] Given this range of meaning, determining the sense of κηρύσσω in 1 Peter 3:19 requires additional clues.

Remember that in chapter two I argued that "spirits in prison" probably refers to evil angels or those otherwise trapped in hell from Noah's day until the Day of Judgment (2 Pet 2:4-10). Given this reality, that Jesus' preaching 1 Peter 3:19 is specifically to evil angels, it seems highly unlikely that κηρύσσω there means anything like "evangelistic preaching." Rather, it makes it all the more likely that Jesus' descent is one in which he

---

[34]Bass, *Battle for the Keys*, 93. It is used in this neutral sense in Lk 4:19; 8:39; 12:3; Rom 2:21; and Rev 5:2.
[35]Bass, *Battle for the Keys*, 92.

proclaims his victory to all those "under the earth" (Phil 2:10), including those "spirits in prison," trapped there until the Day of Judgment. And, as Bass notes, it hardly seems contextually appropriate for Peter elsewhere in the letter to argue for perseverance in persecution (e.g., 1 Pet 4:12-13) if in 1 Peter 3:18-22 he suggests that at least some deceased persons received a postmortem chance to repent.[36] Thus it is not historically or biblically warranted to suppose that the descent implies a postmortem opportunity for salvation. On the contrary, both the biblical data and at least one major version of the historical understanding of the descent do not allow for this interpretation of the doctrine.

Adam and Eve's ascent. An additional reason that some theologians associate the descent with universalism is because many early Christian interpreters portrayed both in writing and in iconography Christ bringing Adam and Eve up from among the dead ones. This, in turn, is interpreted as teaching that Christ's descent healed all of humanity from death's curse. In other words, since Adam is the head of all humanity, by descending to the dead ones and bringing Adam and Eve out with him, Christ's descent is salvifically effective for all humanity. For some theologians, especially contemporary Eastern Orthodox writers,[37] this supposed implicit universalism is portrayed positively. While many Eastern Orthodox theologians are careful not to fully endorse universalism (see text and notes above) there is a strong sense in their writings that Christ's descent effectively destroys death and its effects for all humanity, whether or not they believe in this life.

Other theologians, and especially modern evangelical ones, also believe this imagery concerning Adam and Eve implies universalism.

---

[36] Bass, *Battle for the Keys*, 94.

[37] See on this Alfeyev, *Christ the Conqueror of Hell*, e.g., 166: "Quite often the *octoechos* speaks of Christ raising 'Adam the forefather' and leading him out of hell. Adam is understood not as a concrete personality but rather as a symbol of fallen humanity. As such, his liberation from the chains of hell signifies the renewal of all." An interesting question that I have not pursued in this chapter but that could be related is whether or not one's view of the historical Adam bears on the descent and vice versa. In other words, if "Adam" is understood to be the historical person described in Genesis 1–5 (as I believe him to be), does this impinge on one's understanding of the descent?

Contrary to their Eastern Orthodox counterparts, though, evangelical Protestants are quick to reject universalism (and rightly so), but because they believe the descent implies universalism, they also reject that doctrine.[38] The question is, again, whether or not this is an accurate view of the descent either historically or biblically.

Regarding the biblical argument for universalism, much of what was said above could simply be added here. The primary remaining question in this section is whether the descent, as it has been historically understood, implies universalism via the connection with raising Adam and Eve from the dead. Historically speaking, it should be admitted from the outset that early Christian writers used imagery in their hymns, poems, and devotional works that spoke of raising Adam and Eve in a way that healed humanity. For instance, a Coptic homily, after Jesus descends victoriously to Hades, quotes the earth (underworld) as saying, "Take Thou, then, man [Jesus], the deposit. Take Thou thine image, which Thou has committed as a pledge to me. Take Thou. Adam, being complete in his likeness."[39] Cyril of Alexandria, sometimes employed to defend the notion of a universally salvific descent, similarly often refers to the descent as an event whereby "Christ utterly nullifies the devil's claim on Adam and the human race."[40]

While these examples do, in fact, use generalized language regarding Adam and "all humanity," we need to be careful here not to jump to dogmatic conclusions, especially since many of them clarify elsewhere that by "Adam" they only mean "the saints."[41] Likewise Cyril of

---

[38]E.g., Wayne A. Grudem, "He Did Not Descend into Hell: A Plea for Following Scripture Instead of the Apostles' Creed," *JETS* 34.1 (1991): 109.

[39]E. A. Budge, ed., *Coptic Homilies in the Dialect of Upper Egypt*, Papyrus Codex Oriental 5001 (London: British Museum, 1910), 273-74, as quoted in Alfeyev, *Christ the Conqueror of Hell*, 55.

[40]Daniel Keating, "Christ's Despoiling of Hades: According to Cyril of Alexandria," *St. Vladimir's Seminary Quarterly* 55.3 (2011): 256. For statements that suggest that Christ's descent is in some way effective for all humanity in Cyril's thought, see his *Festal Letter* 2.8, 4.6, passim.

[41]See, e.g., the full text of the Coptic homily cited above, which says prior to the Adam passage quoted, "Then he set free the souls of the saints, and he raised them up with Him." Budge, ed., *Coptic Homilies*, 273-74.

Alexandria, as popular an example of a supposed "universalist" understanding of the descent as he is, does not actually claim universal salvation via the descent in his writings. Instead, if one surveys his entire corpus rather than simply snippets of his work, one finds that he means something more like this: Christ, through his descent, has defeated Death and Hades, and therefore all humanity will rise from the dead in the general resurrection (see more on this below), *but* the descent is only effective in bringing those dead who awaited Christ by faith into the presence of the risen Christ.[42] Additionally, in the more dogmatically oriented works of early Christian writers, many are intent on explaining that the descent does *not* imply universalism. One of the clearest examples comes in Chrysostom, who says,

> This [the bursting of the gates of hell] indicates the destruction of the might of death, not the loosing of the sins of those who had died before his coming. And if this were not so, but he have [sic] delivered all that were before him from hell, how says He, "It shall be more tolerable for the land of Sodom and Gomorrah?"[43]

Thus, according to many early Christian theologians, it is clear that Jesus' descent does not, in fact, provide salvation for all the dead, either at the moment of his descent or at his second coming. Instead, the descent is effective only for those who faithfully looked for the Messiah's coming prior to his first advent. And by "effective" I mean what others

---

[42]So Keating:

> Cyril does not envisage the universal salvation of all human beings. Christ has entirely destroyed Hades as the citadel of Satan and all its inhabitants are now destined to come to "life" in the resurrection of the dead. But the issue of judgment remains—in fact, the reality of judgment can now come fully to light because Satan's hold over the entire human race has been decisively broken.

Keating, "Christ's Despoiling of Hades," 261.

[43]John Chrysostom, *Homilies on Matthew* 36, 3 (*NPNF¹* 10:236), as quoted in Alfeyev, *Christ the Conqueror of Hell*, 67, 84, 86, 89, 91, 94-96, 116. See also the discussion Bass, *Battle for the Keys*, 1-19. Bass mentions a number of examples where early Christian theologians specify that Christ preaches to and releases OT saints, not all those in Hades. For example, Hippolytus, in *Antichr.* 26 (see also Origen, *Fr. Luc.* 23; and Hippolytus, *Antichr.* 45) says that Christ descended, "preaching the Gospel to the souls of the saints." Bass, 13; cf. also 8, 16.

have always meant by the descent's work—that the righteous dead no longer wait for the Messiah but are in his presence, a presence which is now, postresurrection, a bodily one.

Limited versus unlimited descent. The question remains as to whether the descent in any sense is salvific for "all humanity," not just metaphorically but in some real sense. We have already said above that, for many early Christian theologians, it is not salvific for every person; that is, it does not result in the salvation of previously unrighteous dead, or even in a postmortem offer of the gospel to the unrighteous dead. So we want to be clear from the outset that, if the descent can be said to be really for all humanity, that it is not in any ultimately salvific sense, where salvation equals dwelling eternally in a resurrected body on the New Heavens and New Earth in the presence of God in the resurrected Christ. Rather, the question at hand is akin to the debate about limited versus universal atonement in soteriology. There, the argument concerns whether or not Christ's penal, substitutionary death is intended by God to be *potentially* effective for all humankind, but only to be *applied* salvifically to those who believe, or if God intends Christ's death to be only effective for those who are elect. Here, I want to ask a similar question. Is Christ's descent intended for all humankind, but only applied redemptively to those who believe, or is it intended only for those who are elect? To put it in less TULIP-like terms, is Christ's descent intended to bring all the dead out of Hades, only to be separated again based on faith or lack thereof, or is Christ's descent only effective for those who believe?

Before I attempt to answer this question, I should note a couple of relevant scriptural passages that sway some theologians toward a more universal understanding of both the descent and the resurrection. Most prominent is 1 Corinthians 15, and especially verses 12-28. Paul emphasizes here that, if "the dead" are not raised (εἰ γὰρ νεκροὶ οὐκ ἐγείρονται), then Christ is not raised (1 Cor 15:16). In other words, if there is no general resurrection of the dead (νεκρῶν), then there is no hope that

Christ has been raised as the first fruits (1 Cor 15:20).[44] Indeed, "as by a man came death, by a man has come also the resurrection of the dead. For as in Adam all die, so also in Christ shall all be made alive" (1 Cor 15:21-22). The gist of the universalist argument from this section of 1 Corinthians 15 is that Paul seems to imply that the general death caused by Adam's fall will be reversed by a general resurrection, caused by the new Adam's resurrection.[45] Because the resurrection is generally seen as salvific and related to eternally dwelling with God (especially in 1 Cor 15:35-58), these theologians see the general resurrection implied in 1 Corinthians 15:12-28 as universally salvific.

What, then, can we say about the supposed universalist implications of this passage? First, we should acknowledge that it is possible to read Paul here as teaching a general resurrection of the dead that is explicitly caused by Christ's resurrection.[46] Of course, this is not the only way to understand this passage, but for the sake of argument we will grant that this is the way Paul should be understood here. The general resurrection is certainly taught (e.g., Dan 12:2-3, Rev 20:7-15) or implied (e.g., Jn 11:24) elsewhere in Scripture, and it was widely believed in Second Temple Judaism.[47] So it is not out of the question that Paul here assumes a general resurrection and explicitly ties it to Christ's resurrection. Does this, though, mean that the general resurrection is salvific? That is, even

---

[44]Notice that these verses in 1 Cor 15 imply that Christ descended "to/among the dead" since it is "from the dead" (ἐκ νεκρῶν, e.g., v. 12) that he is raised.

[45]This is how some modern commentators take the passage, e.g., Martinus de Boer, *The Defeat of Death: Apocalyptic Eschatology in 1 Corinthians 15 and Romans 5* (Sheffield: JSOT, 1988), 112-13; A. Lindemann, *Der erste Korintherbrief* (Tübingen: Mohr Siebeck, 2000), 344; and Wolfgang Schrage, *Der erste Brief an die Korinther*, vol. 4 (Zurich: Benziger, 2001), 163-66. See also the summary of universalist arguments in Andrew Wilson, "The Strongest Argument for Universalism in 1 Cor. 15:20-28," *JETS* 59.4 (2016): 805-12.

[46]See the discussion in Wilson, "The Strongest Argument for Universalism," 812, for the relationship between Dan 12:2, 1 Cor 15:20-28, and Rev 20:7-15. On this passage and its exegetical, historical, and theological features, see Anthony Thiselton, *The First Epistle to the Corinthians: A Commentary on the Greek Text*, NICGT (Grand Rapids: Eerdmans, 2000), 1222-29.

[47]See the discussions in, for example, John Goldingay, *Daniel*, WBC 30 (Waco, TX: Word, 1989), 308; and Richard Bauckham, *The Fate of the Dead: Studies on the Jewish and Christian Apocalypses*, NovTSup 93 (Atlanta: SBL Press, 1998), 269-89.

if Christ's resurrection is the first fruits of a general resurrection for all humanity, is that general resurrection a general resurrection *to eternal life*? At the very least, 1 Corinthians 15:23 makes a distinction between "those who belong to Christ" and those who do not. Given the coherent nature of the argument of 1 Corinthians 15, this distinction also most likely carries over into Paul's discussion of resurrected bodies and the victory of that resurrection in the rest of the chapter.[48]

In any case, as a first-century Jew and one steeped in the Old Testament and the literature and thought life of Second Temple Judaism, Paul would have known Daniel 12, with its clear bifurcation between those raised to eternal life and those raised to eternal death, as well as other Jewish literature (e.g., *1 En.* 51:1; *4 Ezra* 7:32[49]) that clearly differentiates between the fate of the righteous and unrighteous after the general resurrection. There are also other places in Paul's letters, most notably Romans 5:12-21, where he explicitly and unequivocally says that the salvific benefits of Christ's resurrection are only applied to those who have faith in his redemptive work.[50] The idea, then, that Paul is teaching some kind of universally salvific resurrection in 1 Corinthians 15 does not seem to us to hold up under scrutiny, whether it be through reading the entire chapter carefully (e.g., 1 Cor 15:23), through comparing his statements here with his other letters (e.g., Rom 5:12-21), through reading canonically (e.g., Dan 12:2; Rev 20:7-15), or through understanding Paul's background in Second Temple Judaism (e.g., *1 En.* 51:1-11).

That being said, if Paul still teaches a general resurrection based on Christ's resurrection, what can we say about this general resurrection if it is only salvific for those who believe? First, many Jews in the Second

---

[48]See also Conzelmann's comments on 1 Cor 15:21-22, where he concludes that "'all' does not mean all men together, but all who are in Christ." Hans Conzelmann, *1 Corinthians: A Commentary on the First Epistle to the Corinthians*, Hermeneia (Philadelphia: Fortress Press, 1975), 269.

[49]On the relationship between these texts and Rev 20:13, see Bauckham, *Fate of the Dead*, 269-89.

[50]On this passage and its christological exclusivity, see Thomas R. Schreiner, *Romans*, BECNT 6 (Grand Rapids: Baker Academic, 1998), 267-97.

Temple period, like Paul, would have seen a biblical basis for a general resurrection in texts like Daniel 12. And in Daniel 12, the general resurrection is not salvific for all; some are raised to eternal life, while others are raised only to face final judgment.[51] One's eternal fate is determined by whether or not one's name is written in the book of life. This final judgment scene is recapitulated in Revelation 20:7-15, where, once again, there is a general resurrection of all the dead followed by a sorting of them between those in the book of life and those not in that book.[52] The former are raised to eternal life, the latter to eternal judgment. In other words, the general resurrection is not in and of itself *salvation*. The general resurrection, rather, is the means by which God restores persons to life in an embodied state in preparation for their eternal fate. In this sense, then, it is not problematic to say that Jesus is the first fruits of the general resurrection of the dead, since it by no means implies universal salvation. The general resurrection, begun by Christ, includes all humanity, but not all humanity experiences eternal life because of the general resurrection.[53]

We also need to say, though, that the New Testament does emphasize Christ's resurrection as the first fruits particularly for those who believe. While Paul does seem to refer Christ's resurrection with respect to the general resurrection in 1 Corinthians 15:20-22, everywhere else in his letters he refers to Christ's resurrection with respect to its benefits for believers.[54] It is important to say, then, that while Christ's resurrection

---

[51]So Wilson, "The Strongest Argument for Universalism," 810.

[52]See Beale, *Revelation*, 1035.

[53]This is how, for example, Ambrosiaster takes 1 Cor 15:22, saying,

> Adam died because he sinned, and so Christ, who was without sin, overcame death, in that death comes from sin. Everyone, the righteous and the unrighteous alike, dies in Adam, and everyone, believers and unbelievers alike, will also be raised in Christ. *But the unbelievers will be handed over for punishment, even though they appear to have been raised from the dead*, because they will receive their bodies back again in order to suffer eternal punishment for their unbelief.

Ambrosiaster, *Commentary on Paul's Epistles* 81.171, as quoted in Gerald Bray, ed., *1-2 Corinthians*, ACCS NT 7 (Downers Grove, IL: IVP Academic, 1999), 158, emphasis mine.

[54]See Wilson, "The Strongest Argument for Universalism," 808n17. See also the discussion in David E. Garland, *1 Corinthians*, BECNT 7 (Grand Rapids: Baker Academic, 2003), 706-7.

may provide the basis for the general resurrection, it is only salvific for those who repent and believe, and the New Testament focuses almost exclusively on Christ's resurrection as salvific and beneficial for believers. In other words, while we may be able to speak in some limited sense about Christ's resurrection as the first fruits for the general resurrection, this is not the focus of the New Testament.

Since Christ's exaltation begins at his descent, it, too, is part of the first fruits of his resurrection. Therefore the descent can be said to be in some sense generally effective. But again, the Scriptures make clear that Christ's exaltation is only salvific for those who believe. In what way, then, is the descent effective in a general sense? As the beginning of Christ's exaltation, the descent is of a piece with this study's previous affirmations about the resurrection. It is the beginning of the first fruits of the Christ's resurrection, and therefore of the general resurrection. More specifically, it is the beginning of Christ's binding of the Strong Man (Satan) and the triumph over Death and Hades. Death no longer has any sting (1 Cor 15:54-55). It is therefore effective for those who do not believe only in the sense that it defeats humanity's common enemy, Death, and that it provides a basis for unbelievers' future resurrection to judgment.

Returning to our initial question about a "limited" versus an "unlimited" descent, we should distinguish between the different purposes and effects of the descent. If we are talking about Christ's resurrection, which begins at the descent, as the first fruits of the general resurrection of the dead, then Christ's descent is effective for all the dead. It is, in this sense, unlimited. But if we are talking about the salvific benefits of the resurrection (which begins at the descent), then Scripture makes clear that eternal, resurrected life is reserved for only those who repent and believe in their earthly life. The answer is, therefore, that Christ's descent is effective in both an unlimited and limited manner. It is effective in an unlimited sense in that it is the beginning of Christ's resurrection, the first fruits for the general resurrection prior to the final judgment. But it is effective in a limited sense in that Christ's resurrection is only salvific, and only the salvific first fruits, for those who believe.[55]

CONCLUSION

Part of the impetus among (some) contemporary evangelicals for rejecting the descent is its connection with universalism. This connection is made sometimes through postulating a second chance for those in Hades as Christ's descends there; sometimes through extrapolating Adam and Eve's ascent with Christ to include all humanity; sometimes through assuming that the descent, as the beginning of Christ's exaltation, is included in the first fruits of Christ's resurrection for all humanity; and sometimes through a combination of two or more of these. What we have seen above, however, is that claiming universalism on the basis of the descent doctrine is unwarranted both biblically and historically. Biblically, Scripture does not allow for a postmortem second chance for salvation, and it clearly delineates between those who rise to final judgment and those who rise to eternal life at the general resurrection. Historically, we have seen that early Christian theologians, even though they often used poetic language that could be interpreted as teaching universal salvation, made it clear in their doctrinal disputations that the descent is only effective in a salvific sense for those who believe. If someone rejects the descent, then, it should not be on the basis that it somehow implies or teaches universalism. It simply does not.

---

[55]A passage that I have not discussed but that remains relevant for this conversation is Mt 27:52-53. While some see this as an instance of the effects of the descent, others do not. For an exegetical and narratival interpretation of this passage that considers each option (but ultimately favors the latter), see Raymond Johnson, "I See Dead People: The Function of the Resurrection of the Saints in Matthew 27:51-54," unpublished PhD diss. (Louisville, KY: The Southern Baptist Theological Seminary, 2017). While Mt 27:53 is used by some early Christians to support the descent, I do not see the conclusion about this passage's referent as having much bearing on either the descent in general or the previous discussion on universalism and the general resurrection.

"THE HOLY CATHOLIC CHURCH AND THE COMMUNION OF THE SAINTS"

The Descent and Ecclesiology

> *The Church's one foundation is Jesus Christ her Lord,*
> *She is His new creation by water and the Word.*
> *From heaven He came and sought her to be His holy bride;*
> *With His own blood He bought her and for her life He died.*
> *Yet she on earth hath union with God the Three in One,*
> *And mystic sweet communion with those whose rest is won,*
> *With all her sons and daughters who, by the Master's hand*
> *Led through the deathly waters, repose in Eden land.*

"THE CHURCH'S ONE FOUNDATION," SAMUEL J. STONE

The work of Jesus Christ restores a people—Israel—and thereby creates a people—the church. Jesus' life, death, descent, resurrection, ascension, and gift of the Spirit at Pentecost serve, holistically, as the fulfillment of Israel's exilic hopes and therefore also as her restoration.[1] Because Christ's work is re-

---

[1] See especially the major works of N. T. Wright: *The Climax of the Covenant: Paul and the Law in Pauline Theology* (Minneapolis: Fortress Press, 1993); *The New Testament and the People of God*, Christian Origins and the Question of God 1 (Minneapolis: Fortress Press, 1992), esp. 280-465; and *Jesus and the Victory of*

storative for Israel, the inclusion of the Gentiles should not be seen as supercessionist. The church does not replace Israel but is instead the consummation of Israel. God's people, seeds of the Second Adam, are fruitful and multiply throughout the earth by the proclamation of God's Word in the power of God's Spirit (Acts 6:7; 12:24; 19:20).[2] Theocratic, OT Israel foreshadowed this in their national and ethnically-centered lives in Palestine prior to Christ's coming, but now, in Christ, true Israel includes all those who repent of their sins and confess that Jesus Christ is Lord (Rom 10:9-13), whether Jew or Gentile; Scythian or barbarian; male or female; slave or free (Gal 3:28); native-born or immigrant; American or Iraqi; British or Chinese; Venezuelan or Russian. Christ has, through his work, redeemed for God a people from every tribe, tongue, and nation as the restoration of Israel.

This is because Christ *is* New Israel. He is the Stump of Jesse, the Root of David, the Seed of Abraham and of Eve. He is the recapitulation of all of Israel's history and the fulfillment of all their eschatological expectations. And therefore he is also the restoration of all humanity, since God's covenant with Abraham is meant to restore what was lost in the Fall of Adam. Because Jesus embodies the restoration of Adam and Israel, all those who are united to him are also part of restored Israel, the restored humanity.[3]

It is important to lay this non-supercessionist, non-dispensational ecclesiological framework at the outset of this chapter, because how we understand the relationship between OT Israel, the work of Christ, and the church affects how we understand the descent's relationship to

---

God, Christian Origins and the People of God 2 (Minneapolis: Fortress Press, 1996). However one understands Wright's doctrine of justification, his articulation of Jesus' fulfillment of the hope of Israel is unparalleled in recent scholarship.

[2]G. K. Beale, *The Temple and The Church's Mission: A Biblical Theology of the Dwelling Place of God* (Downers Grove, IL: InterVarsity Press, 2004), 266.

[3]On this framework, see Stephen J. Wellum and Brent E. Parker, eds., *Progressive Covenantalism: Charting a Course Between Dispensational and Covenant Theologies* (Nashville: B&H Academic, 2016), and especially the two initial essays: Jason S. DeRouchie, "Father of a Multitude of Nations: New Covenant Ecclesiology in OT Perspective," 7-38; and Brent E. Parker, "The Israel-Christ-Church Relationship," 39-68.

ecclesiology and eschatology alike. If we take either a supercessionist or a dispensational view of the relationship between the testaments, we will distort Christ's work in general but more particularly what happens with the descent. On the one hand, if we take a supercessionist view, we will neglect how Christ's work, and particularly his descent, is *for Israel*. If, on the other hand, we take a dispensationalist view, we will neglect how Christ's work *in his first coming* is for Israel. While these two views are almost diametrically opposed to one another, it is ironic that they functionally accomplish the same thing: they neglect how Christ's work in his first advent fulfills OT Israel's eschatological hopes.[4] I therefore, in this chapter and the next, want to be clear that Jesus' descent both fulfills Israel's eschatological hopes and, in doing so, also creates new ecclesial and eschatological realities for New Israel, the church.

SOLA FIDE

The reason that Paul can call Christ's church, made of both Jews and Gentiles, "the Israel of God" (Gal 6:16)[5] is because Christ himself is Israel. All those united to the true vine, Jesus, are also a part of that same vine as its branches (Jn 15). And the means by which one is attached to this christological vine is not familial lineage (Jn 3:1-8; 8:31-59; Rom 9), but rather faith. Those who are united to Christ, new Israel and Abraham's seed, are united through faith alone by God's grace alone (Eph 2:4-10; Rom 10:1-11). This may sound predominantly soteriological, but *sola fide* is not only an affirmation concerning how an individual

---

[4]The recent literature on Jesus' work and its fulfillment of Israel's hope is voluminous. N. T. Wright's Christian Origins and the Question of God series has done much to bring the Jewish nature of Christ's identity and ministry to light. See again his *The Climax of the Covenant*; *The New Testament and the People of God*; ad *Jesus and the Victory of God*. Also, see Wright, *The Resurrection of the Son of God*, Christian Origins and the Question of God 3 (Minneapolis: Fortress Press, 2003).

[5]For an introduction to the issues involved in this passage, see Thomas R. Schreiner, *New Testament Theology: Magnifying God in Christ* (Grand Rapids: Baker Academic, 2008), 857-58. For an in-depth exegesis of the passage in support of this phrase as a reference to the church (via allusion to Is 54:10), see G. K. Beale, "Peace and Mercy upon the Israel of God: The Old Testament Background of Galatians 6,16b," *Bib* 80 (1999): 204-23.

might be saved. It is also an affirmation about how Christ's body is constituted, and who belongs in it. Unlike the old covenant, which was ethnically restricted but included both believers and unbelievers within the Abrahamic genealogical line, the new covenant is not restricted ethnically, but it is reserved for only those who believe (Rom 9–11; Eph 2:11-22).[6]

What does this have to do with the descent? I have, in the previous chapter, precluded the idea of a postmortem offer of salvation in the descent and the idea that the descent implies universalism. Here I only wish to further highlight these previously made points by noting that the descent does not supersede or provide an alternative means to the normal process whereby a person is saved—by grace through faith. And, therefore, the descent does not create a portion of God's people outside of God's normal mode of salvation—by grace through faith. This ecclesiological point is important to make in the face of the Roman Catholic doctrine of soteriological inclusivism and its related teachings regarding the descent and purgatory.[7] In some Roman Catholic versions of the descent, it is not just OT saints who are saved, but also "virtuous pagans" (i.e., the Greek philosophers) and, sometimes, infants in limbo. Some Roman Catholic theologians deny this more inclusive salvific and ecclesiological function of the descent, but others, in conjunction with the affirmation that the descent inaugurates the exodus from purgatory to heaven, often think of the descent this way.[8]

Of course, one might object that the descent is only effective for those who respond to Christ's proclamation in Hades by turning to him in

---

[6]On the church as true Israel, see Schreiner, *New Testament Theology*, 717-19, 743-44, 752.

[7]On which see Terence Nichols, *Death and Afterlife: A Theological Introduction* (Grand Rapids: Brazos, 2010), 171-76, for an introduction to the Roman Catholic view. See also the *Catechism of the Catholic Church* §1030 (Mission Hills, CA: Benzinger, 1994), 268. For a Protestant defense of purgatory, see Jerry L. Walls, *Heaven, Hell, and Purgatory: Rethinking the Things that Matter Most* (Grand Rapids: Brazos, 2015). This is a popularized version of his three monographs on heaven, hell, and purgatory, the last of which is *Purgatory: The Logic of Total Transformation* (Oxford: Oxford University Press, 2012). I do not find the case for purgatory to be convincing, either in these volumes or elsewhere. For more discussion on this issue, see chapter five of this book.

[8]On the various Roman Catholic views, see discussion in chapters three and seven.

faith. But we have already demonstrated that a postmortem chance of salvation, whether in the descent or prior to the Final Judgment, is not biblically tenable. So my ecclesiological point is simple: the descent does not provide an alternative means by which a portion of the people of God is constituted. Christ's church, "true Israel," is made up of both Jews and Gentiles who confess that Jesus is Lord during their earthly life.[9] Just as we should reject an extreme dispensational view that OT figures were justified differently (i.e., by obeying the Mosaic Law) than NT persons (i.e., by faith), so also we should reject understanding the descent as an alternative means of entering the people of God. Salvation has always been by grace through faith, for, Abraham "believed the LORD, and [God] counted it to him as righteousness" (Gen 15:6).[10] And since the new covenant people of God consists only of those who have been justified, the descent does not provide an alternative ecclesiological entry point.

DESCENDING RHYTHMICALLY

A second way that the descent affects ecclesiology is with respect to the church's liturgical life. Worship is repeated, rhythmic; it consists of a set of practices that shape and form us in embodied ways.[11] This liturgical formation occurs both in a spiritual sense and in a doctrinal sense. In other words, the repeated worship practices of our corporate gatherings shape how we love God and love neighbor in our individual lives throughout the week and also how we think rightly about God and our

---

[9]On the relationship of the church to Israel and the conception of the people of God as both Jews and Gentiles who express faith in the Messiah, see Gregg R. Allison, *Sojourners and Strangers: The Doctrine of the Church*, Foundations of Evangelical Theology (Wheaton, IL: Crossway, 2012), 61-102.

[10]On the relation between this text, the New Testament, and Christian affirmation of salvation by faith, see Schreiner, *New Testament Theology*, 531.

[11]See James K. A. Smith, *You Are What You Love: The Spiritual Power of Habit* (Grand Rapids: Brazos, 2016). This is an abbreviated version of the arguments made in his Cultural Liturgies project. See James K. A. Smith, *Desiring the Kingdom: Worship, Worldview, and Cultural Formation*, Cultural Liturgies 1 (Grand Rapids: Baker Academic, 2009) and *Imagining the Kingdom: How Worship Works*, Cultural Liturgies 2 (Grand Rapids: Baker Academic, 2013).

neighbor. *Lex orandi est lex credendi et agendi*: the rule of prayer is the rule of belief and action (Celestine I). How, then, does our worship shape our belief about the descent and vice versa? I will argue that the descent affects our worship, and our worship affects our belief in the descent, in at least two areas—baptism and the Sabbath.

Baptism. The earliest understandings of the descent imply or assert that the doctrine is connected to baptism.[12] This is because of at least two spatial understandings of Christ's work. First, Christ's entire work is seen through the pattern of descent to ascent (e.g., Eph 4:9-10). Christ in the incarnation descends to humanity, and this incarnational humbling has a nadir—his death on the cross. From that low point, the rest of Christ's work—namely, his resurrection and ascension—is an ascent back to his Father. The descent stands as the fulcrum between these two movements. It is both the result of his death on the cross, in that he experiences not only the moment but also the state of death. But, as we have repeatedly seen, it is also and primarily understood as the beginning of Christ's exaltation. In this larger schema, then, Christ's descent is both the dénouement of his humiliation and the beginning of his glorification.

Within this larger descent-ascent structure of Christ's life and work, there are three mini-descents, each of which is associated with water. This aquatic association adds another spatial dimension to Christ's

---

[12]On parallels between incarnation, baptism, and the descent, see, for example, Metropolitan Hilarion Alfeyev, *Christ the Conqueror of Hell: The Descent into Hades from an Orthodox Perspective* (Crestwood, NY: St. Vladimir's Seminary Press, 2009), 20; Georgia Frank, "Christ's Descent to the Underworld in Ancient Ritual and Legend," in *Apocalyptic Thought in Early Christianity*, ed. Robert J. Daly, SJ, Holy Cross Studies in Patristic Theology and History (Grand Rapids: Baker Academic, 2009), 217, 224-25 (211-26); Irina Kukota, "Christ, the Medicine of Life: The Syriac Fathers on the Lord's Descent into Hell," *Road to Emmaus* 6.1 (2005): 19-20; Kilian McDonnell, "The Baptism of Jesus in the Jordan and the Descent into Hell," *Worship* 69.2 (1995): 98-109; and Malcolm L. Peel, "The 'Descensus ad Inferos' in the Teachings of Silvanus," *Numen* 26.1 (1979): 35-36. Alfeyev is reliant on Aloys Grillmeier, "Der Gottessohn im Totenreich: Soteriologische und christologische Motivierung der Descensuslehre in der älteren christlichen Überlieferung," *ZKT* 71 (1949): 4-5; and Aloys Grillmeier, SJ, *Christ in Christian Tradition: Volume One—From the Apostolic Age to Chalcedon (451)*, 2nd ed., trans. John Bowden (Atlanta: John Knox, 1975), 74.

descent to the dead. Some early Christian theologians connect these three mini-descents via their association with water,[13] noting the following: the incarnation is a descent of God the Son into Mary's watery womb; Jesus' baptism is a descent into the waters of the Jordan; and Jesus' descent to the dead is a descent into the waters, or abyss, of Sheol.[14] The aquatic nature of these three events provides a common thread by which to tie the entire course of Christ's human obedience together.[15]

Christ's immersions into water are explicit identifications with our humanity—in his incarnation, he identifies with Adam's seed in general; in his baptism, he identifies with Israel in particular; and in his descent to the dead he identifies with and experiences vicariously the result of the first Adam's fall. Christ's descent is therefore the climax of his experience of a fully human life, from birth to vocational baptism to death.

We also should say, though, that, because of the descent's primarily victorious overtones, it serves not only as the climax of his fully human life but also as the explicit beginning point of his proclamation of victory over God's enemies and therefore of his full restoration of humanity. The descent is victorious over the powers and principalities that formerly served under the prince of the power of the air (Eph 2:2). It is thus a declaration of victory, one that begins in the descent and moves upward through the three tiers of the universe: the underworld in the descent, the earth in the resurrection, and the ascension in the heavens.[16] This victorious and restorative aspect could of course also be said of Jesus' incarnation and baptism. It is particularly in the descent, though—after

---

[13]See Kukota, "Christ the Medicine of Life," 20-24.

[14]Sheol is closely connected to the abyss, which in turn is closely connected to the sea. On the synonymous relationship between "the sea," "abyss," and "Hades," see James D. G. Dunn, *Romans 9–16*, WBC 38B (Dallas: Word, 1988), 606.

[15]This phrase is from Thomas F. Torrance, *Incarnation: The Person and Life of Christ*, ed. Robert T. Walker (Downers Grove, IL: IVP Academic, 2007), 79-82.

[16]Recognizing this three-tiered movement does not require one to believe the universe is spatially divided into three separate compartments. Rather, this figurative language is used to communicate spiritual and metaphysical realities about Christ's work.

Christ's active and passive obedience have finished—that Christ begins his victory tour.[17]

This should have profound effects on how we think of baptism. In more liturgically oriented traditions, adult baptism is many times preceded by a renunciation of Satan and all his works by the person to be baptized.[18] While this may be more broadly connected to the new Christian's repentance of sin and faith in Christ as Lord, it is also more particularly a vestige of this ancient connection between the descent and baptism. In ancient iconography, this connection is made more explicit by the images of Christ's feet standing on or over the primordial chaos monster in his baptism. These same chaos monsters, along with Death, Hades, and Satan, are finally and fully defeated in Christ's ultimate descent into the waters of death and bodily resurrection from them.

When Christians remember their own baptisms and baptize others, then, we should explicitly connect it with the victorious elements of Christ's own baptism and descent. It is not as though we, too, defeat the chaos monsters, powers, and principalities in our baptism, but rather that, through union with Christ by faith, we already are ruling and reigning with him (Eph 2:6) and thus participating in his victorious life over them. Christ has achieved the victory over them by his life, death, descent, resurrection, and ascension, and our baptisms are signs and seals that we reap the benefits of it. Our baptisms, though, are also baptisms that unite us with Christ's death, and so they are also reminders that victory is achieved through death. Or, as Paul puts it, "We were buried therefore with him by baptism into death, in order that, just as Christ was raised from the dead by the glory of the Father, we too might

---

[17]See Justin W. Bass, *The Battle for the Keys: Revelation 1:18 and Christ's Descent into the Underworld*, Paternoster Biblical Monographs (Eugene, OR: Wipf and Stock, 2014), 7-11.

[18]Because I am a Baptist, I of course believe that believer's baptism just *is* baptism. Given the connections made here between baptism and the renunciation of powers, it should be obvious why I think believer's baptism is the sensible means of the ordinance. For an introduction to the exegetical and theological arguments for believer's baptism, see Thomas R. Schreiner and Shawn D. Wright, *Believer's Baptism: Sign of the New Covenant in Christ*, NAC Studies in Bible and Theology (Nashville: B&H Academic, 2006).

walk in newness of life" (Rom 6:4). That passage comes in the context of Paul exhorting the believer to die to sin and live in Christ—to put sin, our enemy, to death. Christ's victory over God's enemies came through his own death, and our victory in Christ is achieved only when we also take up our cross, die to self, and follow him. Baptism, then, is connected to the descent both in the sense that it is a symbol of our union with Christ's death and also in the sense that it is a symbol of our participation in the benefits of Christ's victory over Death and Hades.

The descent and communion of the saints. Another implication of the descent for ecclesiology is that Christ's descent is the grounds for the communion of the saints. By "communion of the saints," I mean to affirm that all believers throughout space and time are united to one another by virtue of their union with Christ. This includes not only all believers alive today in a geographic sense, or even just future believers in our own generation in a temporal sense, but *all* believers throughout space and time. That is, this union, this *koinōnia*, includes those who have gone before living Christians to rest in the presence of Christ until he returns.[19]

Here, we draw on Hebrews 12:1 and its reference to the great cloud of witnesses. Not only are these now-dead saints cheering living Christians on, so to speak, in their own races toward glorification in Christ, but deceased saints are also united to living Christians because of their common Spirit-born union to Jesus. And while many may stop here and say that the communion of the saints is only a product of soteriology in general, I want to hasten to add that the descent in particular allows for this kind of communion.

Recall from the previous two chapters that Christ's descent places deceased saints in the presence of the victorious and (then soon-to-be, now fully) risen Christ. Christ's descent changes the nature of paradise,

---

[19]Or, as Horton puts it, "Union with Christ (soteriology) and communion with his body (ecclesiology) form an integral pattern." Horton, *Christian Faith*, 735. See also, on the relationship between geography, time, and the communion of the saints, 800-804, 826-27.

from a place where deceased believers wait for the Messiah to a place where deceased saints are united to and in the presence of the dead-but-soon-to-be-risen Messiah, Jesus. This union to the victorious Christ happens because Christ descends to the place of the righteous dead and changes the nature of that place. It transforms from a place of hope to a place of sight. While these deceased saints still wait for their own bodily resurrection, they see the reality of resurrection in their midst in the person of Jesus, both in his descent and later in his bodily resurrection and ascension. This communion of dead saints with the risen Christ begins with Christ's descent. And therefore, the communion that we living saints enjoy with the risen Christ is also one that unites us with our deceased sisters and brothers in the Lord.

We should also note that this spiritual communion is particularly present in Communion, the Lord's Supper. Whatever one's tradition, at its core the Supper is a memorial of Christ's death and therefore a proclamation of the gospel. Even the most memorialist among us would agree that Christ by his Spirit is present through the proclamation of the gospel,[20] and the gospel is visibly declared in the Supper. And as Paul says in 1 Corinthians 10:16-17, the cup and bread are *koinōnia*, fellowship, sharing, with the blood and body of Jesus.[21] They are also therefore fellowship with one another, making us into one body. Communion thus creates communion with Christ and with one another, a "one another" that necessarily includes all believers throughout time and space who are united to Christ. In communion, then, living Christians

---

[20]For a mostly memorialist understanding of the Supper that nevertheless expresses similar ideas regarding the Supper, gospel proclamation, and the transformation of the Christian, see James M. Hamilton, "The Lord's Supper in Paul: An Identity-Forming Proclamation of the Gospel," in *The Lord's Supper: Remembering and Proclaiming the Lord's Death Until He Comes*, ed. Thomas R. Schreiner and Matthew R. Crawford, NAC Studies in Bible and Theology 10 (Nashville: B&H Academic, 2010), 68-102.

[21]For an exegesis of 1 Corinthians 10, see Hamilton, "The Lord's Supper in Paul," 73-76. For similar views on the Supper as those expressed here, see also Brian J. Vickers, "Celebrating the Past and Future in the Present," 313-40 in Schreiner and Crawford, *Lord's Supper*. Finally, for a fuller expression of my own view of the Supper, see Matthew Y. Emerson and R. Lucas Stamps, "Liturgy for Low-Church Baptists," *CTR* 14.2 (2017): 71-88.

commune not just with those physically near us, or even just those geographically apart but temporally present with us. We commune, because of Christ's descent, with all those who have trusted in Christ throughout space and time.

Sabbath. We will discuss further the eschatological import of Christ's descent for the Sabbath, but here it is sufficient to note that, in terms of corporate worship, a final implication is that the Christian Sabbath should have descent overtones. As usual, we do not want to fragment the work of Christ into bits and pieces, and in one sense Christ's entire exaltation is his Sabbath rest.[22] Perhaps even more importantly, his rest is most explicitly fulfilled in his ascension, because it is at the right hand of the Father that he now sits—rests—in repose. But Christ's descent is also his Sabbath rest. Typically associated with Saturday, the descent comes after the crucifixion on Friday, an event which Jesus culminates by repeating both God's and Moses' words after the creation and completion of the tabernacle: "It is finished" (Jn 19:30). Thus Christ's burial, in which his body lies still, is rest for his human body but also rest for the entirety of his person. His work is completed, and he rests in death. It is interesting that Christ calls death "sleep" a number of times in John—death is no longer final but merely restful, since Jesus is the resurrection and the life and thus defeats Death's power and stay.[23]

While I should not make the descent do more work than it can, I have asked at numerous points throughout this book what kinds of implications it might have on other doctrines within the whole cloth fabric that is Christian theology. Here, it is appropriate to ask how this Sabbatarian element of the descent might matter for the ecclesiological doctrine of the Sabbath. Any conclusions here must be tentative, since we are most

---

[22]On Christ's exaltation, see Michael Horton, *The Christian Faith: A Systematic Theology for Pilgrims on the Way* (Grand Rapids: Zondervan Academic, 2011), 521-47.

[23]John is not the only biblical book to use sleep as a metaphor for death; see also, for instance, 1 Kings 1:21; Job 14:12; Ps 13:3; Dan 12:12; 1 Thess 4:13-18. See the reflection on death as "sleep" in Anthony C. Thiselton, *Life After Death: A New Approach to the Last Things* (Grand Rapids: Eerdmans, 2012), 69-70.

certainly in the realm of speculation at this point. I still want to suggest, though, however tentatively, that because Christ's death and descent are qualified as "restful," they are the fulfillment or recapitulation of the old covenant's Sabbath laws. Jesus is both Lord of the Sabbath (Mt 12:1, 8; Mk 2:28; Lk 6:1, 5) and the one who perfectly rests in the Sabbath in his death and descent. With these facts about Christ's lordship over and recapitulation of the Sabbath, I wonder how tightly churches should hold to Sabbatarianism. Perfect rest has already been enacted by and is found in Christ alone. Certainly there is still creational wisdom in having a day of rest, but the purpose of the old covenant's Sabbath has been fulfilled in Christ's own Sabbath rest—his descent. We will say more about that in the next chapter. For now it is enough to say that, ecclesiologically, the church's rest is found in its members resting in Christ's own work, not their own, and thereby in their union with the Lord and Keeper of the Sabbath.[24] Strict Sabbatarianism thus seems to be an attempt to go back to the old covenant, since Christ has already worked and rested—in his descent—on our behalf.[25]

CONCLUSION

Christ's descent, then, has a number of ecclesiological implications. First, by way of negation, it does not provide an alternative mode of union with Christ. Salvation, and thus inclusion in God's new covenant people, is by grace through faith. The descent is not some sort of intermediate plan B means of salvation or inclusion in God's people. Instead, it is effective precisely and only for those who already awaited the Messiah in their earthly lives prior to Christ's first advent. A second ecclesiological implication of the descent is that it provides the rhythm for our ecclesial lives. To enter into God's church, we descend into the waters of baptism and are thereby united to Christ's own descent into

---

[24]It is possible that this rest in Christ's work and not in our own is portrayed liturgically in the all-night vigils practiced by some traditions on Holy Saturday.

[25]On the Sabbath, see Schreiner, *New Testament Theology*, 653-54.

death (Rom 6:4). And the church's life, particularly its weekly (rhythmic) corporate gatherings, is restful precisely because Christ has worked and rested, in the descent, for us. Additionally, the descent is related to the means by which the communion of the saints throughout space and time occurs. In the descent, Christ transforms paradise, so that the righteous dead now enjoy communion with him and therefore also with us. This communion is especially prevalent in Communion, during which we are spiritually united to Christ's body and blood and so also to one another, including those who are absent from the body but present with the Lord.

"THE RESURRECTION OF THE BODY AND THE LIFE EVERLASTING"

The Descent and Eschatology

Each of the events in Christ's work of salvation, seen cumulatively as the united atoning act of Jesus, is eschatological in character.[1] While Christ's redeeming work is typically located within Christology, soteriology, theology proper, and ecclesiology, this eschatological character is sometimes left to the margins. Perhaps this is due to the modern revision of eschatology to include only "last things" (e.g., death, judgment, the eternal state). And yet the Bible and the early church speak of Christ's work of salvation in terms of the "last days."[2] The economy of salvation—centered on the person and work of Jesus Christ—is eschatological in the sense that it inaugurates the new age of the kingdom of God.

Much of this chapter is taken from my article, "'He Descended to the Dead': The Burial of Christ and the Eschatological Character of the Atonement," *SBJT* 19.1 (2015): 115-31. Used with permission.

[1] See Adrio König, *The Eclipse of Christ in Eschatology: Toward a Christ-Centered Approach* (Grand Rapids: Eerdmans, 1989).

[2] John A. McGuckin, "Eschatological Horizons in the Cappadocian Fathers," in *Apocalyptic Thought in Early Christianity*, ed. Robert J. Daly, SJ, Holy Cross Studies in Patristic Theology and History (Grand Rapids: Baker Academic, 2009), 194-95 (193-210).

This chapter focuses on these two underappreciated aspects of the saving work of Jesus: the descent as a vicarious act of solidarity and the descent as an eschatological event.[3] To anticipate the biblical and theological argument, Christ's time in the tomb on Holy Saturday is an eschatologically charged, vicariously salvific act because at this point in Jesus' work, he takes his Sabbath rest after finishing his new creation, embodies the already/not yet tension inherent in salvation, represents the first fruits of the intermediate state in his sleep, and begins to proclaim his defeat of Death, Hades, and the dragon. The chapter will proceed by examining these four main eschatological implications of Christ's descent, and in doing so will connect the burial of Christ to a number of eschatological doctrines, including the millennium, universalism, and the intermediate state.

ESCHATOLOGICAL VICTORY

We can see a number of eschatological threads running through the various aspects of Jesus' descent. First, there is a strong sense of victory and liberation. The redemptive work accomplished on Holy Saturday is thus eschatological, specifically with respect to the defeat of God's enemies. Typically, victory is left to discussions of the empty tomb, but the descent highlights both of these accomplishments in Jesus' burial. In the OT expectation and the NT explication of the "last days," YHWH's rule over those who oppose him is a major theme.[4] The early church, along with Luther, Roman Catholics, and Eastern Orthodox traditions, emphasizes this eschatological victory, noting that redemption comes in the form of defeating the oppressive powers of sin, death, and Satan and healing humanity.

In Jesus' burial, descent, and resurrection, he defeats the last enemy, which is death (1 Cor 15:26), and crushes Satan's head. Death is swallowed

---

[3]When scholars do tie in atonement with eschatology, it is typically only with respect to the resurrection and its implications for creation and anthropology in the new heavens and new earth.
[4]See, for example, G. K. Beale, *A New Testament Biblical Theology: The Unfolding of the Old Testament in the New* (Grand Rapids: Baker Academic, 2011), 88-116, 129-60.

up in death. Jesus thus accomplishes what will happen on the Day of the Lord: the defeat of Satan, sin, death, hell, and the grave. Indeed, his Passion is the Day of the Lord. The burial of Christ is an eschatological act in its defeat of Hades, both accomplishing that victory and anticipating its culmination at Jesus' return.[5] This victory is of course not yet fully realized, and will not be until Christ's return.[6] Nevertheless, the work necessary for it is accomplished in Christ's death, burial, and descent.

The millennium. Another possible eschatological implication derived from Jesus' descent comes with respect to the millennium of Revelation 20. On the one hand, if Satan is defeated and thrown into the abyss through Christ's victorious descent, this may point to an amillennial reading of Revelation 20:1-6. As we have noted a number of times throughout this book, in the LXX, the word for "abyss" is used on occasion to speak of the place of the dead or as a parallel to Sheol,[7] and in Revelation it is used to speak of the realm where God's enemies dwell and from whence they arise (e.g., Rev 11:7). If Jesus has already descended to the place of the dead and defeated it, it may lead readers of Revelation 20 to assume that Jesus has already cast Satan into the abyss in that eschatologically victorious act. So, perhaps, affirming the descent may lead to affirming a more spiritual or idealistic reading of Revelation 20:1-6.

On the other hand, what about the dead saints who come to life in Matthew 27:52?[8] This seems to be a direct result of Christ's defeat of death, accomplished particularly in his crucifixion in Matthew 27 but also in his burial in the history of doctrine. Both the Eastern Orthodox

---

[5]So Milton McCormick Gatch, "The Harrowing of Hell: A Liberation Motif in Medieval Theology and Devotional Literature," *Union Seminary Quarterly Review* 36 (1981): 78.

[6]See König, *Eclipse of Christ in Eschatology*, 64–96.

[7]On the synonymous relationship of the sea and the underworld in this passage, as well as their equivalency in Jewish thought, see James D. G. Dunn, *Romans 9–16*, WBC 38B (Dallas: Word, 1988), 606.

[8]Ignatius of Antioch, Melito of Sardis, Clement of Alexandria, and Origen make this connection between the descent and the resurrection of the saints in Matthew 27, although they do not then tie it to the question of the Millennium. See Jared Wicks, SJ, "Christ's Saving Descent to the Dead: Early Witnesses from Ignatius of Antioch to Origen," *Pro Ecclesia* 17.3 (2008): 304, 309.

and Roman Catholic versions of the doctrine affirm that Jesus not only descended to the dead but also led captives out of it. We also saw in chapter five that this aspect of the descent, namely, Christ's "release" of the OT saints, can be adopted if it is understood as a shift in the nature of paradise, from a place of messianic hope to one of christological reality. Might it be the case, then, that the resurrected saints in Matthew 27:52 are a foreshadowing of the "first resurrection" in Revelation 20 as seen in a historic premillennial position?[9] The point here is not to use the descent as a solution to the problem of the millennium, but only to note that Jesus' time in the tomb may have implications for this eschatological issue.

Universalism and Cyril of Alexandria. As seen especially in the early church and Orthodox understandings of the descent,[10] there is the question of universalism. Although we have already discussed this issue in chapter seven, it is relevant here as well due to the presence of the general resurrection in Revelation 20. Origen's doctrine of apocatastasis is many times linked in the secondary literature to his understanding of the descent,[11] and Cyril of Alexandria likewise notes the universal implications of Jesus' work on Holy Saturday. As Keating argues, though, Cyril is not a strict universalist.[12] Yes, Christ's descent accomplishes

---

[9]This would entail taking the position on Mt 27:52-53 that it speaks of the time between Christ's death and resurrection, rather than as a parenthetical referent to the second coming and general resurrection. For discussion and analysis, see Raymond Johnson, "I See Dead People: The Function of the Resurrection of the Saints in Matthew 27:51-54," unpublished PhD diss. (Louisville, KY: The Southern Baptist Theological Seminary, 2017).

[10]Of course, there is a strong universalist strain running through Balthasar and his subsequent interpreters as well. See Edward T. Oakes, who has contributed the following to the discussion: "The Internal Logic of Holy Saturday in the Theology of Hans Urs von Balthasar," *IJST* 9.2 (April 2007): 184-99 and "*Descensus* and Development: A Response to Recent Rejoinders, *IJST* 13.1 (January 2011): 3-24, as well as Gavin D'Costa, "The Descent into Hell as a Solution for the Problem of the Fate of Unevangelized Non-Christians: Balthasar's Hell, the Limbo of the Fathers, and Purgatory," *IJST* 11.2 (2009): 146-71. Both Oakes and D'Costa focus on the creation of purgatory (as articulated by Balthasar) and its implications for the solution to the problem of world religions and the unevangelized.

[11]Wicks, "Christ's Saving Descent," 304. Martin F. Connell, "*Descensus Christi Ad Inferos*: Christ's Descent to the Dead," *TS* 62 (2001): 269.

[12]Daniel Keating, "Christ's Despoiling of Hades: According to Cyril of Alexandria," *St. Vladimir's Theological Quarterly* 55.3 (2011): 261-69.

something with universal atoning consequences, but that does not mean, for Cyril, that all will experience life with God in eternity. That is still left to whether or not one is united to Christ in faith. One possible *via media* is that Christ's burial is universally atoning *only in the sense that it defeats death for all humanity.*

In other words, it is possible that the reason that all are raised to life prior to the final judgment (Rev 20:4-5, 12-15; cf. Dan 12:2) is that Christ's defeat of death does in fact defeat what Revelation calls "the first death" for all humanity. But that would not negate final judgment, where one either experiences eternal life or eternal death. Further, as we saw in chapter seven, the recognition of Jesus' descent as eschatologically redemptive may provide a solution to the problem of the resurrection of *all* the dead—believing and unbelieving—at the final judgment, which does not entail universalism. If, as Cyril argued, one still only receives eternal life on the basis of faith in Christ, then the descent is also limited in its application.

THE INTERMEDIATE STATE AND
CHRISTOLOGICAL ANTHROPOLOGY

There are a number of other eschatological aspects of Christ's time in the tomb. One of the intriguing connections between eschatology and the atonement as seen in Christ's burial is the intermediate state. While much has been said on this issue regarding theological anthropology, the burial of Jesus is hardly mentioned in any discussion.[13] And yet in

---

[13]I am here excluding those who affirm some form of the descent doctrine that includes rescuing people from Hades or hell, since those views are necessarily applicable to the interim state. Those who do not affirm either the Roman Catholic or Eastern Orthodox versions of the doctrine, though, do not usually mention Christ's burial as normative for the anthropological makeup in the interim state. For example, the following theologians make no mention of Jesus' time in the tomb in their discussion of the intermediate state: Millard Erickson, *Christian Theology*, 2nd ed. (Grand Rapids: Baker Academic, 2005), 1179-90; Wayne Grudem, *Systematic Theology: An Introduction to Biblical Doctrine* (1996; Grand Rapids: Zondervan, 2000), 810-27; Anthony Hoekema, *The Bible and the Future* (Grand Rapids: Eerdmans, 1979), 92-108; Michael S. Horton, *The Christian Faith: A Systematic Theology for Pilgrims on the Way* (Grand Rapids: Zondervan, 2011), 910-15; John Polkinghorne, *The God of Hope and the End of the World* (New Haven, CT: Yale University Press, 2002), 66-92, 103-112; and Helmut Thielicke, *Death and Life*, trans. Edward H. Schroeder

Christ we see the first fruits not only of the resurrection but also of the intermediate state. Jesus experiences death vicariously for humanity, not only in his descent but also in his simply being dead. His body lying in the grave is redemptive, not only because it evokes Day of Atonement imagery, seen especially in John's echoes of the Holy of Holies in his description of Jesus' tomb,[14] but also because by it he redeems the state of death for all those who united to him. Death for Jesus is not the final word, and thus it is not the final word for those united to him.

Jesus' intermediate state is thus helpful in articulating the intermediate state of those united to him with respect to the question of the unity of the person. The hypostatic union is not severed here. Jesus the God-Man is still fully human and fully divine, and so he experiences death in this united state. His humanity is not severed between body and soul, either, but he experiences death in his humanity as a psychosomatic unity. Further, Jesus experiences death as fully human and fully divine. Here we may wish to appeal to the notion of reduplication, the qua human / qua divine distinctions, so as not to posit that God the Son dies and is separated from the other persons of the Trinity. This, though, is the point: because his Christ qua human fully experiences death *while still hypostatically united* with the divine nature of the Son, death is swallowed up by the Triune God and defeated. Christ vicariously experiences death and conquers it fully and completely precisely because he is the God-Man. Thus, for those who are united with Christ, they too can experience the intermediate state with hope. They can hope and believe, first, that their entire person will still be united when Christ returns. Christ remained fully human—body and soul—during death, and believers will remain fully human during death. They can hope, second, that because this unity is maintained they, like Jesus, will be

---

(Philadelphia: Fortress Press, 1970), 213-17. Although Erickson and Horton do note that Jesus "commends his spirit" to the Father in Lk 23:46, they do not connect this with the burial of Jesus in any way or speak to its anthropological and eschatological implications.

[14]Nicholas P. Lunn, "Jesus, the Ark, and the Day of Atonement: Intertextual Echoes in John 19:38–20:18," *JETS* 52.4 (2009): 731-46.

raised bodily and in continuity with their life premortem (1 Cor 15:35-49). Third, they can hope that the powers that introduced death into the world—sin and Satan—have been crushed by Jesus' own death and descent. And finally, they can hope in the face of their own death because Jesus' descent is an act of solidarity with our own experience of human death. Jesus has gone before us through the Valley of the Shadow of Death (Ps 23:4) and come through the other side to prepare a place for us (Ps 23:5).

Jesus' intermediate state in the grave also speaks to the question of soul sleep. Jesus' death is vicarious and also the first fruits of believers' death, and so whatever we want to say about Jesus' time in the tomb has implications for those united with him. Of course, not everything that happens to Jesus in the tomb is repeated in believers' experience. This is particularly true of his victory over Satan in his burial. Nevertheless, this victory still has implications for those united to Christ, in that they are freed from death and the power of sin. The point here is that what happens to Jesus in his humanity has implications for the intermediate state of those united to Christ. Depending upon how one interprets Jesus' descent, soul sleep is either more or less likely as an option for the intermediate state of humanity. In other words, if one is willing to affirm that Jesus' human soul is "asleep" during his time in the grave due to its unity with his dead body, then soul sleep appears to be a legitimate option for humanity's intermediate state. Likewise, if one is a non-reductive physicalist, one needs to consider the implications of that position for how they view Jesus' time in the grave. If, on the other hand, Jesus' soul is conscious during Holy Saturday, this may preclude soul sleep as an option.[15] For our purposes, because of the view of the descent articulated in chapters two and three, and because of the christological anthropology articulated in chapter six, I do not believe that "soul

---

[15]I find texts such as Lk 16:19-31; 23:43, 46; Phil 1:23; and Rev 6:9 to be indicators that soul sleep is not in accordance with biblical language about death. The point here, however, is to point out that Christ's time in the tomb grounds whatever else we might say about the intermediate state, and specifically here about soul sleep. See also on this issue chapter six.

sleep"[16] or "immediate resurrection" are legitimate options regarding the intermediate state. If a christological anthropology is warranted— that is, if Christ's humanity is paradigmatic for ours—then both soul sleep and immediate resurrection would entail either of those for Jesus himself. And this we cannot adopt by virtue of the biblical and historical case made in chapters two and three.[17] This of course means that one's interpretation of the descent has implications for the intermediate state of believers. So, since Jesus descended only to paradise, and only as part of his "being dead," this tells us about the nature of the intermediate state for the believer,[18] namely, that it is a place where we consciously experience the joyful presence of Christ and await his second coming and our own bodily resurrection.

SABBATH REST

Another eschatological implication of Christ's burial is that it is, is in some ways, his Sabbath rest.[19] Although his ascension also should

---

[16]It is interesting that Luther advocated both for a view of the intermediate state that sometimes sounds like soul sleep and for the more traditional doctrine of the descent. This may be because, though, Luther's doctrine of the descent was bodily, not just soulish. For Luther's comments on the intermediate state, see Martin Luther, *Luther's Works* 28: *Commentary on 1 Corinthians 7 and 15 and 1 Timothy*, ed. Hilton Oswald (St. Louis: Concordia, 1973), 110, 200. His comments there suggest more of a kind of "soul sleep" position, but elsewhere he clarifies that "sleep" is a metaphor and does not deny the consciousness of the soul in the intermediate state. See Martin Luther, *Luther's Works*, vol. 4: *Lectures on Genesis Chapters 21–25*, ed. Jaroslav Pelikan (St. Louis: Concordia, 1964), 312; *Luther's Works*, vol. 8: *Lectures on Genesis Chapters 43–50*, ed. Jaroslav Pelikan (St. Louis: Concordia, 1966), 318; and *Luther's Works*, vol. 15: *Ecclesiastes, Song of Solomon, Last Words of David (2 Samuel 23:1-7)*, ed. Jaroslav Pelikan (St. Louis: Concordia, 1972), 147-50. For interpretations of Luther as explicitly affirming soul sleep, see Jürgen Moltmann, *Is There Life after Death?* (Milwaukee: Marquette University Press, 1998), 47; and Anthony C. Thiselton, *Life After Death: A New Approach to the Last Things* (Grand Rapids: Eerdmans, 2012), 68-69. Calvin, on the other hand, explicitly denies soul sleep.

[17]We also therefore cannot adopt the view, however palatable, of Anthony Thiselton, where our human souls are "asleep" and thus experience time in the intermediate state but are only conscious at the moment of death and the future moment of resurrection. See Thiselton, *Life after Death*, 72-79.

[18]On early Christian views of the hypostatic union and whether Christ descended bodily, see Wicks, "Christ's Saving Descent," 307-309.

[19]One recent theology of Holy Saturday is Alan E. Lewis, *Between Cross and Resurrection: A Theology of Holy Saturday* (Grand Rapids: Eerdmans, 2001). Lewis is heavily dependent upon Balthasar and Moltmann and focuses on Holy Saturday as Jesus' Sabbath. In doing so, however,

ultimately be characterized thus, because Jesus is crucified on the sixth day and in the tomb on the seventh, the burial does have sabbatarian symbolism.[20] Jesus finishes his work of salvation on the cross on the sixth day, rests on the seventh, and then on the eighth day rises again, inaugurating the new creation. The Sabbath for which the people of God hope (Heb 4:1-11)—the eschatological rest promised to Abraham, Isaac, and Jacob—is inaugurated in Christ's burial. Jesus' Passion inaugurates the last days in many ways, but the eschatological Sabbath rest is inaugurated specifically in Christ's burial and descent.[21]

EMBODIMENT OF ALREADY/NOT YET

Finally, Jesus' burial is eschatologically vicarious for all who are united with him because in it he embodies the already/not yet tension inherent to believers in the church age.[22] He sleeps, and in sleeping he takes on the inevitable state of all those who live and die before his return. Although those who are buried with him are also raised to new life (Rom 6:1-4), they still fall "asleep" (1 Thess 4:14) if they die before Jesus' return. There is thus a tension in their hope for the resurrection promised to them. There is hope in that because Christians are united to Christ *in his death*, they also anticipate that they will be united to him in his bodily resurrection (Rom 6:5; also Paul's language of sowing and reaping in 1 Cor 15:42-43). Because Christ has already experienced death, and experienced it *pro nobis*, Christians have hope that death is not the final experience. Rather, "since we believe that Jesus died and rose again, even so, through Jesus, God will bring with him those who have fallen asleep" (1 Thess 4:14). Still, though, this hope is "not yet." Those united to Christ

---

Lewis focuses on Jesus' time in the tomb as a "dark" and "atheistic" Sabbath rather than a positive rest. See Lewis, *Between Cross and Resurrection*, 31, 56, 78.

[20]Paul L. Redditt, "John 19:38-42," *Interpretation* 61.1 (2007): 68-70.

[21]For more on the descent and the Sabbath, see chapter eight.

[22]Note that this tension is inherent in the rest of the eschatological implications we have already mentioned. See, for example, Stefen Lösel, "A Plain Account of Christian Salvation? Balthasar on Sacrifice, Solidarity, and Substitution," *Pro Ecclesia* 13.2 (2004): 155, on the already/not yet tension in Christ's victory through the descent.

have yet to experience physical resurrection. Christ's burial embodies this same tension, with the OT promises of resurrection standing in apparent (but not real) conflict with Christ remaining in the grave. There is much here in common with the previous point about Christ's death being victorious, although here the specific point is that the death believers experience, and the subsequent tension between death and a promised resurrection, is experienced vicariously by Christ. This already/not yet character of Jesus' burial thus demonstrates yet another way in which Christ's descent is eschatological.

CONCLUSION

Christ's descent thus has eschatological import. Because in it he begins to proclaim victory over God's enemies; vicariously experiences the intermediate state; experiences and brings Sabbath rest; and embodies the already/not yet tension, it is a thoroughly eschatological aspect of the one work of redemption. Like the rest of Jesus' work, his descent inaugurates the last days; brings victory over Satan, sin, and death; and is vicarious for those united to Christ. The burial of Jesus is thus an integral piece of his vicarious work and helps to demonstrate the eschatological character of his full work of redemption.

PART THREE

THE DESCENT AND
THE CHRISTIAN LIFE

"AMEN"

Pastoral and Practical Implications of the Descent

Far from being an esoteric or practically irrelevant doctrine, the descent has important consequences for how Christians follow Christ. This is true not only of the descent but of all theology. In fact, the task of systematic theology is to demonstrate how Scripture's teachings bear upon and speak to our world. Therefore we want to conclude by making explicit the descent's impact on our lives as Christians, from how we read the Bible to how we worship to how we approach death.[1]

THE DESCENT AND BIBLICAL INTERPRETATION

Understanding how the two testaments fit together is part of the theological task, and also part of proper biblical interpretation. The descent speaks into this issue, since it is a doctrine that is particularly concerned with the fate of old covenant saints and what happens to them when the new covenant is finally

---

[1] While others, notably Alan Lewis, have attempted to demonstrate the descent's practical implications, here we want to show its implications not just for pastoral care of those facing death but also in other areas of the Christian life. Still, Lewis's work is considered a classic pastoral treatment of the descent. See Alan Lewis, *Between Cross and Resurrection: A Theology of Holy Saturday* (Grand Rapids: Eerdmans, 2001). For my part, while I appreciate Lewis's project, he relies too much on Balthasar's and Moltmann's understandings of the descent.

inaugurated in Christ's life, death, descent, resurrection, ascension, and gift of the Spirit. The definition of the descent upon which this book has relied is one that most closely aligns with progressive covenantalism.[2] This approach to biblical theology argues that, while there is a foundational continuity between the old and new covenants, such that Jesus' work fulfills all the hopes of OT Israel, there is also a progression from the Abrahamic covenant to the new covenant. This progression is effectively one from inclusion in the covenant people based on ethnicity to inclusion based on faith. This is why the sign of the covenant also progresses from circumcision to baptism.[3] The former is related to physical birth in the flesh, while the latter is related to new birth by the Spirit.

A second hermeneutical implication of the descent involves Bultmann's project of demythologization.[4] While we have argued that the spatial terminology of the descent is metaphorical, *metaphorical* does not mean "fictional" or "mythological." On the contrary, the NT writers used spatial, cosmological metaphors to communicate something that is very much true of our spiritual and bodily reality: Christ descended to the dead, his human body lowered into a tomb and his human soul departing to the spiritual realm of the righteous dead. Just because this

---

[2]See on this Stephen J. Wellum and Brent E. Parker, eds., *Progressive Covenantalism: Charting a Course Between Dispensational and Covenant Theologies* (Nashville: B&H Academic, 2016), and especially the two initial essays: Jason S. DeRouchie, "Father of a Multitude of Nations: New Covenant Ecclesiology in OT Perspective," 7-38; and Brent E. Parker, "The Israel-Christ-Church Relationship," 39-68.

[3]For more on this, see chapter eight.

[4]For a recent attempt to retrieve Bultmann's thought from mischaracterization, see David Congdon, *The Mission of Demythologizing: Rudolph Bultmann's Dialectical Theology* (Minneapolis: Fortress Press, 2015). While I am appreciative of any attempt to help readers understand a thinker rightly, and however much Congdon may correct past misunderstandings of Bultmann, this does not negate the fact that demythologization entails the rejection of certain theological and historical realities in the service of existential encounter. Jesus' historical resurrection of the dead is the obvious example, but here we should also mention the cosmological and metaphysical assumptions about the descent—namely, spiritual realms where human souls consciously exist. If Bultmann could not affirm the historicity of the resurrection, I doubt he would be willing to affirm the historicity of the descent or the metaphysic it entails.

spiritual realm is not geographically locatable does not mean it is any less real than Jerusalem or Rome.

DESCENT AND LITURGY

The descent also has implications for our corporate worship. While creedal recitation is not popular among evangelical churches by and large, it is making a resurgence these days in some corners of the evangelical movement. And yet in some cases, recovering a regular recitation of the Apostles' Creed is often ironically coupled with excising the descent clause. This is related to Grudem's argument, outlined and answered in chapters two and three. But it is also sometimes related to an anti-Catholic sentiment that often simmers under the surface of many low-church evangelical congregations and denominations. Both lifelong evangelicals and disaffected Roman Catholics who have left their tradition for evangelicalism often have trouble with anything in the worship service that feels "too Catholic," including creedal recitation. Particularly troubling in many cases is the descent clause. Additionally, many low-church evangelical[5] seminary students are trained to think about the descent almost exclusively in terms of the problematic, late, and idiosyncratic versions discussed in chapter three (e.g., universalist, purgatory-creating, experiencing torment, etc.). Thus the average layperson and church staff both associate the descent with its problematic elements, albeit perhaps for slightly different reasons.

Given this biblical and historical defense of the descent and its implications for the whole of Christian theology, I want to strongly urge evangelical churches and denominations to retain or reinstitute creedal

---

[5]I make this adjectival qualification to acknowledge that the Reformed, Lutheran, and Anglican traditions all have their own understanding of the descent. But in the case of at least the Reformed, the view expressed by Calvin and articulated in Heidelberg Catechism Q. 44 is, in my mind, historically idiosyncratic and biblically unwarranted (that is, in explaining *descendit ad inferos*) in light of the biblical and historical work in chapters two and three. And while many Lutherans and Anglicans would consider themselves evangelical, they seem to have been mostly immune (or at least resistant) to the most anti-liturgical and anti-creedal movements of American evangelicalism.

recitation, and to do so without excising or altering the descent clause. Creedal recitation in general has spiritual benefits, including hermeneutical, catechetical, and communal ones. It teaches Christians their doctrinal heritage, passed down by the church catholic,[6] and gives them the right doctrinal lens through which to read and understand the Scriptures. As we said in chapter one, creeds are only authoritative and beneficial insofar as they are faithful to Scripture, the ultimate authority for Christian faith and practice. But they have been proven over and over again over the course of the last 1500 years to be exactly that. And that includes the descent clause. For this reason, along with others given above, I want to exhort churches to recite the creeds and to include the descent clause in that recitation.

It would be appropriate in this regard, however, to translate *descendit ad inferos/inferna* as "descended to the dead" rather than "descended into hell." Given the ubiquitous use of "hell" in Western culture to mean "place of torment for the unrighteous dead," it is entirely appropriate and perhaps even necessary in our view to avoid confusion in our congregations and denominations by moving away from that particular translation of the Latin and instead using the alternative, "descended to the dead."

The descent and catechesis. This brings up the question of what to do with the Heidelberg Catechism (HC), Q. 44:

> Why is there added: He descended into hell? A: In my greatest sorrows and temptations I may be assured and comforted that my Lord Jesus Christ, by his unspeakable anguish, pain, terror, and agony, which he endured throughout all his sufferings but especially on the cross, has delivered me from the anguish and torment of hell.

As I have stated a few times, I affirm penal substitutionary atonement and so affirm this teaching of the HC. The question is whether or not penal substitution, and therefore HC 44's exposition of the descent, fits within

---

[6]Notice the lowercase "c": I use the word "catholic" here to mean "universal," not as a reference to the Roman Catholic Church.

the biblical, historical, and creedal teaching on Christ's descent to the dead. There are at least two ways to answer that question. One way is to say, based on the biblical and historical evidence presented in chapters two and three, that it is clearly not a reflection of the original intent of the creedal phrase or its reception through the medieval period. Therefore, according to this answer, we should suggest that Reformed churches adjust this answer.

Another way to answer the question, though, is to acknowledge still that the answer to HC 44 does not reflect the original intent or the early and medieval reception of the creedal phrase. Nevertheless, it does affirm something biblical, namely, the penal substitutionary nature of Christ's death. The suggestion that arises from this answer may be something like adding to HC 44, or pointing to the Westminster Shorter Catechism, Q. 27, which reads:

Q. 27. *Wherein did Christ's humiliation consist?*

A. Christ's humiliation consisted in his being born, and that in a low condition, made under the law, undergoing the miseries of this life, the wrath of God, and the cursed death of the cross; in being buried, and continuing under the power of death for a time.

This is almost verbatim from the Westminster Larger Catechism, Q. 50:

Q. 50. Wherein consisted Christ's humiliation after his death?

A. Christ's humiliation after his death consisted in his being buried, and continuing in the state of the dead, and under the power of death till the third day; which hath been otherwise expressed in these words, *He descended into hell* (italics original).

We would disagree that the descent is *exclusively* part of his humiliation, but the point here is that WSC 27 includes one of the main aspects of the descent, which is that Jesus experienced death like all humans do.

Interestingly, Francis R. Beattie, in his exposition of the Westminster Shorter Catechism, explains the descent much in the same vein as this book. He says of WSC 27,

This brings us to the deepest depths of his humiliation. . . . He remained in the state of the dead and under the power of death for a time. It is the midnight of his humiliation now. It seemed as if now, surely, the powers of darkness had gotten the victory, and that Satan had triumphed. Death, the penalty of sin, had laid him low, and the grave held him firmly in its grasp. He was really dead. His spirit had gone to God who gave it, and his body lay cold and lifeless in its rock-hewn tomb.

It is in this connection that the phrase in the Apostles' Creed, "and he descended into hell," which is alluded to in the Larger Catechism, properly comes up for some brief remarks. . . . To understand the phrase, the meaning of the word *hell* must be observed. It does not mean the place or state of the finally lost, but it rather denotes the invisible world of departed spirits. Hence, the meaning of the phrase is, that during the period between his death and his resurrection Christ's human spirit, or soul, was in the region of departed disembodied souls in the unseen world, and at the same time his body was lying in the tomb. In his case, of course, the departed human spirit would go to the estate of the blessed, for he had said to the thief on the cross, who died penitent, that they would be together that day in paradise. And all through even these experiences, the personal union of the human and the divine natures was not destroyed in the God-man. This completes the teaching of the Standards in regard to the humiliation of the Redeemer.[7]

This accords well with the biblical and historical data discussed in chapters two and three, and it provides an appropriate summary of that data. If used in concert with HC 44, then, and perhaps even as the main teaching on the descent (rather than HC 44 as primary, which anecdotally appears to be the case these days), this may serve as an appropriate way to retain HC 44 but also acknowledge that the WSC summarizes the

---

[7]This quote is from the Westminster Shorter Catechism Project website, Francis R. Beattie, "The Presbyterian Standards: Chapter XII. The Humiliation and Exaltation of Christ, i.4," Westminster Shorter Catechism Project, last modified February 12, 2018, www.shortercatechism.com /resources/beattie/wsc_be_027-028.html. See Francis R. Beattie, *The Presbyterian Standards: An Exposition of the Westminster Confession of Faith and Catechisms*, XIII.i.4 (Richmond: The Presbyterian Committee of Publication, 1897), 163-64. See also Charles E. Hill's recent article, "'He Descended into Hell,'" *RFP* 1.2 (2016): 3-10.

biblical, historical, and creedal sense of *descendit ad inferos* better. Of course, all of this is merely suggestion on my part, since I am not part of a Reformed denomination. Deciding how to catechize is ultimately up to those denominations that look to HC, WSC, WLC, and WCF as (derivatively) authoritative confessional documents.

The descent and baptism. The descent, as we have seen, also has strong connections to baptism. In many low-church evangelical contexts, baptism is merely a public affirmation of faith by the baptizand confirmed by some element or practice involving water (usually immersion), and usually it is associated with membership. While these are right and good understandings of baptism, the descent prods us to see other implications of the ordinance, and namely that it unites us to Christ's victorious death and resurrection. It is a visual representation of Christ's work that spiritually unites us to him and to the benefits of that work. There is a reason Luther urged Christians to remember their baptism when faced with temptation: not only does it remind us of our identity in Christ, but it also visually pictures for us Christ descending to defeat the enemies of Death and Hades. Christ achieves victory in his death and proclaims it in his descent. By faith and the regenerating power of the Holy Spirit, we participate in and reap the benefits of that victory. Baptism is victorious, a declaration that Christ has defeated our enemies and so we, too, live in victory over sin, death, and Satan. We should therefore attempt to liturgically recover those victorious aspects of baptism in churches where they have been lost, to remind the baptizand and those already baptized who are present that Christ has won the victory and we are united to him and his benefits by faith as pictured in baptism.[8]

THE DESCENT AND MISSIONS

Perhaps a less obvious implication of the descent is that it should spur on Protestant evangelicals in our evangelism and missions enterprises.

---

[8]For more on this, see chapter eight.

When Christians discuss Christ's atoning work on the cross, we often point to passages like John 14:6, Acts 4:12, all of Romans 10, and other texts that teach the exclusivity of Jesus' saving death. But in many circles, including, increasingly, Protestant and evangelical ones, the descent is treated as a sort of universalist hall pass. Jesus' descent, in this scenario, is a proclamation of victory over Death and Hades *for everyone everywhere.* As we saw in chapter seven, this is closely related to the descent's iconography, which usually includes Christ pulling Adam and Eve out of Hades.

But as I also argued in chapter seven, this understanding of the descent is mistaken on biblical and historical grounds. The descent is not an alternative means of salvation for those to whom Christ descends, nor does it pave the way for universalism.[9] On the contrary, it is one part of the one act of redemption enacted in the person and work of Jesus, a saving act that is exclusively and applied only to those who repent and believe in Christ.

Because the descent is only effective for those who believe; its exclusivity, like the exclusivity of Christ's death and resurrection—of his entire work—should motivate the church to evangelizing with abandon. Those who do not hear the gospel, proclaimed under the earth and on the earth and in heaven, are still under the authority of the prince of the power of the air and are still under the sway of Death and Hades. Christ has defeated these powers, but those who have not trusted Christ are still under the power of these powers. And they are on the road to an eternity in which their masters will not free them but instead be tormented with them in the lake of fire. Only Christ offers freedom from these powers and principalities. Only Christ has defeated them

---

[9] We should draw a connection here between this articulation of the descent's effectiveness and the more common assertion that the resurrection provides the basis for universalism. In that scenario, Christ's resurrection is the beginning of the renewal of all things, including those who in this life oppose Christ. The resurrection of the dead is a resurrection to life, for everyone. But the same critiques of a universalist understanding of the descent apply to a universalist understanding of the resurrection.

and can therefore free us from their clutches. And he only does so for those who repent of their former ways and trust him and him alone for salvation. This is the good news, the good news that Christ won on the cross, proclaimed to the dead ones, and embodied in his resurrection. And this is the good news that we should proclaim to the world, so that those who are now captives of Satan, Death, and Hades can be freed by faith through Christ, the one who has defeated their masters and paid their ransom.

THE DESCENT AND PASTORAL CARE

The most important practical application of the descent, at least in my opinion, is that it means that Christ experienced death in the same way we do and also defeated it. His human body went to the grave and his human soul went to the place of the (righteous) dead. This is not a natural state for humanity. Death is an effect of the fall (Gen 3:17-19; Rom 6:23), and Jesus became fully human to the point that he experienced the fullness of death. He did not die one moment on the cross and rise the next moment but remained dead for three days. This is a great comfort to those who are facing death or those who have lost loved ones. And those two categories encompass everyone on the planet.

When we, or those we love, face death, we can find assurance in the fact that Christ, too, has experienced death in all its fallen fullness. He really, truly died. His soul was separated from his body for three days. This is just as we will remain dead and just as our souls will remain separated from our bodies until Christ returns. Our Savior has gone before us. Just as the Ark of the Covenant went before the people of Israel through the wilderness for three days to find a place for them to rest (Num 10:33), so Christ has gone before us through the wilderness of Hades to prepare a place for us to rest in him.

But he has not only experienced the fullness of human death; he has also defeated it. Death does not have the last word. Those of us who trust Christ do not have hope only because Christ experienced it as we do, but because in it experiencing it as the God-Man he defeated it. And one day he will expel it fully and finally from his presence and from our experience. We do not remain dead, just as Christ did not remain dead, because Christ has defeated death in his death, descent, and resurrection. Because Christ rose, we long for the day when we will rise with him and dwell, bodily, with him forever on the new heavens and new earth.[10] This should also bring believers comfort here on earth as they experience evil, suffering, oppression, and all other effects of sin. Christ's descent answers the problem of evil because in it (and his death and resurrection) he has defeated the principalities and powers (Col 2:15).[11]

The descent, then, ought to be a great comfort to those facing death, whether their own or a loved one's. It is part of the reason we grieve, but not as those without hope (1 Thess 4:13). When we cite Paul's statement in funeral contexts, it is usually to point to the resurrection. And that is right and good, and the ultimate grounds of such hopeful grieving. But in the meantime, while we think of our departed dead, while we walk in their graveyards and look at their ashes and remember their lives, while we ponder our own deaths, and while we consider how long it is, O Lord, until the Second Coming, we do so with hope. We hope because Christ also remained buried in the grave, buried with us and for us. We hope because we have a High Priest who has experienced death as we all will, if the Lord tarries. We hope because we have an advocate who has experienced the pain of death and yet has done so victoriously, rising from it and drawing us with him on the last day. We therefore dig our graves, facing toward the East, knowing that as our bodies decompose, our souls remain with Christ, awaiting the day when he will with loud trumpets return and reunite our bodies and souls so that we

---

[10]For a clear, biblical, and theological exposition of the embodied reality of the new heavens and new earth, see Richard J. Middleton, *A New Heaven and a New Earth: Reclaiming Biblical Eschatology* (Grand Rapids: Baker Academic, 2014).

[11]See on this Fleming Rutledge, *The Crucifixion: Understanding the Death of Christ* (Grand Rapids: Eerdmans, 2015), 376, 413; and Jeremy Treat, *The Crucified King: Atonement and Kingdom in Biblical and Systematic Theology* (Grand Rapids: Zondervan Academic, 2014), 115-19.

can live with him forever by the power of his Spirit to the glory of the Father. Charles Hill summarizes this hope well:

> Christ descended into Hades so that you and I would not have to. Christ descended to Hades so that we might ascend to heaven. Christ entered the realm of death, the realm of the strong enemy, and came away with his keys. The keys of Death and Hades are now in our Savior's hands. And God his Father has exalted him to his right hand, and given him another key, the key of David, the key to the heavenly Jerusalem. He opens and no one will shut, he shuts and no one will open (Rev. 3.7). And praise to him, as the hymn says, "For he hath op'ed the heavenly door, and man is blessed forever more."
>
> All praise and honor and glory to the Lamb who has conquered! "Blessed are the dead who die in the Lord henceforth" (Rev. 14.13). And blessed are we here and now, who even now have this hope, and a fellowship with our Savior which is stronger than death! Thanks be to God. Amen.[12]

Maranatha. Come, Lord Jesus.

---

[12]Hill, "'He Descended into Hell,'" 10.

BIBLIOGRAPHY

Abernethy, Andrew T. *The Book of Isaiah and God's Kingdom: A Thematic-Theological Approach*. NSBT 40. Downers Grove, IL: IVP Academic, 2016.

Alfeyev, Hilarion. *Christ the Conqueror of Hell: The Descent into Hades from an Orthodox Perspective*. Crestwood, NY: St. Vladimir's Seminary Press, 2009.

Allen, Michael and Scott R. Swain. *Reformed Catholicity: The Promise of Retrieval for Theology and Biblical Interpretation*. Grand Rapids: Baker Academic, 2015.

_____, eds. *Christian Dogmatics: Reformed Theology for the Church Catholic*. Grand Rapids: Baker Academic, 2016.

Allison, Gregg R. *Sojourners and Strangers: The Doctrine of The Church*. Foundations of Evangelical Theology. Wheaton, IL: Crossway, 2012.

Anatolios, Khaled. *Retrieving Nicaea: The Development and Meaning of Trinitarian Doctrine*. Grand Rapids: Baker Academic, 2011.

Aquinas, Thomas. *Summa Theologica*. Translated by English Dominican Fathers. Westminster: Christian Classics, 1981.

Arnold, Clinton E. *Power and Magic: The Concept of Power in Ephesians*. Cambridge: Cambridge University Press, 1989. Reprint, Grand Rapids: Baker, 1992.

Aune, David F. *Revelation 1–5*. WBC 52A. Dallas: Word, 1997.

Avery-Peck, Alan J. and Jacob Neusner, eds. *Judaism in Late Antiquity*, vol. 4: *Death, Life-After-Death, Resurrection and the World-to-Come in the Judaisms of Late Antiquity*. Leiden: Brill, 2000.

Ayres, Lewis. *Nicaea and Its Legacy: An Approach to Fourth-Century Trinitarian Theology*. Oxford: Oxford University Press, 2004.

Bales, William A. "The Descent of Christ in Ephesians 4:9." *CBQ* 72 (2010): 84-100.

_____. "The Meaning and Function of Ephesians 4:9-10 in Both its Immediate and More General Context." PhD diss., The Catholic University of America, 2002.

Balthasar, Hans Urs von. *First Glance at Adrienne von Speyr*, 2nd ed. San Francisco: Ignatius, 2017.

_____. *Theo-Drama: Theological Dramatic Theory*, Part IV: *The Action*. Translated by Graham Harrison. San Francisco: Ignatius, 1994.

Barrett, C. K. *Acts 1–14*. ICC. London: T&T Clark, 1994.

Barth, Karl. *Church Dogmatics* II/2. Edinburgh: T&T Clark, 1957. Reprint, 2004.

_____. *Church Dogmatics* IV/1. Edinburgh: T&T Clark, 1967. Reprint, 2004.

Barth, Markus. *Ephesians: Introduction, Translation, and Commentary*. 2 vols. AB 34, 34A. Garden City, NY: Doubleday, 1974.

Bartholomew, Craig G. and Heath A. Thomas, eds. *A Manifesto for Theological Interpretation*. Grand Rapids: Baker Academic, 2016.

Bass, Justin W. *The Battle for the Keys: Revelation 1:18 and Christ's Descent into the Underworld*. Paternoster Biblical Monographs. Eugene, OR: Wipf and Stock, 2014.

_____. "Paradise." Edited by John D. Barry. *The Lexham Bible Dictionary*. Bellingham, WA: Lexham Press, 2016.

Bauckham, Richard. *The Fate of the Dead: Studies on the Jewish and Christian Apocalypses*. NovTSup 93. Atlanta: SBL Press, 1998.

_____. *Jesus and the God of Israel: God Crucified and Other Studies on the New Testament's Christology of Divine Identity*. Grand Rapids: Eerdmans, 2008.

Bauer, Walter and Frederick William Danker. *A Greek-English Lexicon of the New Testament and Other Early Christian Literature*, 3rd ed. Chicago: The University of Chicago Press, 2000.

Beale, G. K. *A New Testament Approach to Biblical Theology: The Unfolding of the Old Testament in the New*. Grand Rapids: Baker Academic, 2011.

_____. *The Book of Revelation: A Commentary on the Greek Text*. NICGT. Grand Rapids: Eerdmans, 1999.

_____. *John's Use of the Old Testament in Revelation*. JSNTSup 166. Sheffield: Sheffield Academic Press, 1998.

_____. "Peace and Mercy upon the Israel of God: The Old Testament Background of Galatians 6,16b." *Bib* 80 (1999): 204-23.

_____. *The Temple and The Church's Mission: A Biblical Theology of the Dwelling Place of God*. NSBT 17. Downers Grove, IL: InterVarsity Press, 2004.

Beattie, Francis R. *The Presbyterian Standards: An Exposition of the Westminster Confession of Faith and Catechisms*. Richmond: The Presbyterian Committee of Publication, 1897.

Bebbington, David. *Evangelicalism in Modern Britain: A History from the 1730s to the 1980s*. Grand Rapids: Baker, 1989.

Beckwith, Roger. *The Old Testament Canon of the New Testament Church and its Background in Early Judaism*. London: SPCK, 1985. Reprint, Eugene, OR: Wipf and Stock, 2008.

Bede the Venerable. *The Commentary on the Seven Catholic Churches of Bede the Venerable*. Kalamazoo: Cistercian, 1985.

Behr, John. *The Mystery of Christ: Life in Death*. Crestwood, NY: St. Vladimir's Seminary Press, 2006.

_____. *The Nicene Faith*, Part I. Formation of Christian Theology 2. Crestwood, NY: St. Vladimir's Seminary Press, 2004.

Bernabé, Alberto. "What Is *Katâbasis?* The Descent into the Netherworld in Greece and the Ancient Near East." *Les Études Classiques* 83 (2015): 15-34.

Best, Ernest. *A Critical and Exegetical Commentary on Ephesians*. ICC. Edinburgh: Clark, 1998.

Bettiolo, P., A. Giambelluca Kossova, C. Leonardi, E. Norelli, and L. Perrone, eds. *Ascensio Isaiae: Textus*. CCSA 7. Turnhout: Brepols, 1995.

Bird, Michael F. *What Christians Ought to Believe: An Introduction to the Apostles' Creed*. Grand Rapids: Zondervan, 2016.

Bloesch, Donald G. "Descent into Hell (Hades)." In *Evangelical Dictionary of Theology*, 2nd ed., ed. Walter E. Elwell, ed. 338-40. Grand Rapids: Baker Academic, 2001.

Blomberg, Craig. *Matthew*. NAC 22. Nashville: Broadman & Holman, 1992.

Borchert, Gerald R. *John 12–21*. NAC 25B. Nashville, Broadman and Holman, 2002.

Bratcher Robert G. and Eugene A. Nida. *A Translator's Handbook on Paul's Letter to the Ephesians*. Helps for Translators. New York: United Bible Societies, 1982.

Bray, Gerald, ed. *1–2 Corinthians*. ACCS NT 7. Downers Grove, IL: IVP Academic, 1999.

_____. "Whosoever Will Be Saved: The Athanasian Creed and the Modern Church." In *Evangelicals and Nicene Faith: Reclaiming the Apostolic Witness*, ed. Timothy George, 45-57. Grand Rapids: Baker Academic, 2011.

Bröse, E. "Der Descensus ad Inferos Eph. 4, 8-10." *NKZ* 9 (1898): 447-55.

Brotherton, Joshua R. "Damnation and the Trinity in Ratzinger and Balthasar." *Logos* 18.3 (2015): 123-50.

_____. "Hans Urs von Balthasar on the Redemptive Descent." *Pro Ecclesia* 22.2 (2013): 167-88.

_____. "The Possibility of Universal Conversion in Death: Temporality, Annihilation, and Grace." *ModTheo* 32.3 (2016): 307-24.

Brown, Raymond E. *The Gospel According to John XIII–XXI: A New Translation with Commentary*. AB 29. New Haven, CT: Yale University Press, 1970.

Brown, Warren S., Nancey Murphy, and H. Newton Malone, eds. *Whatever Happened to the Soul? Scientific and Theological Portraits of Human Nature*. Theology and the Sciences. Minneapolis: Augsburg Fortress, 1998.

Bruce, F. F. *The Epistles to the Colossians, to Philemon, and to the Ephesians*. NICNT. Grand Rapids: Eerdmans, 1984.

Bruns, H. D. *Canones Apostolorum et Conciliorum Veterum Selecti*, t. I. Berlin: G. Reimeri, 1839.

Buchan, Thomas. *"Blessed Is He Who Has Brought Adam from Sheol": Christ's Descent to the Dead in the Theology of Saint Ephrem the Syrian*. Gorgias Dissertation 13. Early Christian Studies 2. Piscataway: Gorgias Press, 2004.

Büchsel, Friedrich. "κατώτερος." In *TDNT* 3:640-42. Grand Rapids: Eerdmans, 1965. Reprint, 1995.

Budge, E. A., ed. *Coptic Homilies in the Dialect of Upper Egypt*. Papyrus Codex Oriental 5001. London, 1910.

Bulgakov, Sergius. *The Orthodox Church*. London: Centenary Press, 1935. Revised and translated by Lydia Kesich. Crestwood, NY: St. Vladimir's Seminary Press, 1988.

Burns, J. Patout, SJ, trans. and ed. *Theological Anthropology*. Sources of Early Christian Thought. Philadelphia: Fortress, 1981.

Buschart, W. David and Kent D. Eilers. *Theology as Retrieval: Receiving the Past, Renewing the Church*. Downers Grove, IL: IVP Academic, 2015.

Cahill, Jonathan. "The Descent into Solidarity: Christ's Descent into Hell as Stimulus for Justice." *JRT* 9 (2015): 237-48.

Caird, G. B. *Paul's Letters from Prison: Ephesians, Philippians, Colossians, Philemon, in the Revised Standard Version*. New Clarendon Bible. Oxford: Oxford University Press, 1976.

Calvin, John. *Institutes of the Christian Religion*, vol. I. The Library of Christian Classics. Edited by John T. McNeil. Translated by Ford Lewis Battles. Louisville, KY: Westminster John Knox, 1960. Reprint, 2006.

Carr, G. Lloyd. *The Song of Solomon*. TOTC 19. Downers Grove, IL: IVP Academic. Reprint, 2009.

Casey, R. P., ed. *The Excerpta ex Theodoto of Clement of Alexandria*. Studies and Documents. Cambridge: Harvard University Press, 1934.

Catechism of the Catholic Church 366. Mission Hills, CA: Benzinger, 1994.

Charlesworth, James H., ed. *The Old Testament Pseudepigrapha*, vol. 2: *Expansions of the 'Old Testament' and Legends, Wisdom and Philosophical Literature, Prayers, Psalms, and Odes, Fragments of Lost Judeo-Hellenistic Works*. New Haven, CT: Yale University Press, 1983. Reprint, Peabody, MA: Hendrickson, 2015.

Connell, Martin F. "*Descensus Christi Ad Inferos*: Christ's Descent to the Dead," *TS* 62 (2001): 262-82.

Conzelmann, Hans. *1 Corinthians: A Commentary on the First Epistle to the Corinthians*. Hermeneia. Philadelphia: Fortress Press, 1975.

Cooper, John W. *Body, Soul, & Life Everlasting: Biblical Anthropology and the Monism-Dualism Debate*. Grand Rapids: Eerdmans, 1989.

_____. "Whose Interpretation? Which Anthropology? Biblical Hermeneutics, Scientific Naturalism, and the Body-Soul Debate." In *Neuroscience and the Soul: The Human Person in Philosophy, Science, and Theology*, ed. Thomas M. Crisp, Steven L. Porter, and Gregg A. Ten Elshof, 238-57. Grand Rapids: Eerdmans, 2016.

Congdon, David. *The Mission of Demythologizing: Rudolph Bultmann's Dialectical Theology*. Minneapolis: Fortress Press, 2015.

Corcoran, Kevin. "The Constitution View of Persons." In *In Search of the Soul: Four Views of the Mind-Body Problem*, ed. Joel B. Green and Stuart L. Palmer, 153-76. Downers Grove, IL: InterVarsity Press, 2005.

Cortez, Marc. *Embodied Souls, Ensouled Bodies: An Exercise in Christological Anthropology and its Significance for the Mind/Body Debate*. London: T&T Clark, 2008.

_____. *Theological Anthropology: A Guide for the Perplexed*. London: T&T Clark, 2010.

Cox, Benjamin D. and Susan Ackerman. "Rachel's Tomb." *JBL* 128.1 (2009): 135-48.

Craig, William Lane and J. P. Moreland. *Philosophical Foundations of a Christian Worldview*, 1st ed. Downers Grove, IL: IVP Academic, 2003.

Crawford, Matthew R. *Cyril of Alexandria's Trinitarian Theology of Scripture*. Oxford Early Christian Studies. Oxford: Oxford University Press, 2014.

Crisp, Oliver D. "Desiderata for Models of the Hypostatic Union." In *Christology Ancient and Modern: Explorations in Constructive Dogmatics*, 19-41. Los Angeles Theology Conference Series 1. Grand Rapids: Zondervan Academic, 2013.

_____. *God Incarnate: Explorations in Christology*. London: T&T Clark, 2009.

_____. and Fred Sanders, eds. *The Christian Doctrine of Humanity: Explorations in Constructive Dogmatics*. Grand Rapids: Zondervan Academic, 2018.

Crisp, Thomas M., Steven L. Porter, and Gregg A. Ten Elshof, eds. *Neuroscience and the Soul: The Human Person in Philosophy, Science, and Theology*. Grand Rapids: Eerdmans, 2016.

Cummings, E. E. "who were so dark of heart they might not speak" (1950). In *Selected Poems*, ed. Richard S. Kennedy, 8. New York: Liveright, 1994.

Cyril of Alexandria. *Commentary on Isaiah*, vol. 3. Translated by Robert Charles Hill. Brookline, MA: Holy Cross Orthodox Press, 2008.

_____. *Commentary on the Gospel According to St John by S Cyril, Archbishop of Alexandria*, vol. 2. Translated by Thomas Randel. London: Walter Smith, 1885.

Daniélou, Jean. *The Theology of Jewish Christianity*. A History of Early Christian Doctrine before the Council of Nicaea 1. Philadelphia: Fortress Press, 1964.

Davids, Peter H. *The First Epistle of Peter*. NICNT. Grand Rapids: Eerdmans, 1990.

Davies, W. D. *The Territorial Dimensions of Judaism*. Berkeley: University of California Press, 1982.

Davis, John Jefferson. *Worship and the Reality of God: An Evangelical Theology of Real Presence*. Downers Grove, IL: IVP Academic, 2010.

D'Costa, Gavin. "The Descent into Hell as a Solution for the Problem of the Fate of Unevangelized Non-Christians: Balthasar's Hell, the Limbo of the Fathers and Purgatory." *IJST* 11.2 (2009):146-71.

de Boer, Martinus. *The Defeat of Death: Apocalyptic Eschatology in 1 Corinthians 15 and Romans 5*. Sheffield: JSOT, 1988.

deClaissé-Walford, Nancy, Rolf A. Jacobson, and Beth LaNeel Tanner. *The Book of Psalms*. NICOT. Grand Rapids: Eerdmans, 2014.

Dempster, Stephen G. "The Servant of the Lord." In *Central Themes in Biblical Theology: Mapping Unity in Diversity*, ed. Scott J. Hafemann and Paul R. House, 128-78. Downers Grove, IL: InterVarsity Press, 2007.

de Vaux, Roland. *Ancient Israel: Its Life and Institutions*. Translated by John McHugh. London: Darton, Longman and Todd, 1961. Reprint, 1998.

Donnelly, Colleen. "Apocryphal Literature, the Characterization of Satan, and the *Descensus ad Inferos* Tradition in England in the Middle Ages." *Religion & Theology* 24 (2017): 321-49.

Duby, Steven J. "Atonement, Impassibility and the *Communicatio Idiomatum*." *IJST* 17.3 (2015): 284-95.

_____. "The Cross and the Fullness of God: Clarifying the Meaning of Divine Wrath in Penal Substitution." *SBET* 29.2 (2011): 165-76.

Dunn, James D. G. *Christology in the Making: A New Testament Inquiry into the Origins of the Doctrine of the Incarnation*. London: SCM, 1980.

_____. *Romans 9–16*. WBC 38B. Dallas: Word, 1988.

Ellingworth, Paul. *The Epistle to the Hebrews: A Commentary on the Greek Text*. NICGT. Grand Rapids: Eerdmans, 1993.

Elwell, Walter E., ed. *Evangelical Dictionary of Theology*, 2nd ed. Grand Rapids: Baker Academic, 2001.

Emerson, Matthew Y. *Christ and the New Creation: A Canonical Approach to the Theology of the New Testament*. Eugene, OR: Wipf and Stock, 2013.

_____. "'He Descended to the Dead': The Burial of Christ and the Eschatological Character of the Atonement." *SBJT* 19.1 (Spring 2015): 115-32.

_____. "'The One Who Trampled Hades Underfoot': A Comparative Analysis of Christ's Descent to the Dead and Trinitarian Relations in Second Century Christian Texts and Hans Urs von Balthasar." *SJT*, forthcoming.

_____. "Mapping Anthropological Metaphysics with a *Descensus* Key: How Christ's Descent to the Dead Informs the Body-Mind Conversation." In *The Christian Doctrine of Humanity: Explorations in Constructive Dogmatics*, ed. Oliver D. Crisp and Fred Sanders, 200-216. Grand Rapids: Zondervan Academic, 2018.

_____. "The Role of Proverbs 8: Eternal Generation and Hermeneutics Ancient and Modern." In *Retrieving Eternal Generation*, ed. Fred Sanders and Scott R. Swain, 44-66. Grand Rapids: Zondervan Academic, 2017.

_____. "Victory, Atonement, Restoration, and Response: The Shape of the New Testament Canon and the Holistic Gospel Message." *STR* 3.2 (2012): 177-94.

_____ and R. Lucas Stamps. "Liturgy for Low-Church Baptists." *CTR* 14.2 (2017): 71-88.

Emery, Gilles, OP. *The Trinitarian Theology of St. Thomas Aquinas*. Translated by Francesca Aran Murphy. Oxford: Oxford University Press, 2007.

Erickson, Millard J. *Christian Theology*, 2nd ed. Grand Rapids: Baker Academic, 2005.

_____. "Did Jesus Really Descend into Hell?" *Christianity Today* 44.2 (2000): 74.

Evans, G. R. *The Language and Logic of the Bible: The Road to the Reformation*. Cambridge: Cambridge University Press, 2009.

Farrow, Douglas. *Ascension and Ecclesia: On the Significance of the Doctrine of the Ascension for Ecclesiology and Christian Cosmology*. Grand Rapids: Eerdmans, 2009.

Feinberg, John S. "1 Peter 3:18-20, Ancient Mythology, and the Intermediate State." *WTJ* 48 (1986): 303-36.

_____. *No One Like Him: The Doctrine of God*. Wheaton: Crossway, 2006.

Feldman, Emmanuel. *Biblical and Post-Biblical Defilement and Mourning: Law as Theology*. New York: Yeshiva University Press/KTAV Publishing, 1977.

Ferguson, Everett. *Baptism in the Early Church: History, Theology, and Liturgy in the First Five Centuries*. Grand Rapids: Eerdmans, 2009.

France, R. T. "Exegesis in Practice: Two Examples." In *New Testament Interpretation: Essays on Principles and Methods*, ed. I. Howard Marshall, 252-81. Grand Rapids: Eerdmans, 1977.

Frank, Georgia. "Christ's Descent to the Underworld in Ancient Ritual and Legend." In *Apocalyptic Thought in Early Christianity*, ed. Robert J., Daly, SJ, 211-26. Holy Cross Studies in Patristic Theology and History. Grand Rapids: Baker Academic, 2009.

Frankfort, Henri, H. A. Frankfort, John A. Wilson, Thorkild Jacobsen, and William A. Irwin. *The Intellectual Adventure of Ancient Man: An Essay on Speculative Thought in the Ancient Near East*. Chicago: University of Chicago Press, 1946. Reprint, 1977.

Friedman Richard Elliott, and Shawna Dolansky Overton. "Death and Afterlife: The Biblical Silence." In *Judaism in Late Antiquity*, vol. 4: *Death, Life-After-Death, Resurrection and the World-to-Come in the Judaisms of Late Antiquity*, ed. Alan J. Avery-Peck and Jacob Neusner, 35-59. Leiden: Brill, 2000.

Garland, David E. *1 Corinthians*. BECNT 7. Grand Rapids: Baker Academic, 2003.

_____. "A Life Worthy of the Calling: Unity and Holiness. Ephesians 4:1-24." *RevExp* 76 (1979): 517-27.

Garrett, Duane. *Song of Songs*. WBC 23B. Grand Rapids: Zondervan, 2004.

Gatch, Milton McCormick. "The Harrowing of Hell: A Liberation Motif in Medieval Theology and Devotional Literature." *Union Seminary Quarterly Review* 36 (1981): 75-88.

George, Timothy. "Introduction." In *Evangelicals and Nicene Faith: Reclaiming the Apostolic Witness*, ed. Timothy George, xvii-xxiv. Grand Rapids: Baker Academic, 2011.

Giles, Kevin. *The Eternal Generation of the Son: Maintaining Orthodoxy in Trinitarian Theology*. Downers Grove, IL: IVP Academic, 2012.

Goldingay, John. *Daniel*. WBC 30. Waco, TX: Word, 1989.

_____. *Psalms*, vol. I: *Psalms 1-41*. BCOTWP. Grand Rapids: Baker Academic, 2006.

Goris, Harm J. M. J. "Thomas Aquinas on Christ's Descent into Hell." In *The Apostles' Creed: 'He Descended into Hell,'* ed. Marcel Sarot and Archibald L. H. M. van Wieringen, 93-114. Studies in Theology and Religion 24. Leiden: Brill, 2018.

Gowan, Donald E. *Theology of the Prophetic Books: The Death and Resurrection of Israel*. Louisville, KY: Westminster John Knox, 1998.

Green, Joel B. "'Bodies—That Is, Human Lives': A Re-Examination of Human Nature in the Bible." In *Whatever Happened to the Soul? Scientific and Theological Portraits of Human Nature*, ed. Warren S. Brown, Nancey Murphy, and H. Newton Malone, 149-73. Theology and the Sciences. Minneapolis: Augsburg Fortress, 1998.

_____. *Body, Soul, and Human Life: The Nature of Humanity in the Bible*. Studies in Theological Interpretation. Grand Rapids: Baker Academic, 2008.

_____ and Stuart L. Palmer, eds. *In Search for the Soul: Four Views on the Mind-Body Problem*. Downers Grove, IL: IVP Academic, 2005.

Gregory the Great. *Letter* VII, 4. In *S. Gregorii Magni Opera, Registrum epistularum*, libri I–VII, ed. D. Norberg, 447-52. CCSL 140. Belgium: Brepols, 1982.

Gregory of Nyssa. *The Soul and the Resurrection.* Popular Patristics 12. Translated by Catherine P. Roth; edited by John Behr. Crestwood, NY: St. Vladimir's Seminary Press, 1993.

Griffiths, Paul J. *Decreation: The Last Things of All Creatures.* Waco, TX: Baylor University Press, 2014.

_____. "Is There a Doctrine of the Descent into Hell?" *Pro Ecclesia* 17.3 (2008): 257-68.

_____. *Song of Songs.* Brazos Theological Commentary on the Bible. Grand Rapids: Brazos, 2011.

Grillmeier, Aloys. *Christ in Christian Tradition* I. Atlanta: John Knox, 1975.

_____. "Der Gottesohn im Totenreich: soteriologische und christologische Motivierung der Descensuslehre in der alteren christlichen Überlieferung." *ZKT* 71 (1949): 1-53, 184-203.

Grudem, Wayne A. "Christ Preaching Through Noah: 1 Peter 3:19-20 in the Light of Dominant Themes in Jewish Literature." *TrinJ* 7 (1986): 3-31.

_____. "He Did Not Descend into Hell: A Plea for Following Scripture Instead of the Apostles' Creed." *JETS* 34.1 (1991): 103-13.

_____. *Systematic Theology: An Introduction to Biblical Doctrine.* Grand Rapids: Zondervan, 1994.

Gundry, Robert H. *Soma in Biblical Theology: With Emphasis on Pauline Anthropology.* SNTS 29. Cambridge: Cambridge University Press, 1976.

Habel, Norman C. *The Land is Mine: Six Biblical Land Ideologies.* Overtures to Biblical Theology. Minneapolis: Augsburg Fortress, 1995.

Habets, Myk. "Putting the 'Extra' Back into Calvinism." *SJT* 62.4 (2009): 441-56.

Hamilton, James M. "The Lord's Supper in Paul: An Identity-Forming Proclamation of the Gospel." In *The Lord's Supper: Remembering and Proclaiming the Lord's Death Until He Comes*, ed. Thomas R. Schreiner and Matthew R. Crawford, 68-102. NAC Studies in Bible and Theology 10. Nashville: B&H Academic, 2010.

_____. *With the Clouds of Heaven: The Book of Daniel in Biblical Theology.* NSBT 32. Downers Grove, IL: IVP Academic, 2014.

Hamilton, Victor P. *The Book of Genesis: Chapters 18–50.* NICOT. Grand Rapids: Eerdmans, 1995.

Hamm, Jeffrey L. "*Descendit*: Delete or Declare? A Defense Against the Neo-Deletionists." *WTJ* (2016): 93-116.

Hanson, Anthony Tyrrell. *The New Testament Interpretation of Scripture.* London: SPCK, 1980.

Harris, W. Hall. *The Descent of Christ: Ephesians 4:7-11 and Traditional Hebrew Imagery.* AGJU 32. Leiden: Brill, 1996.

Harrison, Robert Pogue. *The Dominion of the Dead.* Chicago: The University of Chicago Press, 2003.

Hartog, Paul, ed. *Polycarp's* Epistle to the Ephesians *and the* Martyrdom of Polycarp: *Introduction, Text, and Commentary.* Oxford Apostolic Fathers. Oxford: Oxford University Press, 2013.

Hastings, James, ed. *Encyclopedia of Religion and Ethics,* vol. 4, *Confirmation–Drama.* Edinburgh: T&T Clark, 1912. Reprint, 1981.

Hauge, Matthew Ryan. *The Biblical Tour of Hell.* LNTS 485. London: Bloomsbury, 2013.

Hays, Christopher B. *A Covenant with Death: Death in the Iron Age II and Its Rhetorical Uses in Proto-Isaiah.* Tübingen: Mohr Siebeck, 2011. Reprint, Grand Rapids: Eerdmans, 2011.

Heiser, Michael S. *The Unseen Realm: Recovering the Supernatural Worldview of the Bible.* Bellingham: Lexham, 2015.

Herzog, Markwart. *"Descensus Ad Inferos": Eine religionphilosophische Untersuchung der Motive und Interpretationen mit besonderer Berücksichtigung der monographischen Literatur seit dem 16. Jahrundert.* Frankfurter Theologische Studien 53. Frankfurt: Knecht, 1997.

Hill Charles E. "'He Descended into Hell.'" *RFP* 1.2 (2016): 3-10.

Himmelfarb, Martha. *Tours of Hell: An Apocalyptic Form in Jewish and Christian Literature.* Philadelphia: Fortress Press, 1983.

Hoehner, Harold W. *Ephesians: An Exegetical Commentary.* Grand Rapids: Baker, 2002.

Hoekema, Anthony. *The Bible and the Future.* Grand Rapids: Eerdmans, 1979.

Holmes, Michael W. *The Apostolic Fathers: Greek Texts and English Translations,* 3rd ed. Grand Rapids: Baker Academic, 2007.

Hopkins, Gerard Manley. "41 'No worst, there is none. Pitched past pitch of grief.'" Poems of Gerard Manley Hopkins. Humphrey Milford, 1918.

———. "O Death, Death." Page 61 in *The Major Works,* ed. and with an Introduction and Notes by Catherine Phillips. Oxford World Classics; Oxford: Oxford University Press, 1986; rev. ed., 2002; repr., 2009.

Horton, Michael. *The Christian Faith: A Systematic Theology for Pilgrims on the Way.* Grand Rapids: Zondervan Academic, 2011.

Hughes, Langston. "Drum." In *Selected Poems of Langston Hughes,* 87. New York: Vintage Classics, 1959.

Irwin, William A. "The Hebrews." In *The Intellectual Adventure of Ancient Man: An Essay on Speculative Thought in the Ancient Near East,* ed. Henri Frankfort, H. A. Frankfort, John A. Wilson, Thorkild Jacobsen, and William A. Irwin, 223-362. Chicago: The University of Chicago Press, 1946. Reprint, 1977.

Jobes, Karen H. *1 Peter.* BECNT. Grand Rapids: Baker Academic, 2005.

John of Damascus. *An Exact Exposition of Orthodox Faith* 3, 29. PG 94:1101a.

Johnson, Keith L. "'He Descended into Hell.'" *Christian Reflection* 50 (2014): 27-34.

Johnson, Raymond. "I See Dead People: The Function of the Resurrection of the Saints in Matthew 27:51-54." Unpublished PhD diss. Louisville, KY: The Southern Baptist Theological Seminary, 2017.

Johnston, Philip S. *Shades of Sheol: Death and Afterlife in the Old Testament*. Downers Grove, IL: IVP Academic, 2002.

Jones, David. "To Bury or To Burn? Toward an Ethic of Cremation." *JETS* 53.2 (2010): 335-47.

Jones, Mark. "John Calvin's Reception at the Westminster Assembly (1643–1649)." *CHRC* 91.1-2 (2011): 215-27.

Karmires, I. *He eis haidou kathodos Christou*. Athens, 1939.

Keating, Daniel. "Christ's Despoiling of Hades: According to Cyril of Alexandria." *St. Vladimir's Theological Quarterly* 55.3 (2011): 253-69.

Keener, Craig S. *The Gospel of John: A Commentary*, vol. II. Peabody, MA: Hendrickson, 2003.

King Philip J. and Lawrence E. Stager. *Life in Biblical Israel*. Library of Ancient Israel. Louisville, KY: Westminster John Knox, 2001.

Kingsmill, Edmée. *The Song of Songs and the Eros of God: A Study in Biblical Intertextuality*. Oxford Theology and Religion Monographs. Oxford: Oxford University Press, 2010.

Klann, Richard. "Christ's Descent into Hell." *Concordia Journal* (1976): 43-47.

Kolb, Robert. "Christ's Descent into Hell as Christological Locus in the Era of the 'Formula of Concord.'" *Lutherjarbuch* 69 (2002): 101-18.

König, Adrio. *The Eclipse of Christ in Eschatology: Toward a Christ-Centered Approach*. Grand Rapids: Eerdmans, 1989.

Kreitzer, Larry J. "The Plutonium of Hierapolis and the Descent of Christ into the 'Lowermost Parts of the Earth' (Ephesians 4,9)." *Bib* 79 (1998): 381-93.

Kroll, Josef. *Gott ünd Hölle: Der Mythos vom Descensuskampfe*. Leipzig: Studien der Bibliothek Warburg, 1932. Reprint, Darmstadt: Wissenschaftliche Buchgesellschaft, 1963.

Kukota, Irina. "Christ, the Medicine of Life: The Syriac Fathers on the Lord's Descent into Hell." *Road to Emmaus* 6.1 (2005): 17-56.

Kyrtatas, Dimitris J. "The Origins of Christian Hell." *Numen* 56 (2009): 282-97.

Eric LaRock, "Neuroscience and the Hard Problem of Consciousness." In *Neuroscience and the Soul: The Human Person in Philosophy, Science, and Theology*, ed. Thomas M. Crisp, Steven L. Porter, and Gregg A. Ten Elshof, 151-80. Grand Rapids: Eerdmans, 2016.

Lattke, Michael. *The Odes of Solomon: A Commentary*. Hermeneia. Minneapolis, Fortress, 2009.

Lauber, David. *Barth on the Descent into Hell: God, Atonement and the Christian Life*. Barth Studies. Burlington: Ashgate, 2004.

Laufer, Catherine Ella. *Hell's Destruction: An Exploration of Christ's Descent to the Dead*. Surrey: Ashgate, 2013.

Law, David R. "Descent into Hell, Ascension, and Luther's Doctrine of Ubiquitarianism." *Theology* 107.838 (2004): 250-56.

Leo, Russ. "Jean Calvin, Christ's Despair, and the Reformation *Descensus ad Inferos.*" *Reformation* 23.1 (2018): 53-78.

Levenson, John D. *The Death and Resurrection of the Beloved Son: Transformation of Child Sacrifice in Judaism and Christianity*. New Haven, CT: Yale University Press, 1995.

Levering, Matthew. *Jesus and the Demise of Death: Resurrection, Afterlife, and the Fate of the Christian*. Waco, TX: Baylor University Press, 2012.

Lewis, Alan E. *Between Cross and Resurrection: A Theology of Holy Saturday*. Grand Rapids: Eerdmans, 2001.

Lewis, C. S. *The Voyage of the Dawn Treader*. The Chronicles of Narnia, Book 5. New York: Harper Trophy, 1952. Reprint, 1980.

Lincoln, Andrew T. *Born of a Virgin? Reconceiving Jesus in the Bible, Tradition, and Theology*. Grand Rapids: Eerdmans, 2013.

_____. *Ephesians*. WBC 42. Dallas: Word, 1990.

Lindbeck, George. *The Nature of Doctrine: Religion and Theology in a Postliberal Age*. Louisville, KY: Westminster John Knox, 1984.

Lindemann, A. *Der erste Korintherbrief*. Tübingen: Mohr Siebeck, 2000.

Lints, Richard. *The Fabric of Theology: A Prolegomena to Evangelical Theology*. Grand Rapids: Eerdmans, 1993.

Loftin, R. Keith and Joshua R. Farris, eds. *Christian Physicalism? Philosophical and Theological Criticisms*. Lanham: Lexington Books, 2017.

Longenecker, Richard N. *The Christology of Early Jewish Christianity*. SBT 2/17. London: SCM, 1970.

Loofs, Friedrich. "Descent to Hades (Christ's)." In *Encyclopedia of Religion and Ethics*, vol. 4, *Confirmation–Drama*, ed. James Hastings, 654-63. Edinburgh: T&T Clark, 1912. Reprint, 1981.

Lösel, Steffen. "A Plain Account of Salvation? Balthasar on Sacrifice, Solidarity, and Substitution." *Pro Ecclesia* 13.2 (2004): 141-71.

Lossky, Vladimir. *The Mystical Theology of the Eastern Church*. Cambridge: James Clarke & Co., 1957. Reprint, Crestwood, NY: St. Vladimir's Seminary Press, 2002.

Ludlow, Morwenna. *Universal Salvation: Eschatology in the Thought of Gregory of Nyssa and Karl Rahner*. Oxford Theology and Religion Monographs. Oxford: Clarendon Press, 2001. Reprint, Oxford: Oxford University Press, 2009.

Lundberg, Per. *La typologie baptismale dans l'ancienne église*. Uppsala: Lorentz, 1942.

Lunn, Nicholas P. "Jesus, the Ark, and the Day of Atonement: Intertextual Echoes in John 19:38–20:18." *JETS* 52.4 (December 2009): 731-46.

Luther, Martin. "Christ lag in Todesbanden," (1524). Text and translation from Emmanuel Music. Pamela Dellal, "Cantata for the First Day of Easter" by Johann Sebastian Bach, accessed May 7, 2019. www.emmanuelmusic.org /notes_translations/translations_cantata/t_bwv004.htm.

_____. *Luther's Works 4: Lectures on Genesis Chapters 21–25*. Edited by Jaroslav Pelikan. St. Louis: Concordia, 1964.

_____. *Luther's Works 8: Lectures on Genesis Chapters 43–50*. Edited by Jaroslav Pelikan. St. Louis: Concordia, 1966.

_____. *Luther's Works 15: Ecclesiastes, Song of Solomon, Last Words of David (2 Samuel 23:1-7)*. Edited by Jaroslav Pelikan. St. Louis: Concordia, 1972.

_____. *Luther's Works 28: Commentary on 1 Corinthians 7 and 15 and 1 Timothy*. Edited by Hilton Oswald. St. Louis: Concordia, 1973.

_____. "Third Sermon at Torgau, April 17, 1533." In *Luther's Works*, vol. 57: *Sermons IV*, ed. Benjamin T. Mayes, 127-38. St. Louis: Concordia, 2016.

Luz, Ulrich. *Matthew: A Commentary*. Hermeneia. Minneapolis: Augsburg, 2001.

MacCulloch, J. A. "Descent to Hades (Ethnic)." *Encyclopedia of Religion and Ethics*, vol. 4, *Confirmation–Drama*, ed. James Hastings, 648-54. Edinburgh: T&T Clark, 1912. Reprint, 1981.

_____. *The Harrowing of Hell: A Comparative Study of An Early Christian Doctrine*. Edinburgh: T&T Clark, 1930.

Marcovich, Miroslav. *Iustini Martyris Dialogus cum Tryphone*. Patristische Texte und Studien 47. Berlin: Walter de Gruyter, 1997.

Márquez, Gabriel García. *One Hundred Years of Solitude*. Translated by Gregory Rabassa. Harper Perennial Modern Classics. New York: HarperCollins, 2006.

Marshall, I. Howard. *1 Peter*. IVPNTC 17. Downers Grove, IL: InterVarsity Press, 1991.

_____. *The Gospel of Luke: A Commentary on the Greek Text*. NICGT. Grand Rapids: Eerdmans, 1978.

Martin-Achard, Robert. *From Death to Life: A Study of the Development of the Doctrine of the Resurrection in the Old Testament*. Translated by John Penney Smith. Oliver and Boyd: Edinburgh, 1960.

Maximus the Confessor. *Questions-Answers to Thalassius 7*. PG 90:284bc.

_____. *Questions-Answers to Thalassius 47*. CCSG 7:325, ll. 214-16.

_____. *Questions-Answers to Thalassius 64*. CCSG 22:195, ll. 147-51.

Mays, James L. *The Lord Reigns: A Theological Handbook to the Psalms*. Louisville, KY: Westminster John Knox, 1994.

McCann, J. Clinton. *A Theological Introduction to the Book of Psalms: The Psalms as Torah*. Nashville: Abingdon, 1993.

McDermott, Gerald R., ed. *Oxford Handbook of Evangelical Theology*. Oxford: Oxford University Press, 2010.

McDonnell, Kilian. "The Baptism of Jesus in the Jordan and the Descent into Hell." *Worship* 69.2 (1995): 98-109.

McGrath, Alister E. "Faith and Tradition." In *Oxford Handbook of Evangelical Theology*, ed. Gerald R. McDermott, 81-98. Oxford: Oxford University Press, 2010.

_____. *The Genesis of Doctrine: A Study in the Foundation of Doctrinal Criticism*. Grand Rapids: Eerdmans, 1997.

McGuckin, John A. "Eschatological Horizons in the Cappadocian Fathers." In *Apocalyptic Thought in Early Christianity*, ed. Robert J., Daly, SJ, 193-210. Holy Cross Studies in Patristic Theology and History. Grand Rapids: Baker Academic, 2009.

_____. "Introduction." *On the Unity of Christ* by St. Cyril of Alexandria. Translated and edited by John Anthony McGuckin, 9-48. Crestwood, NY: St. Vladimir's Seminary Press, 1995.

McKnight, Scot. *The King Jesus Gospel: The Original Good News Revisited.* Revised ed. Grand Rapids: Zondervan, 2016.

McMartin, Jason. "Holy Saturday and Theological Anthropology." In *Christian Physicalism? Philosophical and Theological Criticism,* ed. R. Keith Loftin and Joshua R. Farris, 117-36. Lanham: Lexington Books, 2017.

Melito of Sardis, *On Pascha and Fragments.* Translated and edited by Stuart George Hall. Oxford Early Christian Texts. Oxford: Oxford University Press, 1979. Revised reprint, Oxford: Clarendon, 2012.

_____. *On Pascha.* Translated by Alistair Stewart-Sykes. Popular Patristics 20. Crestwood, NY: St. Vladimir's Seminary Press, 2001.

Michaels, J. Ramsey. *1 Peter.* WBC 49. Waco, TX: Word, 1988.

Middleton, Richard J. *A New Heaven and a New Earth: Reclaiming Biblical Eschatology.* Grand Rapids: Baker Academic, 2014.

Moltmann, Jürgen. *The Crucified God: The Cross of Christ as the Foundation and Criticism of Christian Theology.* London: SCM, 1974. Reprint, Minneapolis: Fortress Press, 1993.

_____. "'Descent into Hell.'" *Duke Divinity School Review* 33.2 (1968): 115-19.

_____. *Is There Life after Death?* Milwaukee: Marquette University Press, 1998.

Morgan, Christopher W. and Robert A. Peterson, eds. *Faith Comes by Hearing: A Response to Inclusivism.* Downers Grove, IL: InterVarsity Press, 2008.

Morris, Leon. *The Gospel According to Matthew.* PNTC. Grand Rapids: Eerdmans, 1992.

_____. *The Gospel According to John.* Revised ed. NICNT. Grand Rapids: Eerdmans, 1995.

Mounce, Robert H. *Romans.* NAC 27. Nashville: Broadman & Holman, 1995.

Muller, Richard A. *Dictionary of Latin and Greek Theological Terms: Drawn Principally from Protestant Scholastic Theology.* Grand Rapids: Baker, 1985.

Murphy, Nancey S. *Bodies and Souls, or Spirited Bodies? Current Issues in Theology.* Cambridge: Cambridge University Press, 2006.

Nautin, Pierre, ed. *Homélies Paschales,* I, *Une Homélie inspire du traité su la Paque d'Hippolyte.* SC 27. Freiburg: Herder, 1950.

Nettles, Tom J. "He Descended into Hell." *Modern Reformation* 11 (2002): 38-41.

Nichols, Terrence. *Death and Afterlife: A Theological Introduction.* Grand Rapids: Brazos, 2010.

Nolland, John. *The Gospel of Matthew: A Commentary on the Greek Text.* Grand Rapids: Eerdmans, 2005.

Norelli, E. *L'Ascensione di Isaia: Studi su un apocrifo al crocevia dei cristianesimi.* Origini Nuova Serie 1. Bologna: Centro Editorial Dehoniano, 1994.

Oakes, Edward T. "*Descensus* and Development: A Response to Recent Rejoinders." *IJST* 13.1 (2011): 3-24.

_____. "The Internal Logic of Holy Saturday in the Theology of Hans Urs von Balthasar." *IJST* 9.2 (2007): 184-99.

_____ and Alyssa Lyra Pitstick, "Balthasar, Hell, and Heresy: An Exchange." *First Things* 168 (December 2006): 25-32.

Oberman, Heiko O. *The Harvest of Medieval Theology.* Cambridge: Harvard University Press, 1963. Reprint, Grand Rapids: Baker Book House, 2000.

O'Keefe, John and R. R. Reno. *Sanctified Vision: An Introduction to Early Christian Interpretation of the Bible.* Baltimore: Johns Hopkins University Press, 2005.

Osiek, Carolyn. *The Shepherd of Hermas: A Commentary on the Shepherd of Hermas.* Hermeneia. Minneapolis: Fortress, 1990.

Papaioannou, Kim. *The Geography of Hell in the Teaching of Jesus: Gehena, Hades, the Abyss, the Outer Darkness Where There is Weeping and Gnashing of Teeth.* Eugene, OR: Pickwick, 2013.

Peel, Malcolm L. "The 'Descensus Ad Inferos' in 'The Teachings of Silvanus (CG VII, 4).'" *Numen* 26.1 (1979): 39-49.

Perkins, Pheme. *Ephesians.* Abingdon New Testament Commentaries. Nashville: Abingdon, 1997.

Pitstick, Alyssa Lyra. *Christ's Descent into Hell: John Paul II, Joseph Ratzinger, and Hans Urs von Balthasar on the Theology of Holy Saturday.* Grand Rapids: Eerdmans, 2016.

_____. *Light in Darkness: Hans Urs von Balthasar and the Catholic Doctrine of Christ's Descent into Hell.* Grand Rapids: Eerdmans, 2013.

Polkinghorne, John. *The God of Hope and the End of the World.* New Haven, CT: Yale University Press, 2002.

Pope, Marvin H. *Song of Songs: A New Translation with Introduction and Commentary.* AB. New York: Doubleday, 1977.

Rahner, Karl. "Scripture and Theology." In *Theological Investigations* 6, 89-97. Baltimore: Helicon, 1969.

Ramelli, Ilaria L. E. *The Christian Doctrine of* Apokatastasis: *A Critical Assessment from the New Testament to Eriugena.* VCSup 120. Leiden: Brill, 2013.

Ratzinger, Joseph. *Eschatology: Death and Eternal Life*, 2nd ed. Washington, DC: Catholic University of America Press, 1988.

_____ and William Congdon. *The Sabbath of History.* Washington, DC: William G. Congdon Foundation, 2000.

Redditt, Paul L. "John 19:38-42." *Interpretation* 61.1 (2007): 68-70.

Reno, R. R. *Genesis.* Brazos Theological Commentary on the Bible. Grand Rapids: Brazos, 2010.

Romanos the Melodist. *Kontakion* 44. SC 128, 558.

Rousseau, A. and L. Doutreleau, *Irénée de Lyon: Contre le Hérésies, Livre I* SC 263–64. Paris: Cerf, 1979.

_____. *Irénée de Lyon: Contre le Hérésies, Livre II* SC 293–94. Paris: Cerf, 1984.

_____. *Irénée de Lyon: Contre le Hérésies, Livre III* SC 100, 2 vols. Paris: Cerf, 1974.

Rousseau, A., B. Hemmerdinger, L. Doutreleau, and C. Mercier. *Irénée de Lyon: Contre le Hérésies, Livre IV* SC 210–11. Paris: Cerf, 1965.

Rudman, Dominic. "The Sign of Jonah." *ExpTim* 115.10 (2004): 325-28.

Rutledge, Fleming. *The Crucifixion: Understanding the Death of Christ*. Grand Rapids: Eerdmans, 2015.

Sanders, Fred. *The Triune God*. New Studies in Dogmatics. Grand Rapids: Zondervan Academic, 2016.

Sarot, Marcel, and Archibald L. H. M. van Wieringen, eds. *The Apostles' Creed: 'He Descended into Hell.'* Studies in Theology and Religion 24. Leiden: Brill, 2018.

Saward, John. *Mysteries of March: Hans Urs von Balthasar on the Incarnation and Easter*. Washington, DC: Catholic University of America Press, 1990.

Scaer, David P. "He Did Descend to Hell: In Defense of the Apostles' Creed." *JETS* 35.1 (1992): 91-99.

Schaff, Philip. *The Creeds of Christendom*, 3 vols. Edited by Philip Schaff. Revised by David S. Schaff. New York: Harper & Row, 1931. Reprint, Grand Rapids: Baker, 2007.

_____. *History of the Christian Church*. New York: Scribner's Sons, 1858. Reprint, Peabody, MA: Hendrickson, 1996.

Schnackenburg, Rudolph. *Ephesians: A Commentary*. Translated by Helen Heron. Edinburgh: Clark, 1991.

Schrage, Wolfgang. *Der erste Brief an die Korinther*, vol. 4. Zurich: Benziger, 2001.

Schreiner, Thomas R. *New Testament Theology: Magnifying God in Christ*. Grand Rapids: Baker Academic, 2008.

_____. *Romans*. BECNT 6. Grand Rapids: Baker Academic, 1998.

_____. and Matthew R. Crawford, eds. *The Lord's Supper: Remembering and Proclaiming the Lord's Death Until He Comes*. NAC Studies in Bible and Theology 10. Nashville: B&H Academic, 2010.

_____ and Shawn D. Wright, eds. *Believer's Baptism: Sign of the New Covenant in Christ*. NAC Studies in Bible and Theology. Nashville: B&H Academic, 2006.

Schoedel, William R. *Ignatius of Antioch: A Commentary on the Letters of Ignatius of Antioch*. Hermeneia. Minneapolis, Fortress, 1985.

Selwyn, E. G. *The First Epistle of St. Peter: The Greek Text with Introduction, Notes, and Essays*, 2nd ed. Grand Rapids: Baker, 1981.

Sharley, Lucas W. "Calvin and Turretin's Views of the Trinity in the Dereliction." *RTR* 75.1 (2016): 21-34.

Simonetti, Manlio. "Sull'interpretazione patristica di Proverbi 8, 22." In *Studi sull'Arianesimo*, 9-87. Rome: Editrice Studium, 1965.

Sklar, Jay. *Leviticus*. TOTC 3. Downers Grove, IL: IVP Academic, 2014.

_____. *Sin, Impurity, Sacrifice, Atonement: The Priestly Conceptions*. HBM 2. Sheffield: Sheffield Phoenix, 2015.

Smith Billy K. and Frank S. Page. *Amos, Obadiah, Jonah*. NAC 19B. Nashville: Broadman & Holman, 1995.

Smith, James K. A. *Desiring the Kingdom: Worship, Worldview, and Cultural Formation* Cultural Liturgies 1. Grand Rapids: Baker Academic, 2009.

_____. *Imagining the Kingdom: How Worship Works*. Cultural Liturgies 2. Grand Rapids: Baker Academic, 2013.

_____. *Who's Afraid of Postmodernism? Taking Derrida, Foucault, and Lyotard to Church*. The Church and Postmodern Culture. Grand Rapids: Baker Academic, 2006.

_____. *Who's Afraid of Relativism? Community, Contingency, and Creaturehood*. The Church and Postmodern Culture. Grand Rapids: Baker Academic, 2014.

_____. *You Are What You Love: The Spiritual Power of Habit*. Grand Rapids: Brazos, 2016.

Springer, Carl P. E. "Of Triumph and Triumphalism: Etymological and Poetical Considerations." *Logia* 26.1 (2017): 5-13.

Stamps, R. Lucas. *"Thy Will Be Done": A Contemporary Defense of Two Wills Christology*. Minneapolis: Fortress Press, forthcoming.

Steiner, Richard C. *Disembodied Souls: The* Nefesh *in Israel and Kindred Spirits in the Ancient Near East, with an Appendix on the Katumura Inscription*. Ancient Near Eastern Monographs. Atlanta: SBL Press, 2015.

Stewart, Kenneth J. *In Search of Ancient Roots: The Christian Past and the Evangelical Identity Crisis*. Downers Grove, IL: IVP Academic, 2017.

Stone, Samuel J. "The Church's One Foundation" (1866). Music by Samuel Sebastian Wesley. FBC Radio; accessed May 7, 2019, www.fbcradio.org /lyrics/2845/.

Strawn, Brent A. "My Favorite Part of the Creed: 1 Peter 3:13-22." *Journal for Preachers* 38.3 (2015): 20-25.

Sumner, Darren O. "The Twofold Life of the Word: Karl Barth's Critical Reception of the *Extra Calvinisticum*." *IJST* 15.1 (2013): 42-57.

Suriano, Matthew J. "Sheol, the Tomb, and the Problem of Postmortem Existence." *JHS* 16.11 (2016): 1-31.

Swain, Scott R. "Divine Trinity." In *Christian Dogmatics: Reformed Theology for the Church Catholic*, ed. Michael Allen and Scott R. Swain, 78-106. Grand Rapids: Baker Academic, 2016.

_____. *Trinity, Revelation, and Reading: A Theological Introduction to the Bible and its Interpretation*. T&T Clark Theology. London: T&T Clark, 2011.

Sweeney, Marvin A. *The Twelve Prophets*, vol. 1: *Hosea, Joel, Amos, Obadiah, Jonah*. Berit Olam: Studies in Hebrew Narrative and Poetry. Edited by David W. Cotter. Collegeville: Liturgical Press, 2000.

Ter-Mekerttschian, K. and S. G. Wilson, with Prince Maxe of Saxony, eds. Εἰς ἐπίδειξιν τοῦ ἀποστολικοῦ κηρύγματος; *The Proof of the Apostolic Preaching, with Seven Fragments*. PO 12.5. Translated by J. Barthoulot. Paris, 1917. Reprint, Turnhout: Brepols, 1989.

Thielicke, Helmut. *Death and Life*. Translated by Edward H. Schroeder. Philadelphia: Fortress Press, 1970.

Thielman, Frank S. *Ephesians*. BECNT. Grand Rapids: Baker Academic, 2010.

Thiselton, Anthony. *The First Epistle to the Corinthians: A Commentary on the Greek Text.* NICGT. Grand Rapids: Eerdmans, 2000.

_____. *The Hermeneutics of Doctrine.* Grand Rapids: Eerdmans, 2007.

_____. *Life After Death: A New Approach to the Last Things.* Grand Rapids: Eerdmans, 2012.

Thomas, Heath A. "The *Telos* (Goal) of Theological Interpretation." In *A Manifesto for Theological Interpretation*, ed. Craig G. Bartholomew and Heath A. Thomas, 197-217. Grand Rapids: Baker Academic, 2016.

Torrance, Thomas F. *Incarnation: The Person and Life of Christ.* Edited by Robert T. Walker. Downers Grove, IL: IVP Academic, 2007.

Treat, Jeremy R. *The Crucified King: Atonement and Kingdom in Biblical and Systematic Theology.* Grand Rapids: Zondervan, 2014.

Trueman, Carl R. *The Creedal Imperative.* Wheaton, IL: Crossway, 2012.

Turner, Jr., James T. "How to Lose the Intermediate State Without Losing Your Soul." In *Christian Physicalism? Philosophical and Theological Criticisms*, ed. R. Keith Loftin and Joshua R. Farris, 271-93. Lanham: Lexington Books, 2017.

_____. *On the Resurrection of the Dead: A New Metaphysics of Afterlife for Christian Thought.* Routledge New Critical Thinking in Religion, Theology, and Biblical Studies. Philadelphia: Routledge, 2018.

van der Kooi, Cornelis and Gijsbert van den Brink. *Christian Dogmatics: An Introduction.* Grand Rapids: Eerdmans, 2017.

van Dixhoorn, Chad B. "New Taxonomies of the Westminster Assembly (1643–49): The Creedal Controversy as Case Study." *RRR* 6.1 (2004): 82-106.

van Geest, Paul J. J. "Augustine's Certainty in Speaking about Hell and His Reserve in Explaining Christ's Descent into Hell." In *The Apostles' Creed: 'He Descended into Hell,'* ed. Marcel Sarot and Archibald L. H. M. van Wieringen, 33-53. Studies in Theology and Religion 24. Leiden: Brill, 2018.

Vanhoozer, Kevin J. *The Drama of Doctrine: A Canonical Linguistic Approach to Christian Theology.* Louisville, KY: Westminster John Knox, 2005.

Vickers, Brian J. "Celebrating the Past and Future in the Present." In *The Lord's Supper: Remembering and Proclaiming the Lord's Death Until He Comes*, ed. Thomas R. Schreiner and Matthew R. Crawford, 313-40. NAC Studies in Bible and Theology 10. Nashville: B&H Academic, 2010.

Vidu, Adonis. Opera ad Extra: *The Inseparable Works of the Triune God.* Grand Rapids: Eerdmans, forthcoming 2019.

Walls, Jerry L. *Heaven, Hell, and Purgatory: Rethinking the Things that Matter Most.* Grand Rapids: Brazos, 2015.

_____. *Purgatory: The Logic of Total Transformation.* Oxford: Oxford University Press, 2012.

Walton, John H. *Ancient Near Eastern Thought and the Old Testament: Introducing the Conceptual World of the Hebrew Bible.* Grand Rapids: Baker Academic, 2006.

Bibliography

_____, Victor H. Matthews, and Mark W. Chavalas. *The IVP Bible Background Commentary: Old Testament*. Downers Grove, IL: InterVarsity Press, 2000.

Ware, Timothy. *The Orthodox Church*. London: Penguin, 1963. Revised reprint, 1964.

Webber, Robert E. *Ancient-Future Faith: Rethinking Evangelicalism for a Postmodern World*. Grand Rapids: Baker Academic, 1999.

Webster, John. *Holy Scripture: A Dogmatic Sketch*. Current Issues in Theology. Cambridge: Cambridge University Press, 2003.

_____. *Word and Church*. Essays in Church Dogmatics. London: T&T Clark, 2001.

Wellum, Stephen J. and Brent E. Parker, eds. *Progressive Covenantalism: Charting a Course Between Dispensational and Covenant Theologies*. Nashville: B&H Academic, 2016.

Westphal, Merold. *Whose Community? Which Interpretation? Philosophical Hermeneutics for the Church*. The Church and Postmodern Culture. Grand Rapids: Baker Academic, 2009.

Westra, Liuwe H. *The Apostles' Creed; Origin, History, and Some Early Commentaries*. IPM 43. Turnhout: Brepols, 2002.

White, Thomas Joseph. "On the Universal Possibility of Salvation." *Pro Ecclesia* 17.3 (2008): 269-80.

Wicks, Jared, SJ. "Christ's Saving Descent to the Dead: Early Witnesses from Ignatius of Antioch to Origen." *Pro Ecclesia* 17.3 (2008): 281-309.

Williams, Michael. "He Descended into Hell? An Issue of Confessional Integrity." *Presbyterion* 25.2 (1999): 80-90.

Williams, Rowan. *On Christian Theology*. Oxford: Blackwell, 2000.

Williamson, Paul R. *Death and the Afterlife: Biblical Perspectives on Ultimate Questions*. NSBT 44. Downers Grove, IL: IVP Academic, 2018.

Willimon, William H. *Acts*. Interpretation. Louisville, KY: WJK, 2010.

Wilson, Andrew. "The Strongest Argument for Universalism in 1 Cor. 15:20-28." *JETS* 59.4 (2016): 805-812.

Woodhouse, John. "Jesus and Jonah." *RTR* 43.2 (1984): 33-41.

Wright, N. T. *The Climax of the Covenant: Paul and the Law in Pauline Theology*. Minneapolis: Fortress Press, 1993.

_____. *Jesus and the Victory of God*. Christian Origins and the Question of God 2. Minneapolis: Fortress Press, 1996.

_____. *The New Testament and the People of God*. Christian Origins and the Question of God 1. Minneapolis: Fortress, 1992.

_____. *The Resurrection of the Son of God*. Christian Origins and the Question of God 3. Minneapolis: Fortress Press, 2003.

Wright, Nigel G. "Universalism in the Theology of Jürgen Moltmann." *EvQ* 84.1 (2012): 33-39.

Wyatt, Nicolas. "'Supposing Him to Be the Gardener' (John 20,15): A Study of the Paradise Motif in John." *ZNW* 81 (1990): 21-38.

Wynne, Jeremy J. *Wrath Among the Perfections of God's Life*. T&T Clark Studies in Systematic Theology. London: T&T Clark, 2012.

Yamasaki, Gary. "Jesus and the End of Life in the Synoptic Gospels." *Vision* (5.1): 40-47.

Yates, John. "'He Descended into Hell': Creed, Article and Scripture Part I." *Churchman* 102.3 (1988): 240-50.

_____. "'He Descended into Hell': Creed, Article and Scripture Part II." *Churchman* 102.4 (1988): 303-15.

Yeago, David. "The New Testament and Nicene Dogma." In *The Theological Interpretation of Scripture: Classic and Contemporary Readings*, ed. Stephen Fowl, 87-100. Oxford: Blackwell, 1997.

AUTHOR INDEX

SUBJECT INDEX

SCRIPTURE INDEX

Finding the Textbook You Need

The IVP Academic Textbook Selector
is an online tool for instantly finding the IVP books
suitable for over 250 courses across 24 disciplines.

---

ivpacademic.com
